Solidarity Tibet: Voices of Refugees

Solidarity Tibet:

Voices of Refugees

Brig. S.N.Sinha (Retd.), PVSM

NEHA PUBLISHERS & DISTRIBUTORS
DELHI

Publisher
NEHA PUBLISHERS & DISTRIBUTORS
4832/24,Prahlad Lane,S-207 Ansari
Road, Daryaganj, Delhi-110002
Ph.: 43570976, 23278261
Email: nehapubdistributors@gmail.com

Edition: 2015

ISBN: 978-93-80318-74-5

Laser Typesetting
JEE-VEE Graphics, Delhi

Price: 1195/-

Printed
Vikas Computers, Delhi

Preface

Today, after a long period of life in exile, Tibetan Government and the Tibetan people are transitory through a very crucial period. There are many challenges and issues facing the Tibetan exiled community. The most important being the advancing age of Tibet's spiritual leader, the Dalai Lama. Tibetan government in exile headed by the Dalai Lama has left no stones unturned to resolve the issue of Tibet peacefully with the Chinese government since long, but there has been no positive response from the Chinese side, rather they have strengthened their draconian rule in Tibet imposing strict restrictions on Tibetan people their religious activities and Human Rights.

Under pressure from the Beijing, the Nepalese government has arrested hundreds of refugee Tibetans who cross the border from Tibet to escape persecution by the Chinese regime, refugees say, sending many back to China and earning objections from human rights groups. Kathmandu has also blocked human rights demonstrations led by Tibet support groups and has put a stop to all pro-Tibet activities, refugees who have made it to Dharamsala say, in particular on March 10 when Tibetans sought to commemorate the anniversary of the failed 2008 uprising in Tibet. The 20,000-odd Tibetans who live in Nepal are barred from holding any protests on its soil. Celebrations of the Dalai Lama's birthday are taken as anti-government activities by authorities.

Presently Tibetan people's general standard of living can be comparable to surrounding native rural communities; in some areas the economic conditions are far better than native Indian villages. Almost all the settlements are provided with primary and secondary schools, primary health care centre and cooperative societies. There are also monasteries, nunneries and temples in the settlements. The cooperatives in the settlements play a vital role in settler's life. The cooperatives procure and advance seeds, fertilizers and pesticides, market agricultural produce collectively and provide common services such as tractors, trucks and warehousing. Cooperatives also run small business ventures like carpet weaving workshops and small incense factory.

This work is essentially useful for scholars researchers social activists academics government functionaries and the general reader alike.

—*Editor*

Contents

1

Introduction

TIBET: NEPAL URGED NOT TO RETURN REFUGEES TO CHINA

The Nepalese delegation was responding to the U.S. delegation statement urging them to continue "its long-standing commitment to ensure the safe passage through Nepal of Tibetan asylum seekers and refraining from forcibly returning Tibetan asylum seekers to China." "While we appreciate that the U.S. Administration had raised the plight of Tibetan refugees in Nepal, we remain shocked at the total denial by the Nepalese delegation over the refoulement of Tibetan refugees when cases have been documented by the United Nations High Commissioner for Refugees (UNHCR), Governments, NGOs and the media," Ms. Tsering Jampa, Executive Director of ICT-Europe said.

Although the Nepalese delegation was led by Deputy Prime Minister and Foreign Minister Ms. Sujata Koirala, it was the Nepalese Ambassador who told the UN mechanism: "On the issue of Tibetan refugees, Nepal stated that it does not allow its territory to be used against neighbours or any country. Anyone found in violation of the immigration law or other laws is dealt with according to the law of the land. There are no forceful deportations."

In an advance written question, Switzerland stated: "What measures does the government plan to take, in order to ensure that the status of Tibetan refugees in Nepal is recognized according to international standards?"

As the draft report on Nepal was adopted this afternoon by the Council's Working Group on the Universal Periodic Review (UPR), Nepalese refused to accept the recommendation of the U.S. delegation to: "Protect vulnerable refugee populations by allowing for registration of the refugee population in Nepal and by refraining from forcibly returning Tibetan asylum seekers to China:" In a way to explain their position, Nepal changed its tone by again claiming that "there was no policy of forcibly returning the refugees."

It should be recalled that on 31 May, 2003, the UNHCR in a press statement expressed grave concern about the fate of 18 Tibetan asylum seekers deported to China by Nepal. The statement said that the Nepalese authorities "decided to go ahead with the deportation on Saturday, ignoring last-minute appeals by the UN refugee agency and human rights groups. UNHCR learned that the deported group included eight unaccompanied minors, some as young as 13." UNHCR officials described the move as a blatant violation of Nepal's obligations under international law.

As documented by our annual Dangerous Crossing reports, ICT's written submission to the UPR mechanism "urged Nepal to uphold the principle of non-refoulement by taking adequate policy and administrative steps, including written policy instruction to immigration officials and border police, and training of Nepali police, security forces and immigration authorities about proper procedures and international human rights norms." Nepal also rejected recommendation by Algeria, Moldova, Netherlands, Slovenia and Switzerland who urged the country to become a Party to the 1951 Convention relating to the status of Refugees and its 1967 Protocol. Similarly the call from Netherlands that Nepal adopts national legislation pertaining to refugees that includes the rights of refugees and asylum seekers was not accepted.

ICT's submission expressed concern at the failure of establishment to issue refugee identity certificates to all refugees who met the criteria set by the Government. Thousands of eligible refugees had been waiting for years for processing of the certificates to resume. ICT called for durable solutions for long-staying refugees. Concern was also expressed at the practice of pre-emptive detentions and the wide-scale use of security forces used to intimidate Tibetans residing in Nepal and called on Nepali officials to ensure the fair treatment of Tibetans under Nepali law.

On 13 April, 2007, the UN Committee Against Torture after reviewing Nepal's second report said that the Committee was "disturbed about allegations received concerning cases of refoulement of Tibetan asylum-seekers, given the absolute nature of the prohibition against refoulement" under article 3 of the Convention Against Torture. The Committee also recommended that Nepal "enact legislation aimed at prohibiting refoulement of persons without an appropriate legal procedure...provide to the Committee information on the number of cases of extradition, removal, deportation, forced return and expulsion that have occurred since 1994, as well as information on cases in which deportation was not effected for fear of torture."

On the overall performance of the Nepalese delegation at the UPR examination, the Nepal NGO Coalition for the UPR, representing 235 human rights and civil society organization said in a statement on 25 January that they were disappointed "at the rhetorical statement by the government delegation and their failure to provide any concrete commitments and timelines for the implementation of Nepal's human rights obligations."

The statement added that the Coalition "is troubled by the response of the government delegation who claimed that there is no systematic torture in Nepal, in spite of well documented and credible reports of systematic practices of torture at the hands of the State security forces." According to the Human Rights Council, by the end of the current two-week session of the Working Group on the UPR, 159 States (out of 192 Member States of the United Nations) will have had their human rights records examined and in December 2011 all United Nations' Member States will have been reviewed under this mechanism.

The UPR was created through the UN General Assembly on 15 March 2006 by resolution 60/251, which established the Human Rights Council itself. It is a cooperative process which, by 2011, will have reviewed the human rights records of every country. Currently, no other universal mechanism of this kind exists. The

UPR is one of the key elements of the new Council which reminds States of their responsibility to fully respect and implement all human rights and fundamental freedoms. The ultimate aim of this new mechanism is to improve the human rights situation in all countries and address human rights violations wherever they occur. By the end of the current two-week session of the Working Group on the UPR, 159 States (out of 192 Member States) will have had their human rights records examined and in December 2011 all United Nations' Member States will have been reviewed under this mechanism.

NEPAL'S OFFICIAL POSITION AND ACTIVITIES OF TIBETANS IN NEPAL

Nepalese law does not recognize Tibetan refugees' rights as articulated in the United Nations conventions that form the basis of international refugee law. In recent years China has persuaded the Nepalese government with the notion that Tibetans who flee across the Himalayas are either illegal economic migrants, or criminals.

While Tibetan refugees possessing the RC are allowed to remain in Nepal, RC-holders have no right to an official employment permit, to own businesses or property, or access to colleges and universities on the same basis as Nepalese citizens. For international travel (not including India), RC-holding Tibetans must go through a complex process to obtain a Nepalese government issued travel document.

Although Tibetan refugees livelihood in Nepal lack many basic legal rights that impact their social, economic and cultural life, there is a popular conception among Nepalese citizens that the Tibetan refugee community in Nepal is wealthy and their presence in Nepal has led to difficulties with the Chinese and criticism from western countries. In reality, many Tibetans lack employment opportunities and higher education, forcing many to do manual agricultural work in remote areas in exchange for food. Tibetans living in Nepal typically reside in crowded and poor housing conditions in clustered Tibetan settlements. Increasingly the Nepalese government has denied or curtailed Tibetans' rights to hold cultural, religious, and school events in public and has consistently prohibited peaceful political demonstrations.

Chinese Pressure in Nepal

In August 2004, Nepal's Crown Prince Paras Bir Bikram Shah Dev met China's President Hu Jintao in the Great Hall of the People in Beijing.

During the meeting, Hu said that since the countries recognized diplomatic ties 49 years ago, relations have been growing steadily, and that he particularly appreciated the King of Nepal and the royal family for their "special and important role" in developing the relationship.

He stated that China is "willing to push the good-neighbourly partnership between the two countries to a new level." Crown Prince Paras reiterated Nepal's support for the "one-China" policy, and invited Hu to visit Nepal. Crown Prince Paras' visit resulted in the signing of agreements with Beijing for several new projects – China agreed to provide nearly 450 million Nepalese rupees ($6.4 million) to Nepal to support ongoing projects as well as start new ones. These included laying optical fibre cable from Kathmandu to the border region of Khasa in Tibet for better connectivity; surroundings up an Ayurvedic drugs research centre in Nepal; and building two roads.

These developments followed new trading accords in 2003. On December 3, 2003, China and Nepal opened two new trading posts along the Tibet-Nepal border; one in the Makalu region of east Nepal and the other in west-central part of Nepal. A Chinese development package was also promised to Nepal that will provide over $10 million dollars in aid, some of which will be used for on the ground experts to complete a road linking Nepal and Tibet at Rasuwa in Nepal and Kyirong in Tibet. The trade volume between Nepal and China reached 20 billion Nepalese rupees ($274 million) during Nepal's fiscal year 2003-4, according to Xinhua (September 28, 2004). Kathmandu now has a multi-storey Chinatown shopping centre that opened in March 2003 and sells a wide range of Chinese-made goods, including TV sets, electronics, computer parts, and textiles.

Tibetan Community in Nepal

Nepal states that it will not tolerate "anti-China" activity on its soil, and applies this policy with varying rigor. On the third day of Tibetan New Year, February 23, 2004, local authorities denied Tibetans permission to hold a gathering at the Boudha stupa, an important religious site and centre of the Tibetan community in Kathmandu, with the display of a portrait of the Dalai Lama. A community prayer gathering was held at the nearby Samtenling Monastery compound instead. Nepalese police tolerated a limited commemoration of the Tibetan National Uprising Day on March 10, 2004, at Samtenling Monastery with traditional prayers for those who lost their lives, as permission to hold the event at the Boudha stupa was denied. A spontaneous outburst of slogan-shouting by Tibetan youth as they walked around the Boudha stupa was also tolerated by police.

On July 6, 2004, the 69th birthday of His Holiness the Dalai Lama was observed in the Boudhanath neighborhood on the football grounds of Srongtsen Brikuti Boarding School. Prior permission had been sought from the Chief District Officer (CDO) and the Ministry of Home of the Nepalese government was also informed.

Permission was granted by the CDO with strict orders that Tibetans not engage in any "anti-China" behavior. Representatives of several diplomatic missions in Kathmandu attended the events. On December 10, 2004 Tibetans were allowable to mark International Human Rights Day and the anniversary of the awarding of the Nobel Peace Prize to the Dalai Lama. The occasion was celebrated with a traditional Tibetan prayer meeting at Samtenling Monastery, although permission to display the portrait of the Dalai Lama at the Boudha stupa was again denied.

BEIJING LEANS ON NEPAL OVER TIBETAN REFUGEES

Under pressure from the Beijing, the Nepalese government has arrested hundreds of refugee Tibetans who cross the border from Tibet to escape persecution by the Chinese regime, refugees say, sending many back to China and earning objections from human rights groups. Kathmandu has also blocked human rights demonstrations led by Tibet support groups and has put a stop to all pro-Tibet activities, refugees who have made it to Dharamsala say, in particular on March 10 when Tibetans sought to commemorate the anniversary of the failed 2008 uprising in Tibet. The 20,000-odd Tibetans who live in Nepal are barred from holding any protests on its soil. Celebrations of the Dalai Lama's birthday are taken as anti-government activities by authorities.

The tiny Himalayan nation is caught between Asia's two giants, India and China. Most Tibetans fleeing their homeland cross Nepal to India for shelter in the hill town of Dharamsala where their supreme leader and Tibetan Buddhism's highest religious figure, the Dalai Lama, took refuge in 1959 along with thousands of his followers with the consent of the Indian government. The pressure increased after China's army chief of staff, Gen. Chen Bingde, visited Kathmandu to pledge US$20 million in military and logistical support to the impoverished government of the tiny neighbouring country. It was not the first donation and is unlikely to be the last.

Chen led a 15-member army delegation to Nepal seeking to prevent any additional turmoil by the Tibetans in the country. It was the highest-level military visit from China to Nepal in more than a decade. The People's Liberation Army chief held high-level talks with Nepalese President Ram Baran Yadav, Prime Minister Jhalanath Khanal, Defence Minister Bishnu Paudel and his Nepalese counterpart General Chhatraman Singh Gurung, requesting that the Nepal government block movement of Tibetans across the border.

"The purpose of my visit is to strengthen friendship and cooperation between Nepal and China," Chen told reporters. "This cooperation is not only conducive for our people but also for world peace and the Asia Pacific region." The Nepalese government reassured China of its support and commitment to the 'One China Policy,' and indicated it would bar anti-Chinese activity on its soil. It also agreed to "deepen military ties and ensure peace at the Tibet frontier." "General Chen expressed gladness at the steadily developing relation between two countries and said that economically developing and politically stable Nepal is important not only for the stability of Asia Pacific region but also for the whole world," according to a statement released by the Nepal's Prime Minister's Office in Kathmandu.

Over the years Beijing has vilified any labors by exiles to change the situation inside Tibet, which the Chinese occupied in 1950, terming the invasion a peaceful liberation of longstanding Chinese territory. Tibetans refugees started flocking to Nepal after the failed 1959 uprising against Chinese rule and the Dalai Lama fled over the Himalayas into exile in India. Interestingly Nepal has traditionally been more aligned with India. However, recent moves by Beijing, especially in infrastructure development, have made China a much more influential player in Nepal than India.

"We are treated as criminals in Nepal," said an exiled Tibetan who gave his name only as Tsering. "The Nepalese government does everything the way China wants it do, and we have even lost the right to do a peaceful march." He had lived in Nepal but fled to Dharamsala, he said. Nepal has launched many crackdowns since refugees staged protests against China in the run-up to the Beijing Olympic Games and the deadly 2008 Tibetan riots. Rights groups have declared Tibetan refugees in Nepal to be increasingly vulnerable and at risk of arrest and repatriation to China. Under pressure from China, Nepal has refused to recognize Tibetan refugees who arrived after 1989. They are not allowed to register marriages.

On any major anniversary of that Tibetan exiles attempt to celebrate, dozens are arrested, with reports that even monks are beaten, tear-gassed and kicked. The United Nations' human-rights office says some people are now being arrested purely "on the basis of their appearance" without being demonstrators. Recent Tibetan government-in-exile elections were treated as an unlawful activity by the Nepalese government, depriving a large number of people the right to exercise their vote. "We cannot allow such an illegal activity within our territory," Superintendent of Police Pushkar Karki, who also serves as chief of Kathmandu Metropolitan Police Circle, told local media. "We need to follow the government's policy." Last year the Wikileaks website disclosed US State

Department cables from the embassy in New Delhi, alleging that China pays Nepalese police substantial money to arrest fleeing Tibetans.

"Chinese government rewards (Nepali forces) by providing financial incentives to officers who hand over Tibetans attempting to exit Tibet," said the cable, titled 'Update on Tibetan refugee flow.' Despite the restrictions, more than 2,500 Tibetans cross the border annually, embarrassing the Chinese government, which has sought to portray its administration in Lhasa as benevolent and dedicated to the welfare of the Tibetan people. The Nepalese government since the Wikileaks disclosures has come under fire for bending to pressure from the Chinese government in deporting exiles to China after previously having allowed them unhindered passage.

The Nepalese administration previously honoured a United Nations-brokered "gentlemen's agreement" between Nepal and the UN High Commissioner for Refugees to provide safe transit to Tibetan refugees who wish to travel through Nepal to Dharamsala, where thousands of Tibetan exiles have their base. That agreement has been abrogated under Chinese pressure. Watch groups such as Amnesty International, Human Rights Watch and the International Commission of Jurists have recently warned Kathmandu against breaching its international obligations, instead substituting "preventive arrests and policing restrictions on demonstrations and freedom of movement that deny the right to legitimate peaceful expression and assembly during anniversaries and festivals marked by the Tibetan community." "The link between China's aggression against Tibetans and Nepalese police actions has contributed to an environment of fear and insecurity in Nepal's Tibetan communities," the International Campaign for Tibet, the US based Tibet lobby said. Western countries, particularly the United States, have pressed the Nepalese government to soften its stance. The Undersecretary of State for Democracy and Global Affairs Maria Otero, the White House's special coordinator for Tibetan issues, visited refugee centres in Nepal in February where she met government officials to raise the issues of free passage and problems faced by Tibetans in Nepal itself. She pledged the continued support of the US government for the safety and welfare of refugees. "We have a longstanding policy, as you know, of supporting the needs of vulnerable refugee populations, and consider the Tibetan populations in Nepal to be particularly vulnerable. The U.S. continues to monitor the situation of both newly arriving refugees and the long-staying populations," a State Department official said in a statement on Feb. 18.

The Tibetan government-in-exile has appealed to Western nations to persuade the Nepalese government to allow the Tibetan activities and respect the human rights situation. Analysts believe China's long term plan is to neutralize Tibetans outside Tibet, leaving no voices to speak against them when the Dalai Lama retires completely. Rameshwor Acharya, the former Nepal ambassador to China, told reporters on March 24 that "China's concerns over Nepal are growing" and that "the visit shows that China wants the support of our army to control anti-Chinese activities following the resignation of the Dalai Lama." Thus many of the thousands of refugees wishing to leave their Himalayan homeland are finding that safe passage through Nepal is becoming increasingly unlikely and the future of Nepal's own Tibetan community appears uncertain as well.

TIBETAN REFUGEE CLAIMANTS IN TORONTO

The global prevalence of tuberculosis (TB) infection is predictable to be 32%, with approximately 8 million new symptomatic cases and 1.9 million TB-related deaths annually and a rising incidence of drug-resistant TB (DRTB). Ten percent of new cases of active TB are resistant to at least one first-line agent, and 1% have multidrug-resistant TB (MDRTB) [resistant to at least isoniazid and rifampin]. The annual incidence of new cases varies from > 250 cases per 100,000 in some heavy-burden nations, to < 10 per 100,000 in low-burden countries (including Canada and the United States). Drug-resistance rates are highest in places such as Russia, where rates of DRTB and MDRTB are 30 to 40% and 10%, respectively. Canadian figures correspond to the global median, 10% and 1%, respectively, with slowly increasing levels over the past decade in the province of Ontario.

As the incidence of TB in Canada dropped in the second half of the 20th century, the proportion of cases diagnosed in foreign-born individuals rose steadily, reaching nearly 60% by 1995 and 85% in Ontario. This reflects migration patterns from highly TB endemic countries. Current Canadian screening policy for refugee claimants in Canada requires the initiation of appropriate investigations for TB within 30 days of arrival if their claim was made outside of Canada, or within 60 days of their claim for applicants within Canada. This system could lead to delayed or incomplete screening.

Very high rates of vigorous and MDRTB were reported in a group of Tibetans from India and Nepal who entered the United States in 1990. No publications on subsequent migration of this or similar groups have been reported. Between 1998 and 2000, a group of Tibetan people who had entered the United States as visitors entered Canada and claimed refugee status. Beginning in 1990, as part of a humanitarian effort, there was a resettlement of Tibetans from India and Nepal to the United States. Some Tibetans who initially came to the United States subsequently entered Canada and claimed refugee status. Members of our cohort sought refugee status in Canada after lengthy US stays as visitors, because they were no longer able to maintain their visitor status or otherwise extend their stay in the United States. Most initially settled in Toronto, and many had TB screening completed at our centre. We sought to review TB-related outcomes in this cohort, to compare our experience with the findings of Truong et al, and to assess longer-term follow-up after a stay in a low-incidence region.

Resources and Method

Patients were included for study if they were self-identified as Tibetan, entered Canada between 1998 and 2000, and were referred to St. Michael's Hospital or West Park Healthcare Centre in Toronto. Referrals came from three sources: Canadian immigration officials, the City of Toronto Public Health Department (PHD), or community physicians. Canadian immigration-designated medical practitioners initially assessed all individuals clinically and with chest radiographs (CXRs). Reasons for referral for further assessment included a clinical suspicion of TB, a CXR abnormality consistent with TB, and a history of previous TB. Through discussions with local Canadian immigration designated medical practitioners, we surmised that the majority with an abnormal CXR finding were referred to us. In addition, between July and September 1999, the PHD initiated a campaign to identify and perform a tuberculin skin test (TST) on all recently arrived Tibetan refugees. Individuals with a positive TST result were referred to our centres. We therefore had the opportunity to assess a subgroup of recent Tibetan immigrants deemed to be at high risk for TB, based on an abnormal CXR findings or positive TST results. Data were collected with hindsight from medical records at St. Michael's Hospital, a referral centre for TB cases in Toronto and West Park Healthcare Centre, housing the only inpatient service for complicated TB cases in Ontario. Both are University of Toronto-affiliated teaching hospitals. The St. Michael's Hospital/West Park Healthcare Centre institutional research ethics board approved the study, and all work was in accordance with the Helsinki Declaration of 1975.

Patients were assessed with a history, bodily examination, CXR (reviewed by a pulmonary medicine physician and a radiologist), TST (positive result defined as a e" 10-mm induration 48 to 72 h after intradermal injection of 5 tuberculin units of purified protein derivative), and sputum smear and culture findings (in most patients). Individuals with suggestive symptoms or a CXR finding considered to be consistent with TB were investigated microbiologically, including flexible bronchoscopy if sputum could not be obtained. Latent TB infection (LTBI) was defined by a positive TST result and either a normal CXR finding or negative microbiologic investigations. Active TB was diagnosed when Mycobacterium tuberculosis was recovered (culture-positive TB) or negative culture findings with consistent clinical signs, symptoms, and/or radiographic abnormalities that improved after antituberculous therapy (culture-negative TB). Previous TB, currently inactive, was defined as a history of previous TB treatment, negative microbiologic investigations, and the lack of criteria for culture-negative TB. Individuals unavailable for follow-up before specimens could be sent for microbiologic studies were classified as unknown. Patients were treated in accordance with the contemporary edition of the Canadian standards for the treatment of TB, similar to the American Thoracic Society guidelines.

Accurate figures on the number of Tibetan refugee claimant settling in our area were unavailable. In conjunction with the Ontario Ministry of Health and Long Term Care, members of the Toronto Tibetan community, and the PHD, we estimated that 525 people of Tibetan origin claimed refugee status during the study period. We used this figure as the denominator in rate calculations, and estimated that the true number fell within the plausible range of 450 to 600 people. We calculated confidence intervals using 450 as the sample size, which provides a greater calculated variance and wider and more conservative confidence intervals. Rates of active TB and drug resistance were compared with relevant previously published reports. To facilitate comparisons, we assumed that prevalence from our experience approximated incidence. We used the Yates-corrected and the Wilcoxon test to compare categoric and continuous variables, respectively.

Consequences

An estimated 525 Tibetan people crossed the border into Ontario, Canada between 1998 and early 2001. One hundred eighty-nine individuals were referred for assessment, and records were available for review in 181 patients. The mean age was 29 years, and 123 (68%) were male. Fifty-eight patients (32%) gave a history of previous TB. Two patients each had received a diagnosis of active TB or LTBI in the United States and were still receiving treatment when they entered Canada. History of bacille Calmette-Guérin vaccination status was available in < 10% of patients. Eighty-seven patients (48%) were born in India, 54 patients (30%) were born in Tibet, and 38 patients (21%) were born in Nepal. Information regarding refugee camp residence was unavailable for most patients. New York City was the most common site of previous stay in the United States, with at least 116 of patients (64%) having spent a mean of 11 months there. Other sites of stay included

Chicago, Detroit, Boston, and Minneapolis-St. Paul. The mean durations of stay in the United States and Canada prior to presentation were 11 months and 2.6 months, respectively. All individuals were refugee claimants in Canada.

Conversation

Individuals of Tibetan origin entering Canada from the United States were found to have extremely high levels of active and DRTB. Two contributing factors help explain this alarming finding. These patients originated primarily from northern India, which has some of the highest rates of TB in the world, as well as high levels of drug resistance. Members of this cohort differ from other Canadian immigrants from northern India by their self-identification as Tibetan and their intervening stay in a low-incidence nation. We also believe that many of these people stayed in refugee camps in northern India, but these data are not available to us. Superimposed on this, recent migration and refugee status are recognized risk factors for the development of active TB. Truong and colleagues observed similarly high rates of active and DRTB in a group of Tibetans in Minnesota, and others have reported high rates of DRTB in populations from similarly endemic regions. Our work differs in that we assessed a large group of people after a mean of 11 months in a low-prevalence country, and demonstrated very high rates of active and DRTB at this later time. This finding underscores the high ongoing risk of disease, reported for up to 5 years after migration. TB must therefore always be considered in people who come from high-incidence regions, regardless of intervening stays in low-incidence areas. We considered members of this cohort with the same level of suspicion as Tibetan refugees coming directly from northern India and nearby areas. The particularly high rates observed by us and Truong et al, apparently unique to newcomers of Tibetan origin, also suggest that immigration authorities in both the United States and Canada should be aware of our findings to ensure members of this group receive appropriate screening and surveillance.

High rates of previous TB and inadequate treatment likely also contributed to the high DRTB rate. We were unable to demonstrate an association between a previous history of TB and DRTB, which could relate to an underreporting bias. Members of our cohort may have believed it was in their best interest to not report previous episodes of TB, for fear of jeopardizing success of pending refugee claims and the social stigma often attached to this disease.

It is very likely that a significant figure of the cases of active TB we detected were present while the patients were still living in the United States. That these cases were not detected during US residence may be due to the fact that people entering the United States (or Canada) as visitors may not require screening for TB. This could present a tremendous public health problem. According to an estimate in a US Institute of Medicine report, members of the group of people who entered the United States as visitors in 1996 alone could contribute 2,000 new cases of TB during their stay. In Canada, visitors who have lived in a country with high rates of TB for at least 6 months of the past year and intend to stay in Canada for at least 6 months are required to undergo an immigration medical examination. This stipulation would not require screening of people, like members of our cohort, who maintain a high risk despite an intervening period in a low-incidence region. In both countries, screening is mandated for those seeking to adjust their status after arriving on temporary visas, but this does not address the initial and possibly highest risk period.

The time from entry into Canada and start of screening is concerning, given the very high rates of active TB and drug resistance we observed. The mean time to presentation was 2.6 months, regardless of CXR abnormality or the presence of active disease. This duration falls short of current Canadian screening recommendations, likely reflecting the challenges inherent in achieving timely radiographic and clinical evaluation in people in an unfamiliar environment. We thus support calls to improve the current screening system, and stress its limitations in assessing refugee claimants.

Our findings stress the importance of initial screening, especially in people originating from high-incidence regions and lend support to the Canadian refugee and immigration policy of CXR screening in those > 11 years old. All active cases were detected on initial screening after entry into Canada. As expected, we observed that CXR abnormalities demonstrate an extremely high sensitivity (100% in this series) in detecting active TB cases; however, this finding is likely biased, since the results of the CXR undoubtedly influenced whether or not further investigations were performed.

Given the high continuing risk of disease in newcomers from high-prevalence countries, it must be stressed that initial screening is only the first component in the control of TB in high-risk newcomers. We feel that treating LTBI is important and, consistent with current guidelines, agree strongly that age > 35 years is not a general contraindication to therapy for LTBI. In addition, based on the very high rates of active TB we observed in our cohort, members of similar groups should likely be considered to have a high likelihood of recent infection, and treatment of LTBI should be considered more strongly and pursued more vigorously. Further, we strongly support recommendations regarding medical surveillance of high-risk people who are not treated for LTBI. Identification of people with LTBI currently rests on the use of TSTs. One might consider expanding the screening protocol to include universal TSTs. Decision analysis models in this area have yielded conflicting results, possibly due to differences in patient grouping (all immigrants as a whole vs subsets defined according to estimated risk of LTBI) or estimates of LTBI treatment completion rates. Khan et al found the detection and treatment of LTBI was cost-effective in immigrants to the United States from many developing nations. Schwartzman and Menzies modeled the use of TST screening in immigrants as not cost-effective, primarily reflecting use in low-risk patient groups and poor adherence to LTBI treatment regimens. Including TST in screening becomes more attractive if it is targeted toward high-risk groups and a high rate of LTBI treatment completion is achieved. Our relatively low rates of LTBI treatment and its completion are concerning. Of eligible patients with LTBI, 20% were unavailable for follow-up before treatment, and rates of completion were only 61%. Truong and colleagues reported treatment of LTBI in 58% of a similar cohort, compared with 43% in our series, but did not provide data on completion rates.

The definition of high-risk newcomer may not always be clear. The current Canadian recommendation regarding which visitors require TB screening are based on having lived in a country with high rates of TB for at least 6 months of the past year. We feel that this reflects an inadequate view in identifying high-risk people. When defining TB risk status according to regions of previous residence, we advocate a longer time horizon, possibly 5 years. This threshold may be a more useful one for practitioners assessing people for the presence of active TB, LTBI, and consideration regarding treatment of LTBI.

The choice of optimal regimen for treat LTBI in newcomers from areas with very high rates of DRTB is unknown. During the period when members of our cohort were being assessed, the prevalence of DRTB and MDRTB in this group were not yet clear to us, and we used the most commonly employed regimens for treating LTBI. If the 33% rate of resistance to isoniazid in active TB cases was representative of the prevalence of isoniazid resistance in the cohort as a whole, one would expect that isoniazid LTBI treatment would be effective in < 67%, given its imperfect effectiveness in optimal circumstances. Guidelines have been developed regarding the treatment of LTBI in patients exposed to patients with MDRTB and known resistance patterns, but there is little guidance available for treating patients who are at high risk for DRTB and MDRTB based on other risk factors. Given that the majority of patients with LTBI are likely infected with organisms that are sensitive to isoniazid (even in patients from areas where resistance to isoniazid is high) and the lack of data regarding the efficacy of regimens for treating LTBI in DRTB and MDRTB, we continue to recommend the use of standard regimens but would consider alternative regimens in exceptional circumstances, where we would also advocate systematic follow-up in an attempt to assess effectiveness. This recommendation is supported by Khan et al, who presented a cost-effectiveness analysis addressing this issue. The authors recommend isoniazid, rifampin, or rifampin plus pyrazinamide for treating LTBI in immigrants to the United States who originate from India and the neighbouring nations. Further, the burden of organisms in LTBI is likely low enough that there are no significant concerns of contributing to drug resistance with a single agent to which the organism is sensitive.

Some limitations of our study merit mention. Inherent to its retrospective nature, some data were incomplete. This weakness should be minimized by the presence of standardized history and physical examination forms we employed. Our most important findings, very high rates of active and DRTB, would likely be underestimated by missing data. Our study of cases at St. Michael's and West Park Hospitals introduces a referral bias, potentially inflating disease and drug-resistance rates. This is a difficult bias to address but likely small in magnitude. Given that the Tibetan-targeted PHD TST program referred all patients to our centres, regardless of CXR results, and that we specialize in TB and providing care to refugees and refugee claimants, it is likely that we assessed most members of this population. Precisely estimating the rate of disease was difficult given the uncertainty surrounding the total number of Tibetans arriving in our area. This is not likely a significant source of error for two reasons. First, we found a similar disease rate to the one observed by Truong et al in a similar population. Second, we took measures to provide conservative confidence intervals and the lower bounds still indicated very high rates of disease. It could be speculated that claiming Tibetan ethnic origin may increase the likelihood of a successful refugee claim in Canada, with high-risk patients preferentially claiming Tibetan origin and leading to an overestimate of rates of TB in this population. This is difficult to assess, given the absence of data, but we feel it is not likely significant given the similarity of the rates we observed with those of Truong et al.

TIBETAN DIASPORA

The Tibetan diaspora is a term used to refer to the communities of Tibetan people living outside Tibet. Tibetan emigration happened in two waves: one in 1959 following the 14th Dalai Lama's self-exile in India, and the other in the 1980s when Tibet was opened to trade and tourism. The third wave continues from 1996 to today. Not all emigration from Tibet is permanent; today some parents in Tibet send their children to communities in the diaspora to receive a traditional Tibetan education. In the 2009 census, Tibetans in exile registered are about 128,000, with the most numerous part of the community living in India, Nepal, and Bhutan. However, in 2005 and 2009 an estimation at up to 150,000 was given.

Origins and Numbers

The Central Tibetan Administration (CTA) provides a Green Book-a kind of Tibetan identity certificate-to Tibetan refugees. Based on a CTA survey from 2009, 127,935 Tibetans were registered in the diaspora: in India 94,203; in Nepal 13,514; in Bhutan 1,298; and in rest of the world 18,920. However, their number is estimated at up to 150,000, as mentioned by both Edward J. Mills et al. in 2005 and by the 14th Dalai Lama in 2009.

The larger of the other communities are in the USA, Canada, the United Kingdom, Switzerland, Norway, France, Taiwan and Australia.

First Wave

During the 1959 Tibetan uprising, the 14th Dalai Lama and some of his government fled to India. From 1959 to 1960, about 80,000 Tibetans followed the Dalai Lama to India through the Himalayas. Continued flights, estimated in the numbers of 1,000 to 2,500 a year, increased these numbers to 100,000. The movement of refugees during this time is sometimes referred to as an "exodus", as in a United Nations General Assembly resolution in 1961 that asserted that the presence of Tibetan refugees in neighbouring countries was "evidence" of rights abuses in Tibet.

Second wave

After the opening of Tibet in the 1980s to trade and tourism, a second Tibetan wave of exile took place due to increasing political repression. From 1986 to 1996, 25,000 Tibetans joined and increased by 18% their exiled community in India. This movement of refugees during this second wave is sometimes referred to as a "second exodus". According to a US cable put out by WikiLeaks, from 1980 to November 2009, 87,096 Tibetans arrived in India and registered at the Dharamsala reception centre, whereas 46,620 returned to Tibet after a pilgrimage in India. Most of those staying are children to attend Tibetan Children's Villages school.

Present Emigration

A 2008 documentary directed by Richard Martini claimed that 3,000–4,500 Tibetans arrive at Dharamsala every year. Most new immigrants are children who are sent to Tibetan cultural schools, sometimes with the tacit approval of the Chinese government. Many political activists, including monks, have also crossed over through Nepal to India. Significant cultural gaps exist between recent Tibetan emigrants and Indian-born Tibetans. The more established Tibetans in diaspora reject recent immigrant Tibetans who watch Chinese movies, sing Chinese music, and can speak Mandarin, who are then alienated from the exile community. Newcomers express frustration that the government-in-exile wants to hear only "bad things" about Chinese rule in Tibet, and a lack of economic opportunity in Dharamsala.

In India

Organisations

The main organisation of the Tibetan diaspora is the Central Tibetan Administration of the 14th Dalai Lama based in the McLeod Ganj suburb of the city of Dharamsala in India. One of the people to organize the functioning of Tibetan refugee camps in India and to transform the life of Tibetan refugees into the ways of a diaspora was Polish born Wanda Dynowska (1888–1971), called Umadevi, recalled by the 14th Dalai Lama as the "Polish Mother", along with her friend, Indian citizen of Polish origin, Maurycy Frydman. The CTA maintains Tibet Offices in 10 countries. These act as de facto embassies of the CTA, offices of culture and information and effectively provide a kind of consular help to Tibetans. They are based in New Delhi, India; New York, USA; Geneva, Switzerland; Tokyo, Japan; London, UK; Canberra, Australia; Paris, France; Moscow, Russia; Pretoria, South Africa; and Taipei, Taiwan. The

Tibetan diaspora NGOs deal with the cultural and social life of the diaspora, the preservation of cultural heritage, and the promotion of political Tibetan independence.

Education

The Central Tibetan Schools Administration with a seat in New Delhi is an autonomous organization established in 1961 with the objective to establish, manage and assist schools in India for the education of Tibetan children living in India while preserving and promoting their culture and heritage. According to information on its own website, as of 2009 the Administration was running 71 schools in the areas of concentration of Tibetan population, with about 10,000 students on the roll from pre-primary to class XII, and with 554 teaching staff. According to the information on the website of the CTA, as of 2009.01.13. there were 28 CTSA schools whose enrolment was 9,991 students.

In 2009, The Tibetan Children's Villages established the first Tibetan higher college in exile in Bangalore (India) which was named "The Dalai Lama Institute for Higher Education". The goals of this college is to teach Tibetan language and Tibetan culture, but also science, the arts, counselling and information technology.

2

Tibet Today

In the last decade the Chinese have stepped up their efforts to re-populate Tibet. Today, Tibetans are a minority in their own country — there are now about 7.5 million Chinese to about 6.5 million Tibetans, and inducements of higher pay and other privileges continue to bring a stream of Chinese settlers into the country. The aim of this is to forcibly resolve China's territorial claims over Tibet by means of a massive and irreversible population shift. In May 1993, an official Chinese government document, leaked to the Tibetan Government in Exile, indicated that the Chinese authorities proposed another massive population transfer as one element in what they termed "a final solution" to their "Tibetan problem". In April this year (1996), the *South China Morning Post* reported official sources in Beijing as saying that a further 500,000 ethnic Chinese are to be moved into Tibet.

This large-scale population transfer has resulted in a 300 percent inflation rate in Tibet, a two-class society sharply divided along racial lines, and unprecedented unemployment among Tibetans.

Tibet, once a peaceful buffer state between India and China, has been transformed into a militarized zone. There are at least 300,000 Chinese troops stationed there at any time, as are at least one quarter of China's nuclear arsenal of 350 nuclear missiles at 5 different missile bases.

It is believed that approximately 3,000 religious and political prisoners are held in prisons and forced labour camps where torture is common. There are reports that Tibetan women are subject *en masse* to forced abortions and sterilization. Alexander Solzhenitsyn has described China's administration of Tibet as "more brutal and inhumane than any other communist regime in the world."

There are strong concerns, voiced internationally, that China is using Tibet as a dumping ground for nuclear waste. There were reports that China had made an offer to West Germany in 1984 to dispose of nuclear waste. The offer was not accepted. Recently Tibetan farmers have complained that "fertilizer" they have been forced to use on their fields is destroying crops and killing birds and animals.

Tibet's natural resources and ecology are being irreversibly destroyed. Wildlife, including the rare Tibetan snow leopard and the wild blue Tibetan sheep, has been decimated. Forests have been clear-cut and transported to China (since 1950, 68% of Tibet's forests have been felled, causing grave concern in Bangladesh and India, now both frequently devastated by flooding.)

China severely restricts the teaching and study of Buddhism, an essential core of Tibetan culture. The Communist Party regulates the admission of monks and nuns into the monasteries and "political education" is compulsory. Though for a period after the Cultural Revolution there appeared to be a liberalizing of the Chinese attitude to religious life, a new report released by the International Campaign for Tibet indicates that China has shifted its religious policy to actively suppress and restrict further religious growth. This involves measures to halt unauthorized rebuilding of monasteries destroyed during the Cultural Revolution, setting limits on the number of monks and nuns in all monasteries, enforcing restrictions on youths joining monasteries, prohibiting Tibetan Party members from practising religion, and strengthening the control of the government and the Communist Party over each monastery.

Last year the Chinese authorities reintroduced a ban, current during the Cultural Revolution but lifted in 1979, prohibiting pictures of the Dalai Lama from monasteries and temples. Recently this was widened to include schools and private homes and there are reports of house-to-house searches checking for possession of photographs of the Dalai Lama.

In 1995 the Chinese government kidnapped the six-year-old Gendun Chökyi Nyima and his parents, shortly after he had been recognized by the Dalai Lama as the latest reincarnation of Tibet's second most important spiritual leader, the Panchen Lama. In a resolution of July, 1995, the European Parliament called on China to release the family immediately. This family, like many other groups and individuals who have been detained without trial, remains unaccounted for.

The Chinese authorities meanwhile have appointed another child as the "recognized reincarnation" of the Panchen Lama. In January 1996, nine monks in Tibet were arrested for openly protesting against China's choice.

THE POLITICAL SYSTEM IN TIBET TODAY

Tibet is strictly governed by the Chinese Communist Party, with the active support of the military. The Party rules through branch offices in each province, autonomous region and autonomous prefecture. Subordinate to the Party is the government, which carries out policies designed by the Party. China has established the full panoply of Party and government offices to administer Tibet as exists in China. In Lhasa alone, there are over 60 departments and committees almost all of which are directly connected to their national offices in Beijing. Thus, Tibet is "autonomous" in word only; in fact, the Tibet Autonomous Region has less autonomy than Chinese provinces. The top T.A.R. post, the Party Secretary, has never been held by a Tibetan.

China maintains an occupation army in Tibet of at least a quarter million strong. Military and police are often overwhelmingly present in Lhasa and elsewhere, though as of February 1992, security in Lhasa is dominated by undercover and plainclothes police. The military plays a greater role in the administration of Tibet than any Chinese province, and no Tibetan serves in the leadership of the military district governing Tibet.

Even though the Party still controls Tibet, its control is beginning to slip. There is a pervasive disillusionment with, and contempt for, the Communist Party and the government in Tibet which can even be found among Party members and government functionaries.

Inefficiency and corruption have consumed some government operations to the extent that they barely function and are an enormous waste of government funds. During ICT's one-month tour of eastern Tibet, it became apparent that the Party's goals have been drastically reduced from its once grandiose plans of social, human and economic transformation to simply holding onto power, taking care of Chinese settlers and extracting Tibet's natural resources.

The Party now seems to have little left to offer Tibetans other than the repression which keeps Tibetans from mass rebellion. Nobody in Tibet is talking about how the Party can reform itself, for it has become something that most Tibetans must just tolerate and avoid. Some Tibetans use the Party for their own personal and professional advancement and try to improve conditions for Tibetans from within the system. The late Panchen Lama succeeded in wresting enough power from the system to improve conditions in a number of areas. The Panchen Lama was the only Tibetan who the Chinese feared, unlike current Tibetan leaders such as Ngawang Ngapo Jigme, Mao Rubai and Raidi who have little power. Recent reports from Lhasa indicate increasing alienation and disaffection among middle and lower level Tibetan bureaucrats and a corresponding loss of trust in them by their Chinese superiors.

Human Rights Situation in Tibet

Human rights conditions in Tibet remain dismal. Under the Chinese occupation, the Tibetan people are denied most rights guaranteed in the Universal Declaration of Human Rights including the rights to self-determination, freedom of speech, assembly, movement, expression and travel.

Political Prisoners

China's consistent use of excessive military force to stifle dissent has resulted in widespread human rights abuses including multiple cases of arbitrary arrests, political imprisonment, torture and execution. Human rights groups have documented at least 60 deaths of peaceful demonstrators since 1987. Human rights groups have confirmed, by name, over 700 Tibetan political prisoners in Tibet, although there are likely to be hundreds more whose names are not confirmed. Many are detained without charge or trial for up to four years through administrative regulations entitled "re-education through labor". Also, over the past year unrest has spread from urban areas into the countryside.

Credible reports of mistreatment and torture of detainees and political prisoners in Tibet are widespread, including beatings, shocks with electric batons, deprivation of sleep or food, exposure to cold and other brutalities. Human rights and humanitarian organizations are denied access to prisons and detention centers in Tibet.

Freedom of Religion

Prior to the Chinese invasion of 1950, Tibet was a country steeped in religion. Religious practice permeated the daily lives of the Tibetan people and formed the social fabric connecting them to the land. Recognizing this, the Chinese focused on destroying this cultural base of the Tibetan people in the hopes of quelling dissent to their rule. In 1960 the International Commission of Jurists found "that the Chinese will not permit adherence to and practice of Buddhism in Tibet.... [and] that they have systematically set out to eradicate this religious belief in Tibet."

Over 6000 monasteries and sacred places were destroyed by the Chinese. Despite this and the over 40 years of restrain on their religion, the Tibetans continue to seek to practice their religion. Today the practice of religion continues to be severely limited in Tibet. Although there have been some outward improvements in this area, China maintains strict control over religious institutions and practices and the Tibetans are not free to practice and organize their own religion. ICT published Forbidden Freedom and A Season to Purge which took an in-depth look at the issue of religious freedom in Tibet. China has shifted its religious policy in Tibet to actively suppress and restrict further religious growth.

This shift involves measures to halt unauthorized rebuilding of monasteries destroyed during the Cultural Revolution, setting limits on the number of monks and nuns in all monasteries, enforcing restrictions on youths joining monasteries, prohibiting Tibetan Party members from practicing religion, and strengthen the control of the government and Party over each monastery through "Democratic Management Committees."

The Environment in Tibet

The Tibetan Plateau is the largest and highest plateau in the world. It sustains a unique, yet fragile high altitude eco-system much of which remains unspoiled due to its remoteness and inaccessibility. However, human impact is now taking an unprecedented and devastating toll on the natural resources – the wildlife, forests, grazing lands, rivers and mineral resources are now at a point where they may never recover.

Wildlife

Pre-1950 travelers in Tibet compared it to East Africa, so vast were the herds of large mammals. Today, the herds are all but vanished, wiped out mainly by Chinese soldiers shooting automatic weapons from trucks in the 1960s. Poaching by Tibetans and Chinese continues, threatening the survival of some species. One Tibetan nomad told Dr. George Schaller, the foremost Western specialist on Tibetan mammals, "If the officials obey the law and stop hunting, we will too."

Deforestation

Forests in Tibet are the third largest in China's present day borders and government lumber operations are cutting at an unprecedented rate. Reforestation is neglected and ineffective, leaving hillsides vulnerable to erosion. Rapid and widespread deforestation has life-threatening consequences for the hundreds of millions who live in the flood plains of the major rivers of Southeast Asia, many of which have their headwaters in Tibet. Clear-cutting also threatens the habitat of Tibet's other residents – the rare giant panda, golden monkey, and over 5,000 plant species unique to the planet.

Nuclear Activities

The northern Tibetan Plateau was home to China's "Los Alamos," – its primary nuclear weapons research and development plant, and nuclear weapons were first stationed in northern Tibet in 1972. Today there are at least 3 or 4 nuclear missile launch sites in Tibet housing an unknown number of warheads. Nuclear waste from the research facility is feared to be dumped on the nearby plains where Tibetan nomads allege they have suffered illness and death from strange diseases consistent with radiation sickness. ICT's ground-breaking report Nuclear Tibet, addresses this troublesome area.

Desertification

Government-encouraged population migration into the northern Tibetan plateau, now under control of Qinghai Province, has caused massive and irreparable environmental damage to huge tracts of fragile tableland. Experts attribute the deterioration to overgrazing, irrational land reclamation, and wanton denudation of surface vegetation.

Agricultural Development

Large-scale agricultural development projects are now being carried out in Tibet which are disrupting traditional practices and the ecological balance maintained by farmers for centuries. Motivated by the need to feed the growing Chinese population in Tibet and reduce the costly wheat imports, the projects may ultimately harm Tibetans more than help them. One of the projects, which is funded by the United Nations World Food Program, employs hundreds of Chinese and few Tibetans and is opposed by local Tibetans, ICT and other Tibetan organizations.

Natural Resource Extraction

The extraction of minerals and wood from Tibetan regions is largely done by, or at the direction of, newly arrived Chinese workers and administrators. Some meager benefit may accrue to local Tibetans, but more often than not, the land is left despoiled and traditional Tibetan livelihoods disrupted. Moreover, roads built to access uncut forests or untapped minerals usually result in an increase in local Chinese government administrators who may then assume more control over the local monastery, probably leading to greater restrictions on religious freedom. Implementation of family planning policies may also increase, which could involve coercive methods.

Hydro-electric Construction Projects

China has plans to build dozens of hydro-electric dams on Tibet's rivers and export the electricity to Chinese cities such as Chengdu, Xining, Lanzhou and Xian. The most heated environmental issue in Tibet may be a hydro-electric construction project on Yamdrok Tso, a sacred lake between Lhasa and Shigatse. A correspondent for The Independent wrote, "environmentalists fear this giant project will create one of China's worst ecological disasters of the 21st century."

TIBET IN CONTEXT

The impression of Tibet as an inaccessible highland notwithstanding the region has been witness to human presence for a very long time. Some of the earliest humans who inhabited the Indian subcontinent had passed through the Tibetan high plateau more than 20,000 years ago. It is quite astonishing to find that megalithic rock burials from upto 3,000 years ago exist in the higher reaches of Tibet which, even in our age, are difficult to excavate because of their locations. It must have been some feat for our ancestors who leave us these remarkable monuments to their rugged adaptability.

Tibet had emerged as a unified kingdom from a multiplicity of disparate tribes by the 7th century. The hardy Tibetans, once organized, turned up in the region as a formidable miltary power, striking out from their highland ramparts and spreading Tibetan influence far and wide. Tibetan influence, at its farthest, was felt as far north as the Ferghana Valley in Central Asia, the far reaches of Kashmir in the north-west, with Ladakh and Gilgit-Baltistan still largely Tibetan in their cultural orientation, skirmishing with the Kingdoms of Nepal in the west, threatening the Pala kingdoms of Bengal in the South, of the Asom in the south-east, the Chinese regions of Sichuan and Yunnan in the east, and across the Silk Road routes and cities of the Takla-Makan desert to the frontiers of the Mongol tribes.

The 7th century also brought Buddhism to Tibet. Buddhism was to slowly replace, and in many aspects syncretically assimilate the existing Bon religions and other animistic traditions of the disparate Tibetans and drastically change the nature of Tibetan society, in one possible interpretation, giving rise to a Tibetan nation. Tibetan society gradually also became more settled and inward looking. The spread of Tibetan culture, however, only accelerated with this change with lamaism, the Buddhism of Tibet, becoming the dominant religio-cultural tradition of the soon to be powerful Mongolia.

The Tibetan proto-empire was to come to a rapid end after its heyday. The newly organised Mongolian tribes burst out of their Heartland and went on to create the world empire of the Mongols. The Mongols also went on to conquer China establishing the Sinicized Yuan dynasty. Tibet, too, was conquered by the beginning of the 13th century by the Mongols of the Yuan. With this Tibet became, for the first time, a part of the Heavenly Empire of China.

Since this is a current issue, and a very contentious one at that, one must offer a few comments on the association of Tibet with China. Most debates about whether Tibet was, or is, a part of China begin with a national-territorial frame of reference. This is an anachronism. The Chinese Imperial system was organized not on a national-territorial but what can be called an associational-tributary basis. We can understand this system as having three sets of concentric circles – with the Emperor and the Imperial seat at the centre drawing its legitimacy and authority from Heaven, the cultural core of the Han Chinese civilization forming the second circle around the Imperial seat, and a series of associated kingdoms and other pre-state polities forming the third circle around the cultural core. These polities were in an associational-tributary relationship with the Emperor of China, recognising his overpower, paying tributes and other forms of respect and, often, accepting in their courts the authority of a Resident Agent of the Emperor. The Resident Agent, not to be confused with the role played by an ambassador, was very powerful in these courts when backed by the might of the Imperial army which often intervened when the authority, or commands, of the Emperor were contravened. But whenever the Imperial core was weak or unstable, and unable to impose its authority through arms, the Resident Agents were powerless.

Returning to the narrative, Tibet remained under Yuan suzerainty until the end of the 14th century. From then on, with the power of the Imperial centre weakening, the Yuan dynasty being replaced by the new Ming dynasty after a series of wars, Tibet became more or less autonomous and remained that way till the beginning of the 18th century when it was again brought into the system of the Chinese Empire by the later Qing dynasty.

It was during the interceding years that in Tibet developed the politico-religious organization associated with Tibet during the colonial era. Namely, the Dalai Lama as the head of the state, the 'God-King' as he was called in colonial literature, and the religious bureaucracy of the Buddhist priesthood organizing the functions of the state. Now also began the development of the diplomatic system the region which was so 'irrational' and, consequently, threatening to the new national-territorial order of the British Colonial State.

This system was characterized by a series of overlapping, for want of a better word, authorities. While the individual rulers of the various kingdom represented temporal authority, the Dalai Lama represented both temporal and spiritual authority, somewhat akin to the Pope before Westphalia. So, while temporally his authority was limited within the territories of Tibet, what Charles Bell called political Tibet, even subject to, at times, to external powers, spiritually he was often 'paid respects' by various kingdoms, namely, the Mongols in Central Asia and smaller kingdoms like Sikkim and Bhutan to the south. These relationships were further complicated, for the external observer, when the later Qing dynasty re-asserted Chinese Imperial control over Tibet. Now, a Resident Ambassador – the amban – exercised significant control in Tibet's, especially external, afffairs. This limited, to some extent, the Dalai Lama's overall authority – in both realms. The conflicts of authority manifesting from the relations between political Tibet and the wider cultural Tibet would play a key role in its diplomatic trajectory in the coming years.

Towards the turn of the 18th century, the influence of the Ming Emperor on Tibet began to decline and the amban was reduced to a mere spectator at the court of the Dalai Lama in Lhasa. Now, correspondingly, the Dalai Lama began to assert his authority again. This threatened to come into conflict with British interests especially when the assertion sought to transcend the territorially organized frontier system of British India in the east. Specifically, the frontier buffer-protectorate kingdom of Sikkim. It was a purported Tibetan incursion into Sikkim that was stated as the primary reason for a British invasion of Tibet, under the guise of a diplomatic mission. Subsequent diplomacy ensured Tibet should remain entrenched under the suzerainty of the Chinese Empire, thus, limiting its intentions and operations as an independent actor.

Preliminary Assessment

Before we proceed with the discussion on the British association with Tibet a few comments to set up the frame if reference are in order.

Two factors will be prominent in the British reaction to Tibet. First, a 'cartographic anxiety of blank spaces' – with Tibet being one of the last unknown lands on the British Indian frontier. Second, an Orientalist conception of the inherent duplicitousness of the Asiatic. The first fuels the drive for gaining knowledge of the terrain, the land and its routes of access despite resistance from the Tibetans. The second leads to an implicit denial in dealing directly and honestly with the Tibetans, where British overtures for diplomacy are not diplomacy at all, but an all or nothing demand for accepting the terms they dictate. This is tragically displayed in the so called diplomatic mission, led by Francis Younghusband, to Tibet in 1903-4 which rather than being a diplomatic mission was an expeditionary force with the sole purpose of coercing the Tibetans into accepting British terms and to gain access to Lhasa. The harrowing details of the expedition lead one to wonder whether barbarism and duplicitousness more aptly describe British dealings with Tibet than the other way round.

The details of how these representations and constructions of Tibet played out in actual politics are too vast a subject to be addressed here. However, in British dealings with Tibet these ideas always played very important roles in moulding attitudes and expectations. I leave aside this discussion for now. But a brief mention of these imaginations and attitudes is necessary and should engage ones thought, especially as one considers the shifting narratives of Tibet.

It was a complete ignorance of local realities in Tibet that led to successive British policies towards the country. To the ignorance of terrain, we can add, more importantly, the ignorance of the local lived geographies of Tibet. For example, Tibet's denial of access to Lhasa to any foreigners was fundamentally on the basis of the religio-cultural importance of Lhasa, the seat of the Dalai Lama. This, however, was perceived as evidence of conspiracy and intrigue. One wonders, really, what was behind the desire to reach Lhasa. Was it really strategic or merely an urge to shatter the obstinacy of an Asiatic ruler who refused to treat the British with a privilege they thought they rightfully deserved? Also, one should recognize how the 'in-betweenness' of Tibet continues to remain the primary frame of reference. Tibet is never engaged in its own right.

And nowhere is this more evident than in Lord Curzon's views on the strategic importance of Tibet.

TIBET DISAGREEMENTS

According to John W. Garver, Nehru's policy on Tibet was to create a strong Sino-Indian partnership which would be catalyzed through agreement and compromise on Tibet. Garver believes that Nehru's previous actions (befriending China on such issues as war in Korea, the PRC's U.N. admission, the peace treaty with Japan and transfer of Taiwan to the PRC, Indochina, and decolonization and the Afro-Asian movement) had given Nehru a confidence that China would be ready to form an "Asian Axis" with India. Much misunderstanding between the two nations led to diplomatic spats over Tibet, with Nehru's move to accommodate the Dalai Lama overshadowing his other actions and opinions on Tibet, including the opinion that an armed resistance movement in Tibet would be suicidal and counterproductive. While China treated India's concerns with Tibet as expansionist, Some in India claim that its concerns were in fact sentimental and culturally-linked, as Buddhist Tibet had been under influence of Indian culture for many years.

Top PRC leader Mao Zedong was humiliated by the reception the Dalai Lama obtained in India when he fled there in March 1959. The Tibet disagreements heightened in the Chinese media, with Mao himself asking Xinhua News Agency on 19 April to produce commentary on unknown Indian expansionists operating in Tibet. Mao decided on April 25 to openly criticize Nehru for his Tibet policy:

"Be sharp, don't fear to irritate him [Nehru], don't fear to cause him trouble. Nehru miscalculated the situation believing that China could not suppress the rebellion in Tibet and would have to beg India's help. — Mao Zedong addressing a Politburo Standing Committee

Tensions steadily increased between the two nations when Mao implied that the Lhasa rebellion in Tibet was caused by Indians. On 6 May 1959, Mao published "The Revolution in Tibet and Nehru's Philosophy" where he accused Nehru of openly encouraging Tibetan rebels. This publication was evident of China's perception of India as a threat to its rule of Tibet, which became an underlying reason for triggering the Sino-Indian War. India had become the imperialist enemy, with Nehru and his "big bourgeoisie" striving to "prevent China from exercising full sovereignty over its territory of Tibet" to form of a buffer zone. On the same day, Zhou Enlai lashed out at Nehru's "class nature".

"Nehru and people from the Indian upper class oppose reform in Tibet, even to the extent of saying that reform is impossible...[They want] Tibet to remain for a long time in a backward state, becoming a 'buffer state' between China and India. This is their guiding mentality, and also the center of the Sino-Indian conflict. – Zhou Enlai

India continued negotiations about Tibet. According to the Indian official history, India wished to express goodwill to China and stop the claims of it having a hostile design in Tibet.

In August 1959, the Chinese army took an Indian patrol prisoner at Longju, which falls north of the McMahon Line coordinates drawn on the Simla Treaty, signed in 1914, map (27°44'30''N), but claimed by India to lie directly on the McMahon Line. There was another bloody clash in October at Kongka Pass in Aksai Chin in which 9 Indian frontier policemen were killed. Recognizing that it was not ready for war, the Indian Army assumed responsibility for the border and pulled back patrols from disputed areas.

On October 2, Nikita Khrushchev defended Nehru in a meeting with Mao. The Soviet Union's siding with Nehru, as well as the United States' influence in the region, gave China the belief that it was surrounded by enemy forces. On 16 October, General Lei Yingfu reported on Indian expansionism on the Thag La Ridge. On 18 October, the Chinese government approved the PLA's plan of a "self-defensive counterattack" against India because of its actions in Tibet.

However, Mao decided against further escalation because he feared that India would retaliate by permitting the U.S. to station U-2 surveillance aircraft on its territory. This would allow the CIA to photograph China's nuclear test site at Lop Nor in Xinjiang. A few days after Kongka Pass, Chinese Prime Minister Zhou Enlai proposed that each side withdraw 20 kilometres from a "Line of Actual Control". He defined this line as "the so-called McMahon Line in the east and the line up to which each side exercises actual control in the west". Nehru responded with a proposal to turn the disputed area into a no man's land.

Chinese studies of the 1990s still maintain that India was planning aggression in Tibet. Most Chinese scholars believe that the root cause of the war was India's plan to seize Tibet and turn it into a protectorate or colony of India. The official Chinese history of the war states that Nehru was planning to create a "great Indian empire". It was also insisted that there were right wing nationalist forces that influenced Nehru to pursue the goal of controlling Tibet. Zhao Weiwen, of the Chinese Ministry of State and Security, places emphasis on Nehru's "dark mentality".

China's policy on Tibet did much to heighten the conflict and tensions between the two nations. The perceptions of India as a capitalist expansionist body intent on the independence of Tibet to create a buffer zone between India proper and China was fundamentally erroneous. The negative rhetoric led to what Zhou himself called the Sino-Indian conflict. Because of these false fears, China treated the Indian Forward Policy of the 1960s, which India admits as a fundamental mistake, as the beginning of Indian expansionism into Tibet.

'TIBETAN INDEPEDENCE' BROOKS NO DISCUSSION

The central government has adopted a consistent policy towards the Dalai Lama. It urges him to renounce separatism and return to the stand of patriotism and unity. On December 28, 1978, the Chinese leader Deng Xiaoping said to AP correspondents that "the Dalai Lama may return, but only as a Chinese citizen"; "we have but one demand — patriotism. And we say that anyone is welcome, whether he embraces patriotism early or late." This indicates the central government's attitude of welcoming the Dalai Lama back to the motherland.

The Dalai Lama sent representatives to Beijing to contact the central government on February 28, 1979. On March 12, Deng Xiaoping met the Dalai Lama's representatives and said to them, "The Dalai Lama is welcome to come back. He can go out again after his return." With regard to the central government's negotiation with the side of the Dalai Lama, Deng pointed out, "Now, whether the dialogue to discuss and settle problems will be between the central government and Tibet as a state or Tibet as a part of China? This is a practical question." "Essentially Tibet is a part of China. This is the criterion for judging right or wrong." The central government did everything possible to persuade the Dalai Lama and his followers, through negotiations, to give up their separatism and return to the motherland. The central government leaders have since 1980 met a number of delegations sent back by the Dalai Lama and reiterated on many occasions the central government's policy towards the Dalai Lama.

To satisfy the desire of both local and overseas Tibetans for visits and contacts, the central government has formulated and practiced the policy of free movement in and out of the country. It has also made clear that all patriots belong to one big family, whether they rally to the common cause now or later, and bygones can be bygones. From August 1979 to September 1980, central government departments concerned received three visiting delegations and two groups of relatives sent by the Dalai Lama. Most of the Dalai Lama's kin residing abroad have made return visits to China. Since 1979, Tibet and other Tibetan-inhabited areas have received some 8,000 overseas Tibetans who came to visit relatives or for sightseeing, and helped settle nearly 2,000 Tibetan compatriots.

Regretfully, the Dalai Lama did not draw on the good will of the central government. Instead, he further intensified his separatist activities. At a meeting of the Human Rights Subcommittee of the US Congress held in September 1987, the Dalai Lama put forward a "five-point proposal" regarding the so-called status of Tibet. He continued to advocate "Tibetan Independence," and instigate and plot a number of riots in Lhasa. In June 1988, the Dalai Lama raised a so-called "Strasbourg proposal" for the solution of the Tibet issue. On the premise that Tibet "had always been" an independent state, the proposal interpreted the issue of a regional national autonomy within a country as a relationship between a suzerain and a vassal state, and between a protector and a protected state, thus denying China's sovereignty over Tibet and advocating the independence of Tibet in a disguised way. The central government naturally rejected the proposal, because it was a conspiracy the imperialists once hatched in order to carve up China. The Chinese government solemnly declared, "China's sovereignty over Tibet brooks no denial. Of Tibet there could be no independence, nor semi-independence, nor independence in disguise." Nevertheless, the central government still hopes that the Dalai Lama would rein in at the brink of the precipice and change his mind. In early 1989, the 10th Bainqen Lama passed away. Taking into account the historical religious ties between various generations of the Dalai Lama and the Bainqen Lama as teacher and student, the Buddhist Association of China, with the approval of the central government, invited the Dalai Lama to come back to attend the Bainqen Lama's memorial ceremonies. President Zhao Puchu of the association handed a letter of invitation to a personal representative of the Dalai Lama, providing the Dalai Lama with a good opportunity to meet with people in the Buddhist circles in China after 30 years of exile. But the Dalai Lama rejected the invitation.

As 1989 witnessed a new international anti-China wave, the Nobel Peace Prize Committee in Norway, with clearly political motives, awarded the 1989 Nobel Peace Prize to the Dalai Lama, giving its strong support to the Dalai Lama and the Tibetan separatists. Since then, the Dalai Lama has travelled the world, advocating Tibet's separation from China.

The Dalai Lama simultaneously intensified his efforts to incite and plot riots in Tibet. On January 19, 1990, he said over the BBC: If the Beijing government fails to hold talks with him on his plan of Tibet's autonomy within a year, he will have to change his stand of compromise with China; many young Tibetans stand for the use of force. On April 4, 1991, the Dalai Lama said in the Tibetan language program of the Voice of America, "All matters shall be further strengthened for Tibet's independence." Again on October 10 the same year, he tried instigation in a similar program, "At present, so large a number of Hans are pouring into Tibet that many young Tibetans cannot find jobs. This adds a further element of instability in the Tibetan society. Therefore, new riots are quite possible."

It is because the Dalai Lama sticks to his position of "Tibetan independence" and continues his efforts to split the motherland in and outside China that contacts between the central government and the representatives of the Dalai Lama have yielded no results.

In an interview with Xinhua News Agency reporters on May 19, 1991, on the eve of the 40th anniversary of Tibet's peaceful liberation, Premier Li Peng of the State Council of the People's

Republic of China pointed out, "The central government's policy towards the Dalai Lama has been consistent and remains unchanged. We have only one fundamental principle, namely, Tibet is an inalienable part of China. On this fundamental issue there is no room for haggling. The central government has always expressed its willingness to have contact with the Dalai Lama, but he must stop activities to split the motherland and change his position for 'Tibetan independence.' All matters except 'Tibetan independence' can be discussed."

The central government is willing to contact and negotiate with the Dalai Lama; the door remains open. The central government's policy towards the Dalai Lama is also clear. To be responsible for the history, the Chinese nation and its 1.1 billion people, including the Tibetan people, the central government will make not the slightest concession on the fundamental issue of maintaining the motherland's unification.

Any activity attempting to realize "Tibetan independence" and split the motherland by relying on foreign forces is an ignominious move betraying the motherland and the whole Chinese nation including the Tibetan nationality. The central government resolutely denounces this kind of action and will never allow it to succeed. The central government will continue to implement a series of special policies and preferential measures to promote the construction and development of Tibet so as to enhance national unity, construct a prosperous economy, enrich culture and improve the people's livelihood. Any activity sabotaging stability and unity in Tibet and any unlawful deed creating disturbance and inciting riots runs against the basic interests of the Tibetan people and will be cracked down on relentlessly.

So long as the Dalai Lama can give up his divisive stand and admit that Tibet is an inalienable part of China, the central government is willing to hold talks at any time with him. The Dalai Lama is warmly welcome to return to the embrace of the motherland at an early date and do some work that is conducive to maintaining the motherland's unification, the national unity, as well as the affluent and happy lives of the Tibetan people.

TIBET WORK FORUMS

Having consolidated itself in Tibet by 1960, Mao spent the next two decades establishing the hold over the party in China and elsewhere. The disastrous Great Leap Forward, the Cultural Revolution, skirmishes with USSR and war with Vietnam diverted Chinese attention from Tibet. Tibet was ruled with an iron hand and the party went about its task of assimilating Tibet with the mainland with missionary zeal.

The end of 70s ushered in a period of liberalisation under Deng Xiaoping. The Chinese Government established the Tibet Work Forum, the first forum for policy formulation towards the development in Tibet. The First and Second Forums (1984) were influenced by party moderates such as Hu Yaobang and set out relatively liberal policies for Tibet work. The Third Tibet Work Forum, (1994) post Tiananmen and largescale demonstrations in the 1980s, made major changes in China's Tibet Policy. The leadership felt the Tibet policy was too liberal and made too many concessions to Tibetan nationalists. It ruled out the possibility of any 'Tibetan-ised' form of development and enforced, instead, a policy of assimilating and integrating Tibet into the wider economic and cultural model of the People's Republic of China (PRC).

With China embracing the policy of fast-track economic development and 'opening up', this policy resulted in a massive influx of Chinese Han migrant workers and entrepreneurs into Tibet. The leadership also replaced its moderate policies of encouraging Tibetan culture, religion and participation of Tibetans in government and the economy by enforcing new laws on religion and providing job opportunities to the Tibetans. The consequences were immediate: political repression; tighter internal security, longer sentences for political offences, increased control over monasteries and nunneries, and intensified political education in schools.

Officials at the Third Work Forum described the Tibetan independence movement as a snake, and their attempts to 'cut off the serpent's head' led to restrictions on the spread of Buddhism and a political campaign to destroy the religious as well as the political standing of the Dalai Lama. The Fourth Tibet Work Forum provided a central mandate for the policies currently being implemented and endorsed the general policies decided at the Third Forum and carried them forward. The emphasis of the Fifth Tibet Work Forum, held in January 2010, was on plans for 'leap forward development,' intended to bring levels of income and other economic indicators into line with those in other parts of the PRC.

The large-scale extraction of resources and the strengthening of the state's authority and control over Tibetan areas underpin China's ambitious 'Western Development Strategy'(WDS) which has now been in place for a decade. The Fifth Tibet Work Forum emphasised the scientific concept of development, comprehensively building a moderately prosperous society, a need to build a national ecological security barrier and achieve sustainable development, all this while ensuring national unity, social stability, safeguard to national security and creation of a favourable international environment. The issue of Tibet's ecology and waters also took centre stage as it was important to protect China's influence and control over Tibet's water supply, which is of critical importance to the highly water-dependent societies inside Tibet and millions of people in Asia. President Hu Jintao stated: 'It is all the more necessary to pay attention to turning Tibet into an important national security screen, an important strategic resources reserve base.'

The sustainable management of Tibet's water is increasingly becoming a serious security issue in the region and leading to tensions due to China's economic and environmental policies. However, these Work Forums have not achieved the desired aim of 'assimilating' the Tibetan people. According to Professor Dibyesh Anand, 'The problem with Tibet Work Forums is that they do not address political issues.'

Growth Indicators in TAR

The Central Government has been providing huge amount of aid to Tibet since 2001. During the 10th Five-Year Plan period (2001- 05) alone, it allocated 37 billion Yuan ($5.4 billion) to Tibet in subsidies and 32.2 billion Yuan ($4.5 billion) to 117 projects. In 2011, official figures report that, the Chinese government had earmarked 310 billion Yuan for 188 development projects in Tibet since 2001. Of this, 200 billion Yuan ($29.3 billion) has been allotted in various kinds of subsidies, with an annual average growth rate of 20 per cent, and 110 billion Yuan (16.1 billion dollars) has gone to fixed assets investment, including construction of the Qinghai-Tibet Railway.

With the assistance of the Central Government, Tibet has been able to maintain a double-digit growth in terms of GDP for 17 straight years, outpacing the national average. Jin Shixun, director of the Tibet Autonomous Regional Development and Reform Commission (TARDRC) said that in the past nine years, Tibet has achieved the fastest social and economic development and the Tibetan people have improved their living standard most substantially. According to the Fifth Aid-Tibet Work Conference, Development, Literacy, Health and Public utilities have improved manifold since the 1950s. There has been a massive influx of money to build infrastructure – highways, railways and power projects.

GDP has increased 30 times since 1950. Life expectancy has increased from 35.5 years in 1950 to 67 years. Literacy rates are up from 2 per cent to 30 per cent and the per capita income has doubled in five years from 2078 Yuan in 2005 to 4138 Yuan in 2010. Notwithstanding these indicators, there continues to be a 'trust deficit' between the Chinese Government and the Tibetan people. Despite huge investments by the Chinese Government in Tibet, the vast majority of Tibetans remain severely disadvantaged both socially and economically by the inadequate provision of education, welfare and health care, and marginalised by the influx of Chinese migrants attracted by these strategies. The implementation of policies to settle Tibetan nomads and to resettle Tibetans in towns, is now threatening the livelihoods of hundreds of thousands of people.

The Chinese policies of development, which are based on an urban industrial model in an area that is predominantly rural, are counter-productive; they have increased rather than closed the gap between urban and rural, rich and poor, Chinese and Tibetan, and have degraded Tibet's fragile ecosystem. I argue that this 'trust deficit' is a collective impact of a number of issues of social and religious significance which have been neglected by the Chinese Government. No amount of money inflow or economic progress will win over the Tibetan people. These key issues are; Demographic aggression or Hanisation; Socio – economic inequalities like wage discrimination, unemployment and denial of equal opportunities and; Religious intolerance.

Hanisation of Tibet

The invasion of Tibet by the PLA which commenced in 1950, ostensibly to integrate Tibet with the mainland, culminated in violent attacks and rebellion in 1959. While no official Chinese records or documents are available for the loss of life, livestock and property, during this period, there is sufficient proof and evidence cited by emigrants of Tibet of terrible repression and savagery inflicted by the PLA on the Tibetan people.

Some term it as 'genocide'. The ingrained prejudice against the minorities is a historical truth and Han always treated the minorities with mistrust and disdain. The major policy that the Chinese pursued once Tibet was subjugated was to change its demography. Mao is quoted as saying, 'Tibet covers a large area but is thinly populated. Its population should be increased from the present two or three million to five or six million and then to over 10 million.' This was done by engineering large scale migration of Han Chinese into Tibet with the ultimate aim of reducing Tibetans to a minority in their own land. Clearly Mao wanted to 'Hanise' Tibet. Conflicting reports of population of TAR are available through a number of sources. Official Chinese Government figures are 2.62 million (2000 census) of Tibetans in TAR, but the Dalai Lama's office disputes the official figure and believes that 7.5 million Chinese live alongside six million Tibetans in TAR. The Dalai Lama's office figures seem exaggerated as they include the entire erstwhile state of Tibet. However, in Amdo (Qinghai) and Kham (Sichuan) the Han have already outstripped the locals. Asia Watch in its report in 1990 has disagreed with these figures of 7.5 million given by TGIE but agrees that the migration has been sizeable. Robert McCorquodale and Nicholas Orosz have in a report concluded that, 'a very significant transfer of Chinese to Tibet has taken place since 1949-59.' The report quotes Asia Watch Report 1990 that, 'majority of population in Lhasa is clearly Chinese.'

The report adds, 'in essence, the authorities appear to be applying a discriminatory policy barring Tibetans from coming to Lhasa, while placing no restriction whatever on Chinese migration into the city......a professionally capable and strategically placed Chinese population seems to be the key element in the Chinese Government's plans for the integrated and military development in Tibet.' In June 1987, Deng-Xiaoping admitted that, the Chinese were being encouraged to move to Tibet as the regions two million population is inadequate to develop its resources. Venting his fears at the National People's Congress in 1987, the late Panchen Lama said, 'The expense of keeping one Chinese in Tibet is equal to that of four in China.

Why should Tibet spend its money to feed them?... Tibet has suffered greatly because of the policy of sending a large number of useless people. The Chinese population in Tibet started with a few thousand and today it has multiplied manifold.' So how has this 'demographic aggression' or 'Han migration' affected the average Tibetan in Tibet? To encourage migration from mainland China, the Chinese Government announced a slew of attractive benefits and concessions for its employees and settlers. According to Chinese economists, 'The personnel brought in from developed regions cannot be expected to live on the local fare of tsampi (roasted barley flour) and raw meat. They need good housing, hospitals, cinemas and schools for their children.' The benefits to migrant were: housing, health care, special leave to China, cultural and educational facilities, high altitude allowance; 87 per cent higher wages than in China, special tax exemptions and loans at low interest rates. Above all, the one child policy did not apply to Chinese settled in Tibet. However, to be fair to China's Tibet Policy, Tibet was given favourable treatment. Tibetan businesses enjoyed a preferential tax rate of three per cent lower than mainland China, farmers and herdsmen were exempted from taxes and administrative charges.

Banks have enjoyed a preferential interest rate of two points lower than the mainland as well as low rate on insurance premiums. All this has ensured a double digit growth for TAR for a decade. Has this benefited the Tibetans? In one decade (2000-09) in Tibet, the average savings in rural China were pegged at 1160 Yuan. Yet for Tibet this is 1080 Yuan, well below the national average. Even in business, sales in state owned and individual (largely Han owned in cities) enterprises during the period 2000 to 2009 multiplied five times, but 'others'- smaller/household businesses owned by the common people just trebled over the same period. Large businesses like wholesale and retail, hotels, restaurants etc. multiplied four times over the last decade (2000-09) but 'others'- small business, largely household and small shops stagnated. It may be argued that overall Tibet has benefited but the fruits have not trickled down to 76.2 per cent of the population that is largely rural as per 2009 figures.

During his visit to Lhasa, Professor Dibyesh Anand observed that there were no Tibetan shop owners in Lhasa, only Han and Hui. The smiling and happy Tibetans holding latest mobile phones were only those seen on large posters in Lhasa. The modern Tibetan village was located behind those posters in Lhasa…and that is where Tibetans lived in extreme poverty. Natural growth rate has dropped by 40 per cent in Tibet over the period 1990-09, with birth rate also dropping by 40 per cent over the same period, indicating economic pressures are forcing people to have smaller families to earn a livelihood. There are reports that Tibetans have been relocated to higher reaches in Kham and Amdo areas leaving the fertile valleys for the Han. In 1959 the total area of TAR under farming was 0.2 per cent largely restricted to the river valleys. By 1991 it had increased to 0.3 per cent (almost 50 per cent) largely due to influx of migrants. However, increase in cultivable land was at the cost of pasture land forcing the nomads and the shepherds to look for pastures in higher reaches as also overuse the pastures upsetting the fragile ecology balance. More importantly, this has resulted in a drop in cropland per capita. In Ganze prefecture, for e.g, cropland increased by 4562 hectares while population increased by 255,293 thereby resulting in drop of per capita cropland from 0.17 hectares to 0.11 hectares.

In 2006, a relocation project moved 290,000 Tibetans into urban homes - almost 10 per cent of the whole Tibetan population. Critics of the location policy cited that, China had not researched its urbanisation policy and the effects it would have on employment, jobs and Tibetan culture.

Socio-Economic Inequalities

The condition of 2.21 million Tibetans out of 2.90 million, living in rural areas does not seem to have improved much over the last decade. In 2000, the average number of able-bodied and semi-able bodied labourers in a household of 6.78 persons (say 7) was 3.91 (say 4). By 2009, the average household size had marginally reduced to 6.27 but the average number of labourers barely reduced to 3.88. Assuming that, at least two persons in a family are elders and one child, the pressure on the average Tibetan family in rural areas to work seems to remain unchanged.

All adults have to work to make a living. In 1999, the average rural household saved 542 Yuan a year. A decade later the figure just doubled to 1137 Yuan. The average urban household, largely migrants, on the other hand had an annual disposable income of 5998 Yuan in 1999 and a decade later, 13,544 Yuan - almost 12 times the rural household, indicating a large inequality in the distribution of wealth. Wages of workers in state owned enterprises, largely held by Han and few Tibetans, remain the highest at 50,272 Yuan per annum with certain departments like Public Management and Social Organisation being the most sought after at 55,215 Yuan. In contrast, low end government jobs in urban collective owned units (cooperatives) which are largely reserved for Tibetans average 12,231 Yuan per annum, less than a quarter of state owned enterprises. Interestingly, labour remuneration accounted for two thirds of the GDP in TAR. A closer look at the 'staff and workers' reveals that these group represent upper ranking cadres and workers in public utilities or state owned enterprises. It does not include the migrant or service workers who are from the mainland for a short period of time. Thus, Tibetans have increasingly been marginalised from the areas that generate the GDP in TAR.

The benefits of the increase of wages have been disproportionately captured by non-Tibetans over a period of time. The per capita savings in 2009 in Tibet were 6445 Yuan whereas in comparison, similar provinces like Gansu (9364 Yuan) and Yunnan (8327 Yuan) have a much better record of savings, an indication of the inequality in Tibet versus other similar regions in the mainland. The comparison with cities on the East coast would be too stark and is best avoided. The Tibetans have largely been an agrarian society, and agriculture has been the predominant occupation. The changing economy of Tibet and the policies of the government have forced the Tibetans to change their economic model to shift focus to urban livelihood. In 1999, out of a total GDP of 107 million Yuan, the primary industry (agriculture) earned a GDP of 34.2 million Yuan (31 per cent) whereas tertiary industry, still in infancy (services, rent, hotels, etc) earned 47.4 million Yuan (44 per cent).

A decade later, primary industry doubled to 63.9 million Yuan (reduced to 14 per cent in real terms) but tertiary industry multiplied six times to 240 million Yuan (increased to 54 per cent, substantiating the argument that Tibetans have been forced to abandon their traditional occupation in recent years and take to other means of livelihood. The annual per capita income of a rural household in 2009 in Lhasa was 4149 Yuan, of which 1095 Yuan (about 26 per cent) only was from wages and salaries and as much as 2232 Yuan (53 per cent) from household business operation- an indication that wages alone are highly inadequate to sustain a rural household. In the interiors of Tibet, like Nagqu and Ngari prefectures, the income is almost entirely dependent on household business with almost no wages or salaries. Unemployment among the youth is a rising phenomenon. Since Mandarin is the principle medium of teaching, local Tibetans have lost out on jobs which puts Han settlers at an advantage. Tourism is a booming industry but fluency in Mandarin is a must for people to become local guides.

This has effectively placed local Tibetans at a disadvantage. The entire taxi driver community is Han Chinese as taxi drivers are also supposed to be fluent in Mandarin. Chinese migrants are offered tax concessions, leniency on work permits, bonuses and greater market opportunities. During his visit to China in 1996, Shanker Sharan an Indian, observed, 'For strategic reasons as well as for it's national resources, Chinese rulers do not soften their own grip over Tibet. Chinese logic continues to assert that even after four decades of their rule, Tibet cannot develop it's own ... the situation in Tibet is – Tibetans working, Hans controlling... fear and repression have been internalised among the people.'

The outcome of this has been the marginalisation of Tibetans in their own homeland. When communities are alienated, deprived and denied their rights, they breed dissent. As Barry Sautman says, 'The Chinese government does see economic development as a panacea to cure all problems with ethnic minorities, but economic reforms, with its attendant unemployment, inflation and corruption has set many Tibetans on edge. The potential for inter-ethnic competition that comes with the development is unsettling. Where competition is seen as unfair and occurs in a context of low ethnic interdependence as in Tibet, ethnic conflict and separation are likely to surge'. But as long as Tibetans are without any international support, it does not worry the CPC.

Yan Xuetong, a Chinese scholar says, 'If separatists abroad get no support from China's neighbours, they will become frustrated and fail. And China based separatists without international endorsement are not worth worrying about.' This emboldens the PLA and the CPC to unleash its policy on hapless Tibetans without fear of external intervention or interference. According to Barry Sautman, 'PRC leaders are sure that troops in Tibet will contain any violence initiated by emigrant Tibetans and can accept that as long as China is not fractured, India will not abet Tibetan militancy, since it fears a two front war.'

Religious Intolerance

The average Tibetan is a deeply religious person. Religion has been ingrained in Tibetan society and Tibetan life, culture, festivals and beliefs centre on religion. When China annexed Tibet, 90 per cent of the Tibetans lived in the countryside, and there were only two major professions- farming and religious pursuit- tend to the land and cattle or become a monk. The Chinese policy of religious persecution and religious intolerance has left indelible scars in this deeply religious society.

Samdhong Rinpoche, the Tibetan PM in exile, while speaking on the occasion of the 50 years of Tibetan occupation, summed it up, 'Since the invasion, the Chinese have done everything possible to wipe out the Tibetan identity, culture and religious heritage. But they have not achieved anything; on the contrary, in the last 50 years, we have emerged even stronger and united in our struggle and determination to preserve our Tibetan identity, culture and religious heritage—both inside and outside Tibet'. Kerry Dumbagh, in a Congressional Research Service (CRS) report for the US Congress notes that, while the physical infrastructure of religious institutions in Tibet appears better maintained than five years ago, there are fewer signs of religious devotion at Lhasa's holiest sites than in the past. Controversial issues that have hurt Tibetan religious sentiments are:-

- *Demonisation of the Dalai Lama:* The Dalai Lama has been both the spiritual and temporal head of the Tibetans for centuries. He is at the heart of the Buddhist culture of Tibet. The Chinese Government has made all attempts to demonise and discredit the Dalai Lama as a 'traitor' and a 'wolf in a sheep skin'. This has been a source of deep resentment amongst the Tibetan people. According to Wang Lixiong, 'To Tibetans, the Dalai Lama is not just an individual; he represents the Dalai genealogy and the system has sustained Tibet for more than five centuries…..hostility to the Dalai Lama is not simply seen as hostility to him, but is tantamount to hostility towards the entire Dalai genealogy, the entire Tibetan religious system and the whole Tibetan nation.'
- *Selection of the 11th Panchen Lama:* The Chinese Government has selected their own Panchen Lama - five-yearold Gyaltsen Norbu, son of a yak herder, officially enthroned as the 11th Panchen Lama in a ceremony attended by some Tibetan monks and senior Chinese communist leaders rejecting centuries old tradition of the Dalai Lama's choice. The Chinese have also put the 'real' Panchen Lama, Gedhun Cheokyi Nyima, and his family under arrest and he has never been seen since 1995.
- On August 3, 2007, the State Administration for Religious Affairs (SARA) issued a set of regulations that require all Tibetan lamas wishing to reincarnate to obtain prior

government approval through the submission of a 'reincarnation application.' The 'reincarnation applications' require coming from 'legally registered venues' for Tibetan Buddhism. Management Measures for the Reincarnation of Living Buddhas in Tibetan Buddhism, proclaimed that, 'the reincarnation of Living Buddha's shall not be interfered or dominated by any organisation or individual abroad (read the Dalai Lama) ... the reincarnation of living Buddha's should fulfil the application and approval procedures.' This law attempts to ensure control over the succession of the Dalai Lama by ensuring his successor will be born in China.

- Freedom of movement of monks and nuns has been severely restricted in TAR for purposes of teaching studying or practising religion. All such moves require a lengthy process of permission, reports and approvals from the local government and prefectures.
- Forcible patriotic education of monks and nuns in monasteries: During the 'monastery rectification', many monks chose to be forced out of monasteries rather than obey an order to slander the Dalai Lama in public. According to Tibetan belief, cursing their teacher would take them to hell. China failed to recognise the huge influence that monks and priests have on ordinary Tibetans.

China continues to hold a rigid stance on the issue of religion and the Dalai Lama. Chinese arguments on Tibet are underlined by intention of separatism and threat to national unity, thereby blocking all avenues of rapprochement.

Since February 2009, 21 Tibetans- 19 men and two women- set themselves ablaze protesting against China's religious repression in Sichuan and TAR. 14 out of them were clergy or former clergy persons. Self immolation is increasingly being seen as an accepted expression of religious oppression and the harsh response by the government against such acts has only given this more popularity and publicity.

Nicholas Bequelin, a senior researcher in Hong Kong for Human Rights Watch is quoted in the *New York Times* as saying that, the Chinese Government is trying to prevent incidents by strengthening controls, but too much repression and control provokes these acts suggesting a vicious circle. According to Dibyesh Anand, the immolations are by those monks and nuns who protested and were thrown out of monasteries post 2008. As per the new rules and regulations, no person with criminal record can join monasteries. Since cases were registered against these monks and they had no other place to go, they were left with little option but to immolate themselves.

The Human Rights Watch was also scathing in its report on Chinese intolerance, 'The Chinese authorities have not heeded the demands of Tibetans, but have instead resorted to heavy-handed tactics that can only deepen and further fuel resentment. They must respect the right of Tibetans to practice their religion and to enjoy their culture.' Unable to find a solution to the 'immolation problem', Zhu Weiqun, the Head of United Front Work Department (UFWD), Tibet Section and the official spokesman for Tibet wrote in the *The Study Times* (Xuexi Shibao) that, 'Some of our current educational and administrative policies have unintentionally weakened (the minority people's) sense of nationhood and Chinese nationalism....... The best way to achieve 'national cohesion' is by stopping to give them separate status as an ethnic minority on identity cards, using ethnic labels in the titles of schools and autonomous regions, and giving them privileges reserved for minorities'.

Clearly, China intends to abolish special privileges and preferential policies to its minorities, a radical policy recommendation in China's 'minorities policy'. This is also in violation of the '17-Article Agreement' signed by the Tibetan local Government, often cited as the basis of China's march into Tibet. It stipulates: 'the Central Government will not change the existing political system of Tibet, nor will it change the Dalai Lama's inherent status and position', 'In matters relating to reforms in Tibet, there would be no coercion on the part of the central authorities, and the reform would be carried out by the Tibetan local Government of its own accord. Consultations with local Tibet leaders shall be made when the people show desire for the reform.'

3

Tibetan Refugees' Rights and Services

The Chinese assault of Tibet, and the Dalai Lama's following decision to flee in 1959, resulted in the mass influx of Tibetan refugees into India that continue today.

It has become clear to the Indian government, as well as to the Tibetan community in exile, that repatriation is unlikely in the near prospect. Consequently, an evaluation of India's protection of, and assistance for Tibetan refugees is necessary to ensure their treatment is in accordance with international standards. Unfortunately, such an assessment shows that there is a lack of proper protections and services; this ought to be of particular concern to the international community as India has served on the Executive Committee of the United Nations High Commissioner for Refugees (UNHCR) since 1995.

How can a country be trusted to lead an international organization dedicated to the protection of refugees when it has such unstable and inadequate refugee policies itself? Central to the assessment is India's lack of legal compulsion to provide refugee protections or services. This is largely a consequence of India's abstention from the 1951 Convention relating to the Status of Refugees and the subsequent 1967 Protocol, which, in addition to defining a refugee according to international law, outlines certain rights and services host states must afford them. With the exceptions of the customary international practice of *non-refoulement* and the obligation to provide asylum as outlined in Article 14 of the Universal Declaration of Human Rights (UDHR), India does not have international, regional, or national obligations to refugee populations on its soil (Feller 2006). Despite this, and despite the nation's refusal to accede to the 1951 Convention, India argues its current refugee policy is in accordance with international norms. However, India has no national refugee law, and no regional agreement on the matter exists.

The only mention of foreigners in Indian law are in the Registration of Foreigners Act of 1939, the Foreigners Act of 1946, and the Foreigners Order of 1948— all of which employ the term *foreigner*, broadly defined as "a being who is not a citizen of India." Among other practices, the 1946 Act and the 1948 Order allow the government to limit employment opportunities, freedom of association, and a foreigner's possessions.

These pieces of legislation also restrict movement inside India and prohibit select activities, most of which are political. In fact, Tibetan refugees are only allowed in India on the condition that they abstain from political protests against China – a clear suppression of their right to political expression as afforded by the UDHR. This political suppression was particularly evident during the 1991 visit of then Chinese Prime Minister Li Peng, during which Tibetan refugee leaders were arrested and placed under police surveillance to curtail protests. A similar occurrence was witnessed during Prime Minister Wen Jiabao's 2010 visit. Human rights law grants refugees fundamental civil and political rights, yet the Indian government denies these rights to Tibetan refugees.

India's lack of legal obligation allows it to change refugee policies at will, often to reflect its current political interests. The result is a rather unstable refugee policy, exemplified in the disparity of rights and services afforded to Tibetan refugees according to their date of arrival in the country. The Indian government regarded the first wave of Tibetans arriving in 1959 with the Dalai Lama as refugees and granted them legal asylum. They were allotted land and housing – a privilege not afforded to other foreigners and one that would later be denied to newly arriving Tibetans.

More importantly, these refugees were automatically given a Registration Certificate (RC). According to the Tibetan Government-in-Exile, the Central Tibetan Administration (CTA), the RC is a legal document issued by the Indian establishment that allows Tibetan refugees "the right to enjoy all the privileges enjoyed by any Indian citizen except the right to vote and work in Indian government offices" (Immigration and Refugee Board of Canada 2009).

While many question the extent of the 'privileges enjoyed' by RC-holding Tibetans, the value of the RC is not contested. The RC allows Tibetans to legally travel and work within the country, serves as an identity document, and is a pre-requisite for the Identity Certificate, which is necessary for international travel.

Tibetan refugees arriving between 1959 and the 1970s also benefited from services provided by the UNHCR, which despite its tumultuous relationship with India had a temporary presence in the country. The rights and services afforded to Tibetans inward after the 1970s are scarce and indicative of a changing Indian policy—arguably in an effort to preserve Sino-Indian relations.

In 1963, the Indian government ceased to legally recognize arriving Tibetans as refugees. Consequently, those arriving after 1979 (including some arriving in the late 1960s) have had greater difficulty acquiring RCs.

The newer process to acquire an RC is arduous and particularly concerning because employment, residency rights, and international travel are contingent upon this document. In addition, while the Indian government provided land to the original refugee community, newer arrivals have not been as fortunate. The denial of land by the government is troublesome considering that farming is chief to a Tibetan's income and Indian law prohibits foreigners from purchasing land.

Additionally, the UNHCR closed its office in New Delhi and discontinued its aid to Tibetan refugees in 1975. As a consequence of the Indian government's lack of assistance, the CTA (with substantial assistance from NGOs) has had to shoulder the burden of providing for these refugees. Although the CTA is able to cover basic needs, they are overwhelmed and are unable to effectively address the broader social welfare of this burgeoning community (Adams 2005). Even those with the RC carry on to struggle with their refugee status.

Unable to gain Indian citizenship, they cannot vote, work for local or federal governments, carry an Indian passport, or legally purchase land. Although Tibetans possessing an RC can legally work in pre-approved segments of the economy, many employers often discriminate against them in favor of Indian nationals. This resentment originates from the belief that Tibetan refugees are adversely affecting job opportunities and that they benefit from elevated standards of services not afforded to Indian nationals.

While it is believed that communal relations between the Tibetans and the Indian host community have been improving, there have been isolated reports of aggression and discrimination that have largely gone uninvestigated by local police.

To further exacerbate this issue, Tibetans are not represented in the local and central legislature and thus do not have readily available avenues for redress. In 1949, when the United Nations debated legal protection versus material assistance for refugees, India argued that "the guarantee of legal rights without concomitant material assistance was a hollow concept" (Oberoi 2006, 22).

However, it has become clear that as Tibetans continue to cross the border, India has not only decreased the rights afforded to these newcomers, but too the services provided to them. Given that repatriation for this refugee community does not appear possible in the immediate future, India needs to concern itself with improving its policy toward this population— thereby affording refugees the proper protection and treatment per international standards. Signing the 1951 Convention would be the best avenue by which to accomplish this as it will lessen the burden on India by affording it assistance and services from the UNHCR and HUMAN RIGHTS & HUMAN WELFARE member states. Above all, India's lack of legal obligation should not be understood as an absence of Tibetan refugees' entitlement to proper services and protections.

IMMIGRATION OF TIBETAN REFUGEES IN INDIA

In the initial stage, to accommodate and help Tibetan refugees, the government of India with assistance of the state government of Assam and West Bengal set up various transit camps. In the camps they were given all the necessities. Despite of assistance, Many Tibetan refugees died as a result of living in these highly crowded and unsanitary conditions. This unfortunate state of affairs provoked urgent needs of a long-term rehabilitation program that would serve to bring all the refugees into homogenous Tibetan communities that will facilitate them to perpetrate their culture and traditions and thus preserve their national identity. Thus His Holiness theDalai Lama requested the Government of India to resettle the Tibetans in agricultural-based settlements as most of Tibetans were familiar with agricultural activities. Pt Nehru the then Prime Minister of India accepted and wrote to the government of Indian states, requesting them to make land available to refugees. Accordingly Government of Mysore (as Karnataka state was called at that time) allotted nearly 3,000 acres of land at Bylakuppe in Mysore district in Karnataka in 1960 and the first ever Tibetan exile settlement namely Lugsung Samdupling came into existence in 1961. A few years later another settlement namely Tibetan Dickey Larsoe also called as TDL was established. After that more and more Indian states provided land for Tibetan refugees.

The government of India with requests from His Holiness theDalai Lama builds special schools for Tibetans that provide free education, health care and scholarships for those students who excel in schools. At present there are 35 different Tibetan refugee settlements in India. These settlements are further classified into Agricultural base, Agro-industrial Handicraft based and scattered communities. The total refugee population figures in India according to the report of the survey conducted by the Office of His Holiness theDalai Lama and Department of Home put it at 104686. The Indian government initially provided the Tibetan refugees with excessive amenities including legal Residential Certificates and Identity Certificates.

The second phase of Tibetan refugee mass departure to India was started in late eighties and continues in steady stead till late nineties. Indian government admitted arrival of 25,000 Tibetans refugees between the years of 1986 and 1996 from Tibet. With amplifying power and dominance of Communist China in the stage of world politics and the Indian government, in an attempt to improve its relations with China, declined assistance to these Tibetan refugees, and refused to grant them new allotments of land, denied these new arrival Tibetans both residential and identification certificates.

The statement made by Exile Tibetan Government in late eighties and early nineties says "Tibetans who arrived in India after the initial settlement did not receive official refugee status from the Indian government; they were neither allocated land for housing or farming nor provided with government assistance." Additional to this, a analysis through various figures issued by Tibetan Refugee Reception Centre, a branch of Security department of Exile Tibetan Government who deals with new arrivals from Tibet, states that in an average 2500-3000 Tibetans come to India. Out of these, average of more than 60% stay back in India. This overflowing of Tibetan refugee in India and changes in the treatment of Tibetan refugee in India by Government of India, led to various problems. Central Tibetan Administration of His Holiness the Dalai Lama (CTA) argues that this has lead to overpopulation, unemployment, and food shortages in the Tibetan refugee community. Among them the unemployment among the large youth population seems to be a growing challenge that Tibetan refugee community in India face, as the possible impact it may have on the future of Tibetan fate in general and present refugee community in particular seems highly disturbing.

THE TIBETAN REFUGEES IN SOUTH ASIA

Tibetan art is deeply religious in nature, a form of sacred art. and has created and administered a cohesive and productive community underpinned by a strong and growing civil society. When future generations of Tibetans examine the Tibetan exile experience, they will point to the institutions developed in exile as the single most important element that ensured the survival of Tibet outside the plateau. From the proverb "Every cloud has a silver lining". in the ongoing Tibetan tragedy is the resurgence of Tibetan culture outside of Tibet and the creation of a productive community in exile supervised and serviced by a small but effective bureaucracy. In the introduction to the book Exile As Challenge: The Tibetan Diaspora In 1949 the People's Liberation Army of China marched into Tibet's eastern provinces of Amdo and Kham, occupying the eastern Tibetan headquarters of Chamdo in the following year., its editors, New Delhi-based writer Dagmar Bernstorff and Friedrich-Naumann Foundation director Hubertus von Welck, identify three major reasons why "the Tibetan community in exile is one of the most resilient and successful refugee groups in the world."

First, they point to the ability of individual Tibetans to survive and sustain themselves economically. Second, the educational system created in exile has succeeded in educating sectors of the population who would have been illiterate in traditional Tibetan society.

Finally, the Dalai Lama has introduced democracy to his people and is turning over political power to a directly democratically elected leader, the kalon tripa Noun 1. Kalon Tripa-the chairman of the Kashag and essentially head of the Tibetan government-in-exile Kashag-the advisory board of the Tibetan government-in-exile. Sociologists attribute the success of the rehabilitation of the Tibetan refugees and their tight community to the Central Tibetan Administration The Central Tibetan Administration (CTA), officially the Central Tibetan Administration of His Holiness the Dalai Lama, is a government in exile headed by Tenzin Gyatso, the 14th Dalai Lama, which claims to be the rightful and legitimate government of Tibet.

In this sense, the government has done a great deal for its people despite possessing very few resources. The Tibetan community taking root in exile is all the more remarkable given Tibet's earlier remoteness and isolation, which stemmed mainly from geography but could partially be attributed to choice. For this reason, in the early days of exile, the Tibetan refugees often experienced a sense of wonderment laced with deep anguish; except the selfsame self·same see adaptation. to their new surroundings as much as to catch up with the rest of the world in terms of acquisition of knowledge in all fields. That the refugees are comfortably settled in the modern world these days reflects the quality of leadership provided by the Dalai Lama and the Tibetans' devotion to him, and the tolerance and generosity of the exiles' host countries, especially India.

Indeed, the Tibetan exile community has itself made huge efforts to improve its situation, enabling the Dalai Lama and the Indian government's contributions to amount to something. In particular, other exile communities can look to the Tibetans as they struggle to remain vital, by examining their efforts in community-building, cultural preservation and resurgence and education.

A HOME IN EXILE

The 46 settlements scattered across India, Nepal, and Bhutan form the foundation of the community in exile. These are serviced by welfare officers, either directly elected by the members of the settlements or appointed by Dharamsala, local elected assemblies, schools, hospitals, old people's homes, and cooperatives. According to according to commission, committee-a special group delegated to consider some matter; "a committee is a group that keeps minutes and loses hours"-Milton Berle of the CTA, which published the finding of its first demographic survey in 2000, these settlements are home to most of the 100,451 Tibetan refugees in South Asia This article is about the geopolitical region in Asia.

South Asia, also known as Southern Asia

The idea of the refugees to live in settlements cropped up as a result of the Tibetan leadership's wishthat the Tibetans retains their culture and identity. There was the anxiety that the refugees scattered across India and not organized within structured administrative units would make them submerged within the masses of South Asia. To prevent this, the issue was discussed with then-Indian Prime Minister Jawaharlal Nehru Noun 1. Jawaharlal Nehru-Indian statesman and leader with Gandhi in the struggle for home rule; was the first prime minister of the Republic of India from 1947 to 1964 (1889-1964) Nehru, who allayed fears of Tibetan fracture by ensuring that the settlements would enable Tibetans to practice their own way of life instead of being absorbed into local populations.

The Department of Home of the CTA is responsible for the administration of the 46 Tibetan agricultural and handicraft-based settlements in India, Nepal, and Bhutan. The home department has representatives in all these settlements, all of whom function as the local administrative heads. These administrative heads are either elected locally or appointed by Dharamsala. They look after the day-to-day running of the settlements. All the settlements and those Tibetan communities, which are not organized into settlements, are served by schools, hospitals and clinics, co-operatives, courts to settle civil disputes (although criminal cases are handled by the local police of the host country), old-people's homes, and monasteries.

Keeping One's Own World

A bright spot in the Tibetans' exile experience is the spread of Tibetan Buddhism across the globe. Since 1959 when the Dalai lama, followed by 87,000 Tibetans, fled Tibet, Tibetan masters have travelled around the world to give courses on the teachings of the Buddha. This has resulted in the mushrooming of an interlocking network of Tibetan Buddhist centres. These centres teach Buddhism and Tibetan, conduct intensive meditation courses, and translate Buddhist texts into English and other languages. Some of the bigger centres have established publishing houses that produce books on Buddhism, catering to an expanding market.

Aided by the growing appreciation of their culture by non-Tibetans, the Tibetan refugees have managed to rebuild and reconstruct in exile what the Chinese authorities destroyed in Tibet. Monasteries in old Tibet served as universities and libraries, the repositories of the wisdom of Buddhist India and centres of learning where successive generations of monks inherited and passed on this knowledge to new generations. This model of monastic education, based on Nalanda, ancient India's Buddhist university, enabled the Tibetans to keep intact the complete body of Buddhist knowledge down the centuries. However, since the Chinese invasion of Tibet between 1949 and 1950 and the Cultural Revolution (1966-1976), about 6,000 Tibetan monasteries have been razed to the ground and its monks defrocked, jailed or sent to labour camps. This is the equivalent of a western country waking up to discover all its universities have disappeared overnight and their students and brilliant faculty members vanished.

Half a century years later, the Tibetan refugees have managed to rebuild the core monasteries of all the traditions of Tibetan Buddhism and that of Bon, Tibet's homegrown religion. All the heads of Tibetan Buddhism's four schools, Nyingma, Sakya, Kagyu, and Gelug, and the Bon religion, are in exile. Under their guidance, the same standard of monastic education as that which characterized ancient Tibet has been maintained. Examples abound.

Sherab Gyatso, an Englishman who has been ordained in the Tibetan Buddhist order, relates that at Gomang College of Drepung Monastery in South India, a monk's day begins between 5 to 5:30 a.m. with morning prayer. Breakfast is served at 8 a.m. The rest of the day is spent on attending philosophy classes, text memorization, and debate sessions. Lunch is served at noon. After lunch, rest. Classes start after rest. For others, there is private study. This goes on till 5:30 when the evening meal is served. Argumentation and debate are seen as the keys to attaining greater knowledge

In exile, Tibetans have not only rebuilt monasteries but have opened secular institutions of learning, research, and training in the fields of traditional Tibetan medicine Tibetan medicine is a centuries-old traditional medical system that employs a complex approach to diagnosis, incorporating techniques such as pulse analysis and urinalysis, and utilizes behavior and dietary modification, medicines composed of natural materials (e.g., astrology, language, painting, metal and wood crafts, sculpture, and performing arts. These efforts have enabled the Tibetan exiles to maintain the integrity of their culture and spiritual heritage. More importantly, they have contributed to the revival of the cultural heritage of non-Tibetans who share the same culture as the Tibetans. Through the length of the Buddhist Himalayas from

Ladakh, Lahaul and Spiti in Himachal Pradesh in the west, Mustang, Dolpo and Solo Khumbu in Nepal, Sikkim, Bhutan and Arunachal Pradesh in the east, students flock to Tibetan monasteries and institutions to learn Tibetan language, Buddhism, and medicine.

Partly in response to this worldwide interest in Tibetan culture, but mainly to maintain the integrity of their culture, Tibetans have established important cultural centres and educational institutions in India. Hundreds of Tibetan and non-Tibetan students graduate from the Central Institute of Higher Tibetan Studies The Central Institute of Higher Tibetan Studies (CIHTS) is a university institute founded in Dharamsala, India in 1967. The CIHTS was founded by Pt. Jawahar Lal Nehru in consultation with Tenzin Gyatso the Dalai Lama with the aim of educating the youths of Tibet in exile in Benares (funded and recognized by the Indian government as a university), Tibet House in New Delhi, the Library of Tibetan Works and Archive, the Norbulingka Institute, and the Amnye Machen Institute in Dharamsala. Here, classes are conducted on Buddhism and Tibetan, traditional thangka painting, and metal works. These institutions also provide Tibetan and non-Tibetan scholars facilities to research 'Tibetan history and culture. They publish books and journals in Tibetan and English. The Dharamsala-based Tibetan Astro and Medical Institute trains young Tibetans in the traditional Tibetan medical system and runs clinics in all the Tibetan settlements and big cities to provide health care to Tibetans and non-Tibetans who wish to be treated traditionally.

To promote international outreach, the relatively new Sarah College of Higher Tibetan Studies in Dharamsala teaches young Tibetans and students from the West, South Korea, Japan, Taiwan, and Mongolia the Tibetan language, the country's literature and history, as well as the Buddhist philosophy. Sarah College has established exchange programs with Emory and Miami Universities in the United States. Every year, accompanied and supervised by their professors, 10 to 15 students from these two universities spend an entire semester studying Tibetan culture and history, Buddhism, the exile community, administration, and media. Since the break-up of the Soviet Union, monks and students from

Mongolia and Kalmykia, Burytia and 'Tuva in Russia have been streaming to India to study the Tibetan language, Buddhism and medicine and to re-connect with the source of their cultural heritage, disrupted during the years of the Soviet Union. All this has resulted in a fresh flowering of the culture and spiritual traditions of Tibet outside of the country.

REFUGEES IN INDIA: LEGAL FRAMEWORK, LAW ENFORCEMENT AND SECURITY

There are numerous aspects pertaining to refugees which are of major importance both to India, as a country and to the refugees, particularly in the context of law enforcement. Given the security scenario prevailing in the country, particularly arising out of the role of some of the neighbours in this regard, an utterly humanitarian matter like the 'refugees' has come to be influenced by considerations of national security. It is a reality that we can ill-afford to overlook this aspect of the matter in any dispassionate deliberation of the subject under review in this article. While law and order is a State subject under the Indian Constitution, international relations and international borders are under the exclusive purview of the Union government. This has resulted in a variety of agencies, both of the Central as well as the State governments, having to deal with refugee matters connected with law enforcement. Also, all policies governing refugees are laid down by the Union government though the impact of the refugee problem as such has to be borne by the State administration to a greater degree if not wholly.

Security personnel at the international borders, immigration personnel at the land check posts, international airports and seaports, besides a host of state police personnel, are all intimately connected with law enforcement affecting refugees one way or another. As the very term 'security' denotes, all the above categories of personnel are entrusted with the onerous responsibility of ensuring national as well as internal security of the country as their first and foremost charge. They have to make sure that the laws of the land are enforced in regard to refugees without in any way ignoring or neutralising security considerations. But, at the same time, it is also their responsibility that the humanitarian overtones so characteristically and inseparably associated with refugees in general, are not lost sight of. It is also well known that every single situation pertaining to 'refugees' is replete with human rights aspects as well. It is obvious that these have also necessarily to be taken due care of by law enforcement personnel.

A proper understanding of the circumstances pertaining to specific refugee situations by the concerned law enforcement agency or even by an individual official, would pave the way for taking care of both the security as well as the humane aspects- from both the humanitarian as well as the human rights angle. At the same time, knowledge on the part of all those who handle refugees- whether they are part of the government machinery or outside it (including international agencies, NGOs etc) of the laws of the land and also how the security and enforcement personnel function, would considerably facilitate looking after the refugees.

4

Tibetans Permanent Refugees in India

That Tibetans can now renew Indian residency permits every 5 years provides a measure of security, but it still consigns Tibetans to refugee status, which prevents many educated, talented and integrated individuals from fully participating in Indian society. In the 1970's the Indian government offered to make all Tibetan refugees citizens of India, but the CTA declined the offer. Wangyal, a retired CTA official said; "Many of us who were involved in those discussions now think turning down the generous offer from the Indian government was a mistake. But there was still a belief that we would soon go back to Tibet, which, in hindsight, was unrealistic even then. If this third generation of Tibetans in exile had Indian citizenship, the Tibetan community would have far more resources and be much stronger today."

Previous CTA administrations did not pursue Indian citizenship for Tibetan refugees. A number of Tibetans acquired Indian citizenship on their own, but research indicates that only 1-3% of Tibetans who are eligible for Indian citizenship apply. The Immigration and Refugee Board of Canada and the United States Bureau of Citizenship and Immigration Services report that both Tibetans born in Tibet who escaped to India and those born in India to Tibetan refugee parents, face legal obstacles to obtaining Indian citizenship.

Many Tibetans, Indians and international supporters agree; the exile community should commence a new dialogue with the

Indian government on securing citizenship for Tibetans, especially those born in India. In a highly publicized 3-year court case, Namgyal Lagyari of Dehradun attained Indian citizenship, which has inspired other Tibetans born in India to do the same.

Tibetans in India need better access to legal resources and education, to fully understand UN and Indian refugee charters and laws, to know the full scope of rights and restrictions that apply to refugees, and to pursue citizenship or immigration through legal processes.

The Quest for the West

Switzerland was the first nation to grant citizenship to a small number of Tibetan refugees in the 1960's. In the 1970's a visionary Canadian Ambassador in New Delhi took an especial interest in the Tibetan refugees and managed a resettlement project, which brought whole families together. The US Immigration Act of 1990 approved 1000 immigrant visas to Tibetans in India and Nepal. But in the American system, a single individual is selected by a lottery. Many relatives spent years waiting for reunification visas, straining ties already injured by separation from kinfolk in Chinese Occupied Tibet.

Today, after 23 years, an estimated 10,000 Tibetans have legally immigrated to the USA to join the relative who went first. But the "quest for the west" as it is often termed in the *chai* stalls of McLeod Ganj and Majnu ka Tila, has caused serious dislocations and fractures. Many in India, constrained by permanent refugee status into a third generation, feel great pressure to try to go west by any means possible.

Most Tibetan refugees are poorly informed about immigration laws and procedures, and are therefore easily misinformed, exploited and harmed by visa brokers.

Visa Brokers, Passport Rings

Refugee groups are especially vulnerable to exploitation, bribery and coercion, and Tibetans are no exception. There are numerous passport and visa brokers operating throughout the Tibetan exile world, from New Delhi to New York. In many cases large sums are paid to visa brokers, who frequently vanish with the cash. Many "clients" of brokers arrive in Manhattan or London, owning a huge debt, which can take several years to pay off. Tibetans who enter Germany as asylum seekers are given a tiny stipend and must live in restricted housing for months or years before they are granted residency, which was not what they expected when cutting the deal with the broker back in Asia.

The US State Dept. has concerns about passport rings operating from Tibet and India, with a well-worn trick, familiar to consular officers; a passport with a US visa is sent back, the photo is changed and a new person enters the USA without having an interview at any consulate.

In recent years, trends have emerged that have caused considerable harm; newly arrived refugees fabricating their date of birth or parentage, to pass as children of Tibetans who entered India before issuance of resident permits for Tibetans was suspended, and Tibetans from India who enter the US and are lured by brokers to claim asylum by fabricating abuse at the hands of Indian officials, or alter documents to pretend they were born in Tibet and thereby qualified for political asylum. Falsifying one's identity invites disastrous consequences, including deportation and arrest; there are documented cases of INS officials discovering fabricated information and deporting Tibetans back to India.

In the late 1990's aggressive brokers began collecting funds from Tibetans in India promising a green card based on bogus asylum claims. I was asked to write supporting letters for persons who had advanced money to brokers, so I had the opportunity to read many of these narratives, which alleged relentlessly cruel treatment at the hands of Indian officials. When I asked if the narratives were true, I was told they were not: they had been written by the broker.

I did not support these claims; I was concerned they would cause problems in the future. If the Indian government learned of the schemes, it would be rightly offended — to this day India is the largest donor to the Tibetan refugees — and it would offend HH Dalai Lama, who has never sought to leave his exile home and proudly states; "I am a son of India."

The Damage Done

In 1998 I received a call from an official at the fraud department of the US Dept. of State in Washington DC, inquiring about a spike in Tibetan refugee asylum claims from India, asking if Tibetans were indeed at risk in India. I forwarded documents from the Indian Home Ministry and the CTA and independent monitoring agencies, with the history of India's generous care for the Tibetan people and their great esteem for HH Dalai Lama. Surely there are individual cases of exploitation and abuse, but the Indian government deserves praise for its humanitarian service to the Tibetan people and its concern for the preservation of Tibetan culture and religion.

Shortly thereafter, I received a letter from a one Mr. Pema Gashon, then a leader of the Tibetan Youth Congress of New York and New Jersey, and a familiar presence at all New York Tibetan gatherings. Mr. Gashon described his plan to get asylum for Tibetans from India, writing; "we know that our case is not strong so we will pay you any fee you wish if you will get members of Congress and President Clinton to support us." I made several copies of the letter, provided them to CTA officials and urged them to investigate the matter and question Mr. Gashon about offering a bribe to a relative of a US Senator, in exchange for false information about India, a country where my father had served as the US envoy in the 1970's.

I was not privy to any information about what if any action was taken, but I know of several individuals who obtained green cards via Mr. Gashon, and others who paid him large sums of cash but did not obtain papers.

Over the past 15 years, such brokers have multiplied. The Tibet Justice Center and other groups have gathered anecdotal evidence of how the brokers operate; inducing their clients to lie to officials, withholding passports to obtain more funds, threatening to deport clients back to India or Tibet: persuading US law firms to work pro bono while taking large sums of cash from anxious clients; stealing passports from clients for the broker's relatives and friends. There are reports of Tibetan women sold into prostitution rings to pay off the debt. (This is how illegal passport/ visa rings operate around the globe).

And now, sadly, Tibetans in India who have legitimate opportunities to visit the USA, for education, business or family reunification, cannot obtain visas. Most are automatically rejected without having any review of their files. Even Fulbright scholars cannot get a fair hearing. Addressing the Tibetan Community at the Kalachakra in Washington, DC, in 2011, HH Dalai Lama asked that people follow legal procedures and not falsify any information for the purpose of obtaining asylum.

The CTA and other US based Tibet support groups in the USA should work with the US Embassy in New Delhi to grant Tibetan visa applicants fair hearings, and with the US congress to pass a new senate resolution authorizing a second US resettlement project. During the 1990 project the US offered to take more than 1000, but the CTA declined. The US is in the process of resettling 60,000 Bhutanese refugees of Nepali origin who have been in UNHCR camps since the early 1990's. The Tibetan refugees are a small population with longstanding support in the US Congress, thus a strong case can be made for issuing more immigrant visas, which would put a lot of unscrupulous visa brokers out of business.

A great many Tibetan refugees are now stranded in the USA without papers, manipulated by brokers and scammers, living on the fringes of a struggling immigrant network. Most immigrant groups in the US have legal advisory teams and legal defense funds; the CTA could also establish a program that provides counsel to refugees, educating them about their legal status, rights and options. The CTA can also open dialogues with embassies in New Delhi about resettlement, to research procedures whereby Tibetans can legally immigrate.

THE REFUGEE SCENE IN INDIA

A brief look at the refugee scenario in India will help appreciate in the proper perspective, the complexities of law enforcement in a variety of situations impinging upon the refugees.

India has been home to refugees for centuries. From the time when almost the entire Zorastrian community took refuge in India fleeing from the persecution they were then subjected to on religious grounds in Iran, India has, from time to time continued to receive a large number of refugees from different countries, not necessarily from the neighbouring countries alone.

The most significant thing which deserves to be taken note of is that, there has not been a single occasion of any refugee originating from the Indian soil except the transboundary movement of the people during the partition of the country in 1947. On the other hand, it has invariably been a receiving country and in the process, enlarging its multi-cultural and multi-ethnic fabric.

In keeping with its secular policies, India has been the home to refugees belonging to all religions and sects. It is relevant to point out that since its independence India has received refugees not only from some of its neighbouring countries but distant countries like Afghanistan, Iran, Iraq, Somalia, Sudan and Uganda.

The South Asian sub-continent has often witnessed situations where refugees from one or the other neighbouring countries have crossed over to India. Considering the sensitivities of national and regional politics in the sub-continent, the problem of refugees crossing over to India cannot be totally disassociated from the overall security issues relevant locally. At the end of 1999, India had well over 2,51,400 refugees, who do not include those from countries like Afghanistan, Iran, Iraq, Somalia, Sudan and Uganda.

RECENT TIBETAN REFUGEES IN INDIA

Fifty years ago, in 1949, the People's Republic of China moved its troops into Tibet. As a result of Chinese acts of war, imprisonment, labor camps, executions, and starvation, approximately 1.2 million Tibetans have died in Tibet (Planning Council, 1994). Nuns and monks who since 1987 have been actively demonstrating against Chinese occupation have been imprisoned. Released pris-oners find it difficult to continue to live in Tibet where they face pervasive discrimination and feel unsafe. More than 120,000 Tibetans, including 18,000 Buddhist clergy, have sought refuge in Bhutan, Nepal, and India. Among the recent refugees, approximately 45% are clergy (Planning Council, 1994).

The Tibetan refugees belong to the 70% of the world's refugees who are displaced within the developing world (United Nations High Commission for Refugees, 2000). Most of the literature on mental health of refugees has, however, focused on the selected refugees who managed to find refuge in the West (Ager, 1993; Boehlein & Kinzie, 1995). Studies conducted in the West have shown high rates of traumatic events and physical complaints among tortured refugees (Goldfeld, Mollica, Pesavento, & Faraone, 1988; Hougen, Kelstrup, Petersen, & Rasmussen, 1988; Priebe & Esmali, 1997; Ramsay, Gorst-Unsworth, & Turner, 1993). The few studies on refugees displaced within the developing world have shown relationships be-tween traumatic events and physical and mental seque-lae, including depression, anxiety, and posttraumatic stress disorder (PTSD; de Jong et al., 2001; Holtz, 1998; Mollica et al., 1993; Shrestha et al., 1998; Summerfield & Toser, 1990; Van Ommeren et al., 2001).

In a previous study on Tibetan refugees in India, Holtz (1998) compared 35 imprisoned and tortured refugees—28 nuns and 7 lay men—with 35 closely mat-ched, nonimprisoned, nontortured refugees. The nuns had been receiving room and board as well as social and cul-tural support within their nunnery. Using the Hopkins Symptom Checklist-25 (Mollica, Wyshak, de Mameffe, Khuon, & Lavelle, 1987), Holtz (1998) found that those who had been imprisoned and tortured were more likely to suffer from elevated anxiety. The groups did not differ in terms of depression or number of somatic symptoms. Holtz' study contributes to the knowledge of impact of history of torture and imprisonment on Buddhist nuns liv-ing in a stable institution—acknowledging that the ex-periences of other imprisoned Tibetan refugees may be different. Depression and anxiety may be higher among imprisoned refugees who do not live in such relative ideal circumstances. Research into the consequences of trauma among Tibetans is especially relevant because of Tibetan leadership claims that symptoms related to traumatic stress are rare among Tibetan torture survivors (e.g., Brown, 1997).

The Tibetan Transcultural Psychosocial Organiza-tion Mental Health Program in Dharamsala, Himachal Pradesh, India, conducted the present study on request by and in collaboration with the Department of Health of the Tibetan government-in-exile. The study's objective was to examine the impact of trauma history on the mental health of recent Tibetan refugees and involved a carefully trans-lated instrument and interviews with newly arrived nuns, monks, lay men, and lay women. We hypothesize elevated rates of traumatic events, somatic complaints, anxiety, and depression among imprisoned and tortured refugees com-pared to refugees who have not experienced these events.

Method

The study was conducted in 1995 in Dharamsala, a village in the foothills of the Himalayas in India. Be-fore settling in one of the various Tibetan settlements in South Asia, the vast majority of new refugees first travel to Dharamsala for blessing by His Holiness the Dalai Lama, the exiled religious and political leader of Tibet.

Participants: A sample of Tibetan refugee participants was se-lected using the following criteria: (a) arrival in India between 1991 and 1995, with an equal number of par-ticipants in each year, (b) age 18 or older at the time of escape, (c) equal numbers of imprisoned and never im-prisoned refugees, and (d) equal numbers of men and women in the imprisoned and nonimprisoned groups. Par-ticipants were selected from handicraft centers, monaster-ies, and lists provided by the Government's Refugee Re-ception Center and Security Department in Dharamsala. Initial participants were asked to refer other imprisoned and nonimprisoned Tibetans, who were also interviewed. We approached 195 people, and one person refused to be interviewed. Twenty-four interviews were randomly ex-cluded to ensure equal number of participants from each arrival year. Our final sample consisted of 76 imprisoned and 74 nonimprisoned refugees, after excluding those who were younger than 18 at time of escape (n = 2), those who had been imprisoned for criminal reasons (n = 12), and those who had been political prisoners but not in Tibet (n = 6).

Instruments: The interview schedule, administered to all partici-pants, consisted of demographics, the Hopkins Symptom

Schedule-25 (HSCL-25; Mollica et al., 1987), a list of eight somatic complaints, and a list covering 27 traumatic events, covering flight from Tibet, imprisonment and tor-ture in Tibet, and deprivation during imprisonment or flight. In addition, imprisoned refugees were asked to com-plete the trauma symptom section of the Harvard Trauma Questionnaire (HTQ; Mollica et al., 1992).

Both the HSCL-25 and the HTQ have been shown to be valid and reliable screening instruments for screen-ing anxiety, depression, and PTSD among Indochinese refugees in the United States (Mollica et al., 1987, 1992). Among the Indochinese refugee population, the instru-ments are both sensitive and specific to identifying diag-noses made by an independent, highly experienced psychi-atrist. The 1 -week test-retest reliability and the interrater reliability of the HSCL-25 were.89 and .98 (Mollica et al., 1987); the 1-week test-retest reliability and the interrater reliability of the HTQ were .92 and .98 (Mollica et al., 1992).

The Tibetan translation and cultural adaptation of the instruments took 8 months. First, two translations of the HSCL-25 into written Tibetan language were tested. We found that illiterate patients of our program could not fully comprehend written Tibetan language when the items were read to them, because the language used in written Tibetan tends to differ from spoken Tibetan. Also, wide variations between Tibetan dialects resulted in com-munication difficulties. Moreover, translations of words involving direct expression of emotion were poorly un-derstood because Tibetans typically communicate without such words.

Second, three bilingual Tibetan nurses independently translated the English items into verbal Tibetan language, that is, they were instructed to provide an audio record-ing of how they would ask the questions to patients in an empathic manner. The three nurses discussed their translations, compared them with the two available writ-ten Tibetan translations, and, based on consensus, pro-vided one version and a list of items of which they felt uncertain. Third, three bilingual Tibetans provided a blind-back translation of the nurses' version. Fourth, focus groups were organized to discuss those items that had changed meaning during the translation process and those items of which the nurses had been uncertain. Focus groups typically consisted of six people, including both newly arrived and already settled Tibetans. To test un-derstanding of items, focus group members were asked to provide examples. Whenever one of the focus group mem-bers did not understand an item, the facilitator stimulated the group to formulate a translation that was understood by all. After each focus group discussion, discussed items were back-translated to identify errors in translation and to determine the need for further focus groups. Each of the HSCL-25 and the HTQ items were discussed by three focus groups. The final version of the interview schedule was tested by 20 pilot participants and found satisfactory. Process notes on the translation of each item are avail-able upon request. The list covering traumatic events is displayed verbatim in Table 1 and was—without special instructions—administered to respondents. The HSCL-25 consists of 25 Likert-type questions ranging from 1 *(not at all)* to 4 *(extremely)*. The first 10 questions cover anxiety (scale range 10-40), and the remaining 15 questions cover depression (scale range 15-60). In previous work with refugees displaced within the developing world, an average score of 1.75 or more on the HSCL-25 anxiety or depression subscales was used to identify people with high depression and anxiety (Holtz, 1998; Mollica et al., 1993; Shrestha et al., 1998). How-ever, as the 1.75 cut-off score has never been validated for the Tibetan population, we did not use the cut-off score. The Cronbach's alpha internal consistency coefficients were .83 for the HSCL-25 anxiety subscale, .79 for the HSCL-25 depression subscale, and .86 for the HTQ items.

Procedure: The instruments were interviewer-administered rather than self-administered because a significant pro-portion of Tibetan refugees is illiterate. The interview was split in two parts and administered at separate times to reduce interviewee fatigue. During the first interview, all questions were asked except the HTQ. During the second interview, the HTQ was administered. The gap between the two interviews was on average 1 week. However, only 65 out of 76 imprisoned refugees (86%) attended the sec-ond interview. The less than perfect participation rate for the second interview is possibly because of refugees hav-ing moved away from Dharamsala, a transit center for Tibetan refugees. The two Tibetan interviewers, one male and one female, were not blind to group status. They had received a half-day of training and had administered the 20 pilot interviews under supervision. Interviews were conducted in a confidential setting. After complete de-scription of the study to the participants, informed oral consent was obtained. We did not obtain written consent because of illiteracy and distrust of forms.

Statistics: We used two-tailed x^2 and *t* tests for univariate com-parisons between imprisoned and nonimprisoned refu-gees. We used the two-tailed Fisher's Exact Tests when the expected frequencies were less than 5.0 for 2 or more cells of a 2 x 2 table. For these analyses, alpha was set at .01, rather than at .05, to reduce chance significance caused by multiple tests. All analyses were performed with com-mercially available software (SPSS Inc., 1995).

Results

Demographics: Sampled imprisoned and nonimprisoned refugees did not differ on most demographic variables, including sex, age, and year of escape. The average imprisoned refugee was 27.2 years old (*SD* = 8.3; range = 19-68); the av-erage nonimprisoned refugee was 26.6 years old (*SD* = 7.3; range = 9-62). The average imprisoned refugee es-caped in April 1993 (*SD* = 17.3 months), and the av-erage nonimprisoned refugee escaped May 1993 (*SD* = 17.9 months). Imprisoned refugees were more likely to have been a nun in Tibet and to be currently a nun in In-dia (Table 2). Forty-five percent of the total sample had been clergy in Tibet, which is representative of the recent refugee population (Planning Council, 1994). Although the two groups did not differ in terms of marital status, the previously imprisoned refugees had fewer children (0.2 [S£> = 0.6] vs. 0.5 [*SD* = 1.0]), /(120.6) = -2.4; $p < .05$.

Reasons for Leaving Tibet: Thirty-eight percent of refugees reported more than one reason for leaving Tibet. Refugees who had been imprisoned were more likely to report leaving Tibet be-cause of perceived danger to their life or because of dif-ficulties living in Tibet as a result of past political ac-tivities. Refugees who had never been imprisoned were more likely to report leaving Tibet to obtain an educa-tion (Table 2). The vast majority of refugees escaped with others (91%) and without permit (99%).

Traumatic Events: Traumatic events were frequently reported by both imprisoned and nonimprisoned refugees. As expected, the imprisoned refugees reported more traumatic events (11.5 [*SD* = 3.8] vs. 4.5 events [*SD* = 2.7]), /(137.0) =13.1, $p < .001$. All imprisoned and 89% of nonimprisoned refugees had experienced at least one traumatic event. Female imprisoned refugees compared to male impris-oned refugees were more likely to report that they had been kept naked as a form of torture (68% vs. 36%), X^2(1,JV=76) = 7.6, $p < .01$.

Sequelae: Imprisoned refugees had significantly higher HSCL-25 anxiety scores (22.5 [*SD* = 6.5] vs. 18.7 [*SD* = 6.8]), r(148) = 3.6, $p < .001$. The groups did not differ in terms of HSCL-25 depression scores (28.5 [*SD* = 7.4] vs. 27.6 [*SD* = 7.4]), r(148) < 1, and number of somatic complaints (3.7 [*SD* = 2.1] vs. 3.2 [*SD* = 2.3]), /(148) = 1.4, $p > .05$.

The 65 imprisoned refugees who completed the HTQ symptom list most frequently reported: having re-current thoughts or memories of the most hurtful or terri-fying events (92%), difficulties concentrating (74%), sud-den emotional or physical reactions when reminded of the most hurtful or traumatic events (71%), spending time thinking why these events happened to me (68%), feeling irritable or having outbursts of anger (65%), feeling on guard (60%), and recurrent nightmares (52%). Accord-ing to the HTQ assessment, 20% of imprisoned refugees met diagnostic criteria for PTSD (American Psychiatric Association, 1987).

Discussion

We compared previously imprisoned Tibetan refu-gees with never imprisoned refugees. We found that imprisoned refugees had experienced more traumatic events and currently experienced more anxiety. The groups did not differ in terms of depression and somatic com-plaints. Both groups experienced significant stressors and symptoms.

This study has several limitations. The sample covers many participants residing in institutions— underrepresenting those who settle freely. This overrep-resentation may be especially true for the subsample that completed the HTQ, which was administered 1 week af-ter the HSCL. Some refugees in transit may have moved outside Dharamsala shortly after the first interview and may not have completed the HTQ. Another limitation is that the HTQ was only administered to the imprisoned refugees and not to the comparison group. A further lim-itation is that female refugees may have been inhibited to disclose imprisonment because of stigmatizing experi-ences. Also, especially for women, the list of traumatic events was limited. For example, it did not include forced abortion and sterilization, a product of China's birth con-trol policy and potentially a highly traumatic event that may have occurred to some of the imprisoned and nonim-prisoned female participants in our study. Moreover, be-cause of sociocultural stigma women may have felt very uncomfortable to endorse the item *rape or sexual abuse,* which nonetheless may have taken place. Even in the West, the wording of sexual assault items greatly impacts en-dorsement rates (Resnick, Kilpatrick, Dansky, Saunders, & Best, 1993). Since female imprisoned refugees were more likely to endorse the item *being kept naked,* sexual assault may have occurred more often than reported. An unusual strength of this study is the thorough translation with special concern for comprehensibility and semantic equivalence. Nevertheless, whether the translation is ex-actly equivalent to the original was not established.

The pattern of results is similar to that of Holtz (1998), who also noted a difference in anxiety and no differ-ences in depression and somatic complaints in his study of tortured and imprisoned Tibetan refugees. Holtz did not report HSCL-25 scale scores, but instead he reported rates of elevated anxiety and depression (defined as mean HSCL-25 scale scores greater than 1.75). If we defined elevated anxiety and depression similarly, we would find that 63% of our total sample had elevated anxiety and 57% had elevated depression. Holtz (1998), in contrast, observed much lower rates (41 and 14%, respectively). The difference between our and Holtz' results are perhaps due to the use of different translations of the HSCL-25. Alternatively, the difference may be explained by dif-ferences in sample composition, because the nuns inter-viewed by Holtz live in a well-financed and stable insti-tution. Our clinical experience suggests that high anxiety and depression rates among both imprisoned and non-imprisoned refugees may be related to: experience of trau-matic events among both groups, material, social, and cul-tural losses associated with being a refugee, acculturative stress, disappointment with life in exile, and experience of culture-bound syndromes and idioms of distress (Ketzer & Crescenzi, 2002).

The high levels of anxiety and depression in the Tibetan community is consistent with our clinical experi-ence. Patients typically seek help by presenting headaches, stomach pain, bodyaches, fits, medically unexplained paralysis, feelings of unhappiness, palpitations, insomnia, discomfort with anger, and difficulties concentrating and learning. Although we observed a 20% prevalence rate of PTSD in the previously imprisoned refugees, we find that this diagnosis does not go far enough to describe the complexity of symptoms that follow the traumatic events experienced by our Tibetan patients. As the transcultural literature suggests (Kirmayer, 1996), PTSD symptoma-tology is often mixed with depressive, anxiety, and so-matic symptoms. The 20% prevalence rate may seem low compared to other victimized groups living in the West (de Girolamo & McFarlane, 1996). However, the observed prevalence rate is similar to other studies of atrocities out-side the West. Differences in method-ology, in sociocultural context, and in nature and extent of atrocities may all account for the variance in findings across studies.

Tibetans are rightly proud of their traditional col-lective coping and spiritual mechanisms that help many people—but not all. These coping mechanisms are mostly cognitive and spiritual: reciting mantras, visualizing His Holiness the Dalai Lama, and focusing on *Karma,* pa-tience, compassion, impermanence, and the suffering of others. Our clinical experience in Dharamsala indicates that these traditional mechanisms tend to work especially well for coping with loss, death, and other events within the usual range of suffering. However, the traditional, cog-nitive forms of coping do not always seem to reach tortured refugees. Severe emotional arousal may cloud the access to the cognitive and spiritual coping system. Without ac-cess to the collective coping mechanisms, the refugee ap-pears to be left isolated—especially since display of emo-tion is socially discouraged. During treatment we try to provide space for emotional expression and to bridge be-tween the patient's emotional experience and the available cultural forms of coping (cf. Ketzer & Crescenzi, 2002). Research involving detailed assessment of various tradi-tional ways of coping among Tibetan refugees may help us understand to what extent different practices mediate mental well-being among Tibetan trauma survivors.

REFUGEES AND THE INDIAN LEGAL FRAMEWORK

Refugees encounter the Indian legal system on two counts. There are laws which regulate their entry into and stay in India along with a host of related issues. Once they are within the Indian territory, they are then liable to be subjected to the provisions of the Indian penal laws for various commissions and omissions under a variety of circumstances, whether it be as a complainant or as an accused. These are various constitutional and legal provisions with which refugees may be concerned under varying circumstances.

Constitutional Provisions

There are a few Articles of the Indian Constitution which are equally applicable to refugees on the Indian soil in the same way as they are applicable to the Indian Citizens.

The Supreme Court of India has consistently held that the Fundamental Right enshrined under Article 21 of the Indian Constitution regarding the Right to life and personal liberty, applies to all irrespective of the fact whether they are citizens of India or aliens. The various High Courts in India have liberally adopted the rules of natural justice to refugee issues, along with recognition of the United Nations High Commissioner for Refugees (UNHCR) as playing an important role in the protection of refugees. The Hon'ble High Court of Guwahati has in various judgements, recognised the refugee issue and permitted refugees to approach the UNHCR for determination of their refugee status, while staying the deportation orders issued by the district court or the administration.

In the matter of *Gurunathan and others vs. Government of India* and others and in the matter of *A.C.Mohd.Siddique vs. Government of India and others,* the High Court of Madras expressed its unwillingness to let any Sri Lankan refugees to be forced to return to Sri Lanka against their will. In the case of *P.Nedumaran vs. Union Of India* before the Madras High Court, Sri Lankan refugees had prayed for a*writ* of mandamus directing the Union of India and the State of Tamil Nadu to permit UNHCR officials to check the voluntariness of the refugees in going back to Sri Lanka, and to permit those refugees who did not want to return to continue to stay in the camps in India. The Hon'ble Court was pleased to hold that "since the UNHCR was involved in ascertaining the voluntariness of the refugees' return to Sri Lanka, hence being a World Agency, it is not for the Court to consider whether the consent is voluntary or not." Further, the Court acknowledged the competence and impartiality of the representatives of UNHCR. The Bombay High Court in the matter of *Syed Ata Mohammadi vs. Union of India,* was pleased to direct that "there is no question of deporting the Iranian refugee to Iran, since he has been recognised as a refugee by the UNHCR." The Hon'ble Court further permitted the refugee to travel to whichever country he desired. Such an order is in line with the internationally accepted principles of '*non-refoulement*' of refugees to their country of origin.

The Supreme Court of India has in a number of cases stayed deportation of refugees such as *Maiwand's Trust of Afghan Human Freedom vs. State of Punjab* ; and, *N.D.Pancholi vs. State of Punjab & Others.* In the matter of *Malavika Karlekar vs. Union of India,* the Supreme Court directed stay of deportation of the Andaman Island Burmese refugees, since "their claim for refugee status was pending determination and a *prima facie* case is made out for grant of refugee status." The Supreme Court judgement in the Chakma refugee case clearly declared that no one shall be deprived of his or her life or liberty without the due process of law. Earlier judgements of the Supreme Court in *Luis De Raedt vs. Union of India* and also *State of Arunachal Pradesh vs. Khudiram Chakma*, had also stressed the same point.

Arrest, Detention and Release

There is yet another aspect of *non-refoulment* which merits mention here. The concept of 'International Zones' which are transit areas at airports and other points of entry into Indian territory, which are marked as being outside Indian territory and the normal jurisdiction of Indian Courts, is a major 'risk factor' for refugees since it reduces access of refugees to legal remedies. This legal fiction is violative of the internationally acknowledged principle of *non-refoulement*. In the matter of a Palestinian refugee who was deported to New Delhi International Airport from Kathmandu was sent back to Kathmandu from the transit lounge of the Airport. He was once more returned to New Delhi International Airport on the ground of being kept in an 'International Zone'. Such detention is a classic case on the above point barring legal remedies to the detained refugee. The only relief in such a case is through the administrative authorities.

Articles 22(1),22(2) and 25(1) of the Indian Constitution reflect that the rules of natural justice in common law systems are equally applicable in India, even to refugees. The established principle of rule of law in India is that no person, whether a citizen or an alien shall be deprived of his life, liberty or property without the authority of law. The Constitution of India expressly incorporates the common law precept and the Courts have gone further to raise it to the status of one of the basic features of the Constitution which cannot be amended.

The Indian Constitution does not contain any specific provision which obliges the state to enforce or implement treaties and conventions. A joint reading of all the provisions as well as an analysis of the case law on the subject shows international treaties, covenants, conventions and agreements can become part of the domestic law in India only if they are specifically incorporated in the law of the land. The Supreme Court has held, through a number of decisions on the subject that international conventional law must go through the process of transformation into municipal law before the international treaty becomes internal law. Courts may apply international law only when there is no conflict between international law and domestic law, and also if the provisions of international law sought to be applied are not in contravention of the spirit of the Constitution and national legislation, thereby enabling a harmonious construction of laws. It has also been firmly laid that if there is any such conflict, then domestic law shall prevail.

INDIA'S INTERNATIONAL COMMITTMENTS

India does not have on its statute book a specific and separate law to govern refugees. In the absence of such a specific law, all existing Indian laws like The Criminal Procedure Code, The Indian Penal Code, The Evidence Act etc. apply to the refugees as well. Even though India is not a signatory to the 1951 Convention on refugees and also the 1967 Protocol, India is a signatory to a number of United Nations and World Conventions on Human Rights, refugee issues and related matters. India's obligations in regard to refugees arise out of the latter. India became a member of the Executive Committee of the High Commissioner's Programme (EXCOM) in 1995. The EXCOM is the organisation of the UN, which approves and supervises the material assistance programme of UNHCR.

Membership of the EXCOM indicates particular interest and greater commitment to refugee matters. India voted affirmatively to adopt the Universal Declaration of Human Rights which affirms rights for all persons, citizens and non- citizens alike. India voted affirmatively to adopt the UN Declaration of Territorial Asylum in 1967.

India ratified the International Covenant on Civil and Political Rights (ICCPR) as well as the International Convention on Economic, Social and Cultural Rights (ICESCR) in 1976. India ratified the UN Convention on the Rights of the Child in 1989. India ratified the Convention on the Elimination of All Forms of Discrimination Against Women (CEDAW) in 1974 under which Article 1 imposes legally binding obligation. India accepted the principle of *non-refoulement* as envisaged in the Bangkok Principles, 1966, which were formulated for the guidance of member states in respect of matters concerning the status and treatment of refugees. These Principles also contain provisions relating to repatriation, right to compensation, granting asylum and the minimum standard of treatment in the state of asylum.

In order to get a clear understanding of the rights which devolve on the refugees on account of India's international commitments mentioned above and their relevance to law enforcement, it is pertinent to enumerate some of the more important rights accruing to refugees under the above mentioned Conventions. Article 13 of the Universal Declaration of Human Rights guarantees 'Right to Freedom of Movement', Article 14 'Right to Seek and Enjoy Asylum' and Article 15 the 'Right to Nationality.' Article 12 of the ICCPR deals with 'Freedom to leave any country including the person's own' and Article 13 'Prohibition of expulsion of aliens except by due process of law'. Under Article 2 A of the UN Convention on the Rights of the Child, the State must ensure the rights of "each child within its jurisdiction without discrimination of any kind"; Article 3 lays down that "In all actions concerning children the best interest of the child shall be a primary consideration"; Article 24 relates to 'Right to Health'; Article 28 to 'Right to Education' and Article 37 to 'Juvenile Justice'.

INDIA NEEDS TO RE-VISIT ITS TIBET POLICY

The continuing border incursions by the Chinese PLA into the Indian borders with growing frequency, Chinese cartographic aggression as a part of well-calibrated strategy and openly showing areas of other neighbouring countries including India as parts of China in the passports issued by China, denying Indian military officers posted in J&K to be included in the delegations, declaring the visit of Indian PM to Arunachal Pradesh as illegal, etc. are factors that demand a change in India's policy towards Tibet. Their aggressiveness has crossed all limits as they are indulging in highly provocative acts of stopping the Indian patrols from covering their area. These constitute a direct challenge to India's sovereignty. In addition, the continuing human rights violations in Tibet resulting in Tibetans resorting to extreme step of committing suicide, which have crossed 100 in the last four years, themselves provide sufficient ground for India to change its policy towards Tibet.

A look at the history of Tibet too would reveal that the China invaded Tibet and has virtually converted it into its colony. Since the Chinese Revolution of 1911, when the Chinese forces were withdrawn from Tibet, Tibet had enjoyed de facto independence and had opposed Chinese attempts to reassert control. Even prior to 1911, Tibet had only acknowledged suzerainty (and not sovereignty) of the Manchu Emperors and their control fluctuated between military presence to a nominal link. It is interesting to note that in history there were periods when China was under the suzerainty of the Tibetan Emperor. The Tibetan Emperor Trisong Detsan (755-797 A.D.) invaded parts of China including Chengan (now Xian) and forced China to pay tribute to Tibet and accept Tibetan suzerainty. In 1821 a treaty between Tibet and China was concluded that accepted that both the nations were independent.

The British, noting the situation, had always been treating Tibet as an autonomous region under the nominal Chinese suzerainty. British made several attempts after 1911 to bring China and Tibet together to accept this situation but the attempts always broke down on the issue of boundary between China and Tibet and not between Tibet and India.

Eventually, the British presented the Chinese government in 1921 with a declaration to the effect that they did not feel justified in withholding any longer their recognition of the status of Tibet as an autonomous state under the suzerainty of China, and that they intended dealing on that basis with Tibet in the future. The British, after 1921, promised support to the Tibetan government in maintaining the latter's practical autonomy which was considered important to the security of India and to the tranquillity of India's north-eastern frontier. The above policy was clearly mentioned in the memorandum issued by the British government on 23rd June 1943. The British PM Antony Eden on November 5, 1945 reiterated this in writing to the Chinese foreign minister Dr. TV Soong.

After 1947, the Indian authorities too continued with this policy. When China invaded Tibet in 1950, Sardar Patel then Deputy PM of India, in a note to the then secretary general in the external affairs ministry, Sir Girja Shankar Bajpai noting the implications of the Chinese moves in Tibet stated that the Chinese invasion had completely changed the security calculations and clearly pointed out that a serious danger was developing in the north and north east. He also agreed with the latter that 'a reconsideration of our military position and a redisposition of our forces were inescapable.' Sardar Patel later sent this note to the then Indian PM J L Nehru outlining the need for taking suitable action for India's defence. He clearly spelt out the strategic implications in the following lines-

"We have also to take note of a thoroughly unscrupulous, unreliable and determined power practically at our doors. The invasion of Tibet in my judgment, entitles us to treat them with a certain amount of hostility, let alone a great deal of circumspection. In these circumstances, one thing, to my mind, is quite clear; and, that is, that we cannot be friendly with China and must think in terms of defence against a determined, calculating, unscrupulous, ruthless, and unprincipled and prejudiced combination of powers, of which the Chinese will be the spearhead." He certainly had Pakistan in mind when he talked of combination of powers. In the detailed note to Bajpai, he had mentioned that the threat from the West and North West had not reduced. How accurate his assessment was can be seen in the present context.

Unfortunately India's policy of non-interference allowed the Chinese government to impose 17-Point Agreement on Tibet under duress. The immediate consequence of this was that the Indo-Tibetan border became Sino-Indian border – a situation the British had tried to avoid at all costs. The trade agreement signed in 1954 was based on Panchsheel principles and that in effect buried the de facto independent Tibet nation. After this, India in the hope of managing China, signed a number of agreements that showed that India had accepted Tibet as an autonomous region of China. These included Agreement on Maintenance of Peace and Tranquillity along the Line of Actual Control in the India-China

Border of 1993, Agreement between China and India on the Confidence Building Measures in the Military Field along the Line of Actual Control in the India- China Border Areas of 1996, Declaration on Principles for Relations and Comprehensive Cooperation of People's Republic of China and Republic of India of 2003 and Agreement between the Government of Republic of India and the Government of the People's Republic of China on Political Parameters and Guiding Principles for the Settlement of India-China Boundary Question of 2005. The text of these high sounding agreements would reflect that both sides would not do anything that would increase tension on the border and that both sides are sincere in resolving the issue through peaceful means. However, the Chinese actions have been contrary to the contents of agreements.

In addition to the lack of sincerity on the part of the Chinese in making these agreements, these agreements could not be implemented as there was no agreement on the length of the Sino-Indian border. While China does not include the area of J&K and considers Arunachal Pradesh as part of Tibet, India considers the entire length of the border between Tibet and India as Sino-Indian border. With this ambiguity, there are bound to be problems in the resolution of the issue. However, these agreements placed India in a disadvantageous position. India in these agreements accepted the Tibetan Autonomous Region as a part of China without obtaining any commitment from China on the issue of J&K or Arunachal Pradesh. Even after 2003 agreement, which agreed to the establishment of a trading mart in Nathula in Sikkim, Chinese maps continued to show Sikkim as an independent nation. Whenever, this issue was raised, the Chinese authorities brushed it aside by saying that they had inherited this from history and there was no need to give importance to the issue.

Basic issue is not what China is projecting through various statements and agreements but it is the intention of China towards India, which needs to be analysed in the light of its activities. Several experts have pointed out that China has encircled India by developing its strategic relations in our neighbourhood and desires to keep India under pressure so that it may it may not emerge as a strong nation. The Chinese activities certainly reveal this intention. China in the name of "Four Modernization" focussed on developing its armed forces and building infrastructure along the border. The recent aggressiveness shown in all the bordering areas reflects the intents of grabbing all the disputed areas along the Chinese borders. Its continued assistance in nuclear and missile fields to Pakistan is certainly affecting India's security and this cannot be regarded as a friendly act.

On the other hand some writers point out that Xi Jinping the Chinese President has told the Indian PM that China wants to settle the boundary question soon and therefore India should give some time more to China. Chinese President Xi Jinping in the "Five Point" proposal had committed that both sides would accommodate each other's core concerns and would reconcile bilateral disagreements amicably is underlined by them. To strengthen their argument they highlight that the fact that China had settled the boundary disputes with 12 other nations and there was give and take. Hence they argue that there is a possibility that China with the changed leadership may make serious efforts to resolve the boundary dispute with India.

On balance when the Chinese motives are analysed in the backdrop of continued anti-India activities, the view of the first category of experts appears to be correct. The Chinese leaders in the past had also made statements indicating their desire to amicably settle the issue. Late Sri Brijesh Mishra as the Indian envoy was told by Mao himself that the two countries should continue to fight. Deng also told the then Indian PM Rajiv Gandhi that the two countries should forge closer relations. Even Hu Jintao had expressed similar views. However the Chinese activities reflect that they have different plans and the Chinese continue with their intrusions without paying any attention to the Indian core concerns. The talks of the Chinese leaders when seen in the light of their activities only reveal their duplicitous nature.

The justification for the change in the policy towards Tibet is in fact provided by the Chinese themselves. Notwithstanding so many agreements, if the Chinese authorities are not considering the J&K as a part of India, India is fully justified in not treating the Tibet Autonomous Region as part of China. What India needs to discuss is the return of the territory illegally occupied by China in J&K. Rest is the border between India and Tibet, which should be discussed with the latter. India should declare that the length of India-China border is only limited to the J&K part that touches China. India at the same time stop policy of accommodating Chinese wishes by not sending officers from J&K or Arunachal Pradesh. Such acts actually go against our national interests by giving the impression that India is prepared to accept such demands. This does not mean that India and China would go to war but would establish that India can react against unjust demands of China. India –China trade, which is highly in favour of China, is yet another leverage against China and can be effectively used. The India-China trade deficit increased by 34% against India in the first five months of this year over the last year. The Chinese PM had recently come to India with a large delegation of the Chinese companies. The Chinese companies should be placed in the category of companies from the countries of concern and should not be given facilities to operate.

In addition, the continued human rights violations in Tibet demand suitable response from India. India being the neighbouring country cannot turn a blind eye to the happenings in Tibet. In fact this in itself is a sufficient reason for changing our policy towards Tibet. The Tibetans today remain marginalised. China has settled Hans by giving them incentives, with the result that in Lhasa and other urban centres Hans are in majority. The Asia Watch Report of 1990 had pointed out that in Amdo (Qinghai), Kham (Sichuan) and Lhasa Hans had outstripped the locals. The Tibet Youth Congress has also noted that recently that about 2 million Tibetans have been relocated since 2006. The unemployment among the Tibetans is increasing. The Tibetans cannot join as guides for tourists as the fluency in Mandarin is essential. In addition, as the locals have been moved to rural areas, they are not in a position to take advantage of the flourishing tourism in Tibet. Recently, Tibetans in Canada had protested against the Chinese policy of removing the Tibetans from urban areas and settling them in rural areas.

However, what is hurting the Tibetans most is the attack on religion of Tibetans. Dalai Lama, who is the spiritual head of Tibetans, is being demonised by the Chinese authorities. The real Panchen Lama, Gedhun Cheokyi Nyima, was imprisoned along with his family in 1995 and they selected their own man as Panchen Lama. In addition laws have been imposed which say that no one with criminal cases can join monasteries. The Chinese slap charges on all those who are considered to be anti-Chinese. And by the State Administration for Religious Affairs bill of 2007, all Lamas who wish to re-incarnate are required to obtain permission from the Government and that re-incarnation has to take place only in China.

The Chinese authorities are getting concerned about their vulnerabilities and therefore are trying to project that they intend to take necessary steps by changing their policies. The Chinese are aware that much of the economic development of China is due to the exploitation of natural resources of Tibet and they need them. Recent comments of Professor Jin Wei in Yazhou Zhoukan (Asia Weekly), a Chinese weekly in Hong Kong on June 9, 2013, and the reported proposals for new approach suggest that the current hard-line policy on Tibet is being questioned. The Chinese authorities may also be worried about the continued latent militancy in Tibet and suicides by Tibetans.

In sum, the security and foreign policies should be dictated by the strategic vision. The border incidents should not be treated as localized affairs. By saying this, Indian leadership is encouraging China to continue with their intrusions. The security establishment of the country and experts have been demanding a change in the policy to protect our national interests. It is well known that there are no permanent friends and no perennial enemies, what is permanent are our national interests. Tibet is not merely a strategic card against China but also the responsibility of India to support Tibetans against the continued human rights violations.

TIBETAN REFUGEES' RIGHTS AND SERVICES IN INDIA

The Chinese invasion of Tibet, and the Dalai Lama's subsequent decision to flee in 1959, resulted in the mass influx of Tibetan refugees into India that continues today. It has become clear to the Indian government, as well as to the Tibetan community in exile, that repatriation is unlikely in the near future. Consequently, an evaluation of India's protection of, and assistance for Tibetan refugees is necessary to ensure their treatment is in accordance with international standards. Unfortunately, such an assessment shows that there is a lack of proper protections and services; this ought to be of particular concern to the international community as India has served on the Executive Committee of the United Nations High Commissioner for Refugees (UNHCR) since 1995. How can a country be trusted to lead an international organization dedicated to the protection of refugees when it has such unstable and inadequate refugee policies itself?

Central to the assessment is India's lack of legal obligation to provide refugee protections or services. This is largely a consequence of India's abstention from the 1951 Convention relating to the Status of Refugees and the subsequent 1967 Protocol, which, in addition to defining a refugee according to international law, outlines certain rights and services host states must afford them. With the exceptions of the customary international practice of *non-refoulement* and the obligation to provide asylum as outlined in Article 14 of the Universal Declaration of Human Rights (UDHR), India does not have international, regional, or national obligations to refugee populations on its soil (Feller 2006). Despite this, and despite the nation's refusal to accede to the 1951 Convention, India argues its current refugee policy is in accordance with international norms. However, India has no national refugee law, and no regional agreement on the matter exists.

The only mention of foreigners in Indian law are in the Registration of Foreigners Act of 1939, the Foreigners Act of 1946, and the Foreigners Order of 1948— all of which employ the term *foreigner*, broadly defined as "a person who is not a citizen of India." Among other practices, the 1946 Act and the 1948 Order allow the government to limit employment opportunities, freedom of association, and a foreigner's possessions. These pieces of legislation also restrict movement inside India and prohibit select activities, most of which are political. In fact, Tibetan refugees are only allowed in India on the condition that they abstain from political protests against China – a clear suppression of their right to political expression as afforded by the UDHR. This political suppression was particularly evident during the 1991 visit of then Chinese Prime Minister Li Peng, during which Tibetan refugee leaders were arrested and placed under police surveillance to curtail protests. A similar occurrence was witnessed during Prime Minister Wen Jiabao's 2010 visit. Human rights law grants refugees fundamental civil and political rights, yet the Indian government denies these rights to Tibetan refugees.

India's lack of legal obligation allows it to alter refugee policies at will, often to reflect its current political interests. The result is a rather unstable refugee policy, exemplified in the disparity of rights and services afforded to Tibetan refugees according to their date of arrival in the country. The Indian government regarded the first wave of Tibetans arriving in 1959 with the Dalai Lama as refugees and granted them legal asylum. They were allotted land and housing – a privilege not afforded to other foreigners and one that would later be denied to newly arriving Tibetans. More importantly, these refugees were automatically given a Registration Certificate (RC). According to the Tibetan Government-in-Exile, the Central Tibetan Administration (CTA), the RC is a legal document issued by the Indian authorities that allows Tibetan refugees "the right to enjoy all the privileges enjoyed by any Indian citizen except the right to vote and work in Indian government offices" (Immigration and Refugee Board of Canada 2009). While many question the extent of the 'privileges enjoyed' by RC-holding Tibetans, the value of the RC is not contested. The RC allows Tibetans to legally travel and work within the country, serves as an identity document, and is a pre-requisite for the Identity Certificate, which is necessary for international travel. Tibetan refugees arriving between 1959 and the 1970s also benefited from services provided by the UNHCR, which despite its tumultuous relationship with India had a temporary presence in the country.

The rights and services afforded to Tibetans arriving after the 1970s are scarce and indicative of a changing Indian policy—

arguably in an effort to preserve Sino-Indian relations. In 1963, the Indian government ceased to legally recognize arriving Tibetans as refugees. Consequently, those arriving after 1979 (including some arriving in the late 1960s) have had greater difficulty acquiring RCs. The newer process to acquire an RC is arduous and particularly concerning because employment, residency rights, and international travel are contingent upon this document. In addition, while the Indian government provided land to the original refugee community, newer arrivals have not been as fortunate.

The denial of land by the government is troublesome considering that farming is chief to a Tibetan's income and Indian law prohibits foreigners from purchasing land. Additionally, the UNHCR closed its office in New Delhi and discontinued its aid to Tibetan refugees in 1975. As a consequence of the Indian government's lack of assistance, the CTA (with substantial assistance from NGOs) has had to shoulder the burden of providing for these refugees. Although the CTA is able to cover basic needs, they are overwhelmed and are unable to effectively address the broader social welfare of this burgeoning community (Adams 2005).

Even those with the RC continue to struggle with their refugee status. Unable to gain Indian citizenship, they cannot vote, work for local or federal governments, carry an Indian passport, or legally purchase land. Although Tibetans possessing an RC can legally work in pre-approved segments of the economy, many employers often discriminate against them in favour of Indian nationals. This resentment originates from the belief that Tibetan refugees are adversely affecting job opportunities and that they benefit from elevated standards of services not afforded to Indian nationals. While it is believed that communal relations between the Tibetans and the Indian host community have been improving, there have been isolated reports of aggression and discrimination that have largely gone uninvestigated by local police. To further exacerbate this issue, Tibetans are not represented in the local and central legislature and thus do not have readily available avenues for redress.

In 1949, when the United Nations debated legal protection versus material assistance for refugees, India argued that "the guarantee of legal rights without concomitant material assistance was a hollow concept" (Oberoi 2006, 22). However, it has become clear that as Tibetans continue to cross the border, India has not only decreased the rights afforded to these newcomers, but also the services provided to them. Given that repatriation for this refugee community does not appear possible in the immediate future, India needs to concern itself with improving its policy towards this population— thereby affording refugees the proper protection and treatment per international standards. Signing the 1951 Convention would be the best avenue by which to accomplish this as it will lessen the burden on India by affording it assistance and services from the UNHCR and member states. Above all, India's lack of legal obligation should not be understood as an absence of Tibetan refugees' entitlement to proper services and protections.

TREATMENT OF THE REFUGEES

In the beginning, two large transit camps were set up in consultation with the Government of India: one at Missamari, located ten miles from Tezpur in the Indian State of Arunachal Pradesh; the other at Buxa Duar, a former British prisoner-of-war camp situated near the Bhutanese border in West Bengal. Within a few weeks after the setting up the camps, 6,000 refugees arrived at Missamari and 1,000 at Buxa Duar. As the camps could accommodate not more than 9,000 persons between themselves, simultaneous efforts were made to disperse the refugees for road building works in the cooler regions of North India to prevent fatalities due to intense heat, overcrowding, and epidemic of amoebic dysentery. The first batch of 3,394 people was sent for roadwork in Sikkim in September 1959 in several groups.

Agricultural base Settlements

The Dalai Lama's vision of exile society took root in his new headquarters, an abandoned British hill station called Dharamsala. On 29 April 1960, after a little more than a year's stay, the Dalai Lama moved to his new headquarters from Mussoorie. In Dharamsala, the Dalai Lama revitalized his small administration in exile and called a special meeting of the people's deputies and staff members on 2 September 1960 to formulate new strategy and plan. As a part of the new plan, he established a bureau (now known as Bureau of H.H. the Dalai Lama) in New Delhi to serve as the Tibetan link with the Indian Government and various international relief agencies that were coming to the refugees' aid. Similarly, the Office of Tibet in New York was also set up in 1964 to raise the issue of Tibet at the United Nations and to disseminate information on Tibetans inside and outside Tibet. Rehabilitation, however, was the instant task at hand.

Although the roadwork had provided the much-needed temporary employment for the refugees, it turned out to be not only dangerous, but also hard. The migratory and unsettled nature of the roadwork proved to be extremely hard, particularly on the children and old people. Apart from this, many road-workers suffered from tuberculosis and other communicable diseases due to lack of nutrition and sanitation, compounded by hard labour. As such, the Dalai Lama approached Prime Minister Nehru for assistance for the permanent rehabilitation of the refugees. Nehru, on his part, canvassed the State Governments for vacant countryside for the purpose. Karnataka State (in South India) immediately responded, offering initially 3,000 acres of uninhabited stretch of jungle in gently rolling hills 52 miles west of Mysore City, situated at the altitude of 2,6000 ft. above sea level. It agreed to accept initially 3,000 Tibetan refugees and provide a grant of four million Indian rupees to execute the rehabilitation project.

Soon after this, the first Tibetan agricultural resolution was set up in the middle of December 1960 at Bylakuppe, accommodating a total of 3,217 Tibetan refugees by the end of 1965. For administrative reasons, the settlement was divided into six camps, each with 500 acres. In the first few years, the settlers engaged in reclaiming land, digging wells, and constructing houses, during which they were paid daily wages and given regular rations. The settlers were divided into artificial families of five people, relatives or not, and each family was given five acres of agricultural land. They were accommodated in the three-room brick-walled, tile-roofed single story house, built on a 500-sq. ft., part of which also served as their kitchen garden. A cooperative society was set up in 1961 and later formally registered. The cooperative society procured and advanced seeds, fertilizers, and pesticides; marketed agricultural produce collectively; and provided common services such as tractors, trucks, and warehousing. Besides, the cooperative society later played crucial role in managing carpet weaving centres, flour mills, poultry farms and other ventures such as retail outlets in the settlements. In the same year, a school was opened in the settlement. When the Bylakuppee settlement was first started, a small dispensary was set up in a tent to cater to the emergency medical needs of the refugees. Later in 1964, a special complex of concrete houses was built with assistance from foreign organizations to accommodate a dispensary with inpatient facilities.

For the first five years, the settlers cultivated cotton, tobacco, rice, millet, paddy, lentils and oilseeds, all of which failed miserably. Farming in South India was so different from Tibet's unique high-altitude agronomy that many settlers became totally discouraged and helpless. However, the agony of the repeated crop-failure was solved in 1965, when a Swiss technical adviser, in consultation with the Agriculture University of Bangalore, conducted soil tests and also tested the yields of bullock-ploughed and tractor-ploughed fields. This test resulted in the cultivation of maize crop instead of cotton, tobacco, and other crops and also replacement of bullock plows by tractor plows. The new crop and methods proved so successful that, by the end of 1966, the settlement became self-supporting. Bylakuppe settlement had served as a model for planning other agriculture based settlements later. By mid-seventies, 26 agricultural-based settlements were established in India, Nepal and Bhutan, accommodating a majority of the Tibetan refugees.

Agro-Industrial Settlement

It was apparent that it was not viable to restore all the refugees in agriculture-based settlements. Not only was it hard to find relatively large tracts of land, it was also not practical to rehabilitate all the refugees in agriculture-based settlements. Many of the refugees were traditionally nomads and traders, and had no idea of farming. With this in view and also to expedite the process of rehabilitation, it was found necessary to seek other avenues of resettlement.

Thus, a plan was made to rehabilitate many of the refugees in small-scale industries. To facilitate this, the Tibetan Industrial Rehabilitation Society (TIRS) was established in October 1965, with its headquarters in New Delhi. For the next three years, the TIRS launched several small industrial projects. These included woolen mill at Bir, tea estate in Bir and Chauntra, Tibetan crafts at Bejnath, limestone quarry at Kumrao, hydrated lime plant at Sataun, fiberglass factory at Poanta Sahib, and handicraft centre in Puruwala.

These projects accommodated more than 4,000 refugees. These projects were meant not only to provide adequate employment opportunities to the inmates, but also skills in different trades. In each industrial project, school and health care facilities were provided by the TIRS with funds raised from foreign agencies. Besides, the TIRS established a Himalayan Marketing Society, based in New Delhi, to market the produce of these settlements. However, many of these industrial efforts failed due to lack of technical and managerial skills. The majority of the industrial settlements gradually began to depend more on traditional carpet weaving, roadwork in summer, and woolen garment trade in Indian towns and cities in winter.

Handicraft-based Settlements

Over the centuries, Tibet had shared intimate cultural and deal relationship with its neighbouring countries. Through these interactions resulted in the development of many traditional crafts in Tibet. The traditional crafts included metal work, woodcraft, clay modelling, applique work, thangka painting, hand-made paper, leather work, woolen cloth and carpet weaving, etc. Although there were no major institutes in the traditional society to promote these trades, these arts and crafts were practiced in individual households and the products were sold out locally, or through traders to different part of Tibet. When the Tibetan refugees came into exile in early 1960s, some of the Tibetan craftsmen settled in Kalimpong, traditional Tibetan trading post in the North

India, and others settled temporarily in Darjeeling and Nepal. Thus, with hope of preserving and promoting the traditional Tibetan crafts as well as to provide employment options for the refugees, the CTA, in consultation with the Government of India, set up several handicraft-based settlements as a part of rehabilitation scheme.

The first handicraft-based settlement was set up on a four-acre estate in Darjeeling in October 1959. The 13th Dalai Lama, during his exile from Tibet in 1910-11, had used the site as his temporary residence and therefore, has a special sentimental value for the Tibetans. The settlement or centre provided shelter and employment for 450 people. Education and medical needs of the inmates were also taken care of. Besides, the centre also ran old people's home and a crèche for small children.

The centre's produce, such as carpets, woolen sweaters, Tibetan women's aprons, wood carved decoration items, wooden toys, leather goods, etc. were marketed locally as well as abroad with the help of aid agencies. Encouraged by the success of the first handicraft-based settlement, other similar settlements or centres were set up in the following years.

These included the handicraft centre in Dalhousie, Dharamsala, Kalimpong, Simla, Clement Town, Rajpur, and Dehradun–all in India. Similar settlements were also set up in Nepal. In these handicraft-based settlements, cooperative units were established to procure raw materials and market produce. While the cooperatives marketed the settlement's produce both in India and abroad, the settlers engaged also in individual trade of sweaters–knitted initially by themselves, but later bought from the factories in Ludhiana City in Punjab, India–to supplement their income. Each winter they set up makeshift bamboo-walled and plastic-topped stalls on the sidewalks of bazaars and marketplaces all across India. By the later half of the sixties, sweater selling became the supplementary trade of the majority of Tibetan refugees.

By 1980, only 30,000 Tibetan refugees remained on road construction work. By 1992, a total of 52, 500 people were rehabilitated in the agricultural settlements, 7,700 in Agro-Industrial settlements, and 6,400 in handicraft-based settlements, and 39,800 refugee remained outside the organized units, earning livelihood in petty private enterprises or in the Indian service industries.

New Challenges

The death of Mao Zedong in 1976 and the end of the Cultural Revolution in China and Tibet resulted in opening China to the outside world. This dramatic change also led to the opening of Tibet and the first-post 1959 contact between Beijing and Dharamsala, which took place in March 1979. Many Tibetans, both inside and outside Tibet, took the advantage of the situation to undertake the arduous cross-Himalayan journey to visit their family members and relatives. Many families met for the first time after two decades of separation. With the passage of time, a steady stream of new refugees from Tibet came to seek asylum in India and Nepal.

From 1987 to 1994, Tibet was rocked by a series of pro-independence demonstrations. The Chinese authorities reacted by escalating the machinery of repression, especially against those involved in demonstration. This made life in Tibet all the more difficult, resulting in a mammoth increase in the flow of refugees. Between 1986-1996, some 18,700 refugees arrived in India and Nepal. The situation became still worse after 1994 when the Chinese government introduced harsher policy to deal with the Tibetan nationalism in Tibet.

In order to cater to the needs of these new refugees, the CTA opened a Reception Centre in Dharamsala in 1990. Later, its branches were opened in Kathmandu and Delhi. While the Kathmandu Reception Centre is supported jointly by the UNHCR and CTA, the centres in Dharamsala and Delhi are funded by the CTA with a support from the United States' Government. The rehabilitation of the children below the age of 18 and monks and nuns is comparatively easier as the children can be sent to existing boarding schools and the monks and nuns to the monasteries and nunneries in India. The rehabilitation of adult refugees is problematic. This is because most of the adult new refugees are unskilled and most of the existing settlements are overcrowded.

As such, the CTA opened a special Adult Education Centre in the outskirts of Dharamsala in 1993 to provide vocational and language training to the new refugees.

MIGRATION FROM SETTLEMENTS IN INDIA

Migration of young people from Tibetan settlements in India is a serious cause of concern as it threatens Tibetan identity and culture in exile with marginalization. According to Tenzin Lekshay, most exile settlements are guarded by old aged people, some established schools in the settlements are on the verge of closing for lack of pupils, and graduates are scattering to Indian cities because of the lack of employment opportunities in the community. According to Nawang Thogmed, a CTA official, the most oft-cited problems for newly migrating Tibetans in India are the language barrier, their dislike for Indian food, and the warm climate, which makes Tibetan clothing uncomfortable. Some exiles also fear that their Tibetan culture is being diluted in India. Indian television runs in Hindi and English.

In Bhutan

Few Tibetans settled in Bhutan after 1959, as the country was used mainly as a transit route to India. However, in 1961, following growing tensions between China and India, India sealed its northern border with Bhutan, prompting Bhutan to arrange an emergency meeting with the Government of India (GOI) and the CTA to deal with the Tibetans stuck in the country. The government of Bhutan agreed to take in 4000 settlers, although ordinary Bhutanese became increasingly resentful of the Tibetan immigrants because of their refusal to assimilate into Bhutanese culture. In 1974, 28 Tibetans, including the representative of the Dalai Lama in Thimphu, were arrested and accused of a conspiracy to assassinate King Jigme Singye Wangchuck. When the CTA refused to provide evidence of their innocence, relations between Bhutan and Dharamshala soured, and in 1979, the Government of Bhutan announced that any Tibetan in the country that did not take Bhutanese citizenship would be repatriated back to China. Despite the CTA's opposition, 2300 Tibetans applied for citizenship; most of the remainder resettled in India.

In Europe and North America

Tibetans in Europe and North America are not as politically active or unintegrated into the host society as Tibetans in India, because they do not live in concentrated communities, and are educated in local schools instead of living under a special Tibetan jurisdiction as Tibetan Indians do.

In Europe, Tibetans have been received more positively than other immigrants to Europe, and are stereotyped as spiritual and victims. Politically, organizations such as the Tibetan Youth Association in Europe attempt to cultivate a Tibetan identity for Tibetans in Europe. However, many Tibetan youths in Europe cannot speak a Tibetan language and do not feel they belong to a wider Tibetan community; such identity crises have on occasion led to drug dependency and crime.

INDIA'S REFOULEMENT POLICY

India's ability to *refoule* persons seeking asylum in India violates international customary law on the treatment of refugees, as well as the standards codified in the Refugee Convention.

As part of customary international law, the policy of *non-refoulement* prevents a country from expelling refugees to countries where their lives or liberties would be threatened. The majority of states, including the 137 signatories to the Refugee Convention, consistently practice *non-refoulement* in its determination of whether to grant entrance to people seeking asylum.

Furthermore, states consider *non-refoulement* an obligation to all persons seeking asylum, regardless of whether they are in countries that are signatories to the Refugee Convention. Most states, regardless of whether they are parties to the Refugee Convention, hold that non-refoulement transcends the Refugee Convention and observe this rule. The practice of *non-refoulement* by most states, as well as their respect for the policy as a legal obligation, has rendered *non-refoulement* customary international law. India consequently violates customary international law, as well as the Refugee Convention, when it returns groups at the border.

Incongruent Policy Toward Refugee Groups

India bases its treatment of various refugee groups on political grounds, resulting in an unstable and ever-changing domestic policy. India grants privileges to certain refugee groups based on bilateral and multilateral political relations with other states, as well as domestic political opinion.

An examination of India's treatment of Tibetan refugees arriving in the 1960s and 1970s versus Tibetan refugees arriving since the 1980s provides an example of India's discriminatory policies. Tibetan refugees began to enter India in 1959, after Communist China's invasion of Tibet and its violent repression of a Tibetan rebellion, forcing the Dalai Lama, the spiritual leader of Tibet, to flee across the Indian frontier. 85,000 Tibetan refugees followed the Dalai Lama when China annexed Tibet in 1959.

By 1998, according to the Tibetan Administration in India, the number of Tibetan refugees in India had reached more than 118,000. The Indian government conditioned the entry of any Tibetan refugees on the Dalai Lama's pledge to personally abstain from violent and political activities.

India gave Tibetan refugees arriving in the 1960s and 1970s preferential treatment compared to the other refugee communities living in India for a variety of reasons. The first group of Tibetan refugees to enter India had several exigencies that other refugee groups did not.

First, a head of state of a previously independent country, the Dalai Lama, asked for shelter for himself and his people. Second, China's invasion of Tibet played a role in relations between Democratic India and Communist China and focused the world's attention on the Tibetans' plight. Third, Tibetan refugees were then, and still are, the largest body of refugees in India, and were thus too large a group to ignore. Fourth, Tibetan refugees are members of a society and culture that is eager to re-establish itself in its home territory and were viewed as only having a temporary reliance on India. As a result of these exigencies, India allowed the Dalai Lama to establish a Tibetan government-in-exile called the Central Tibetan Administration (CTA), seated in the northern

Indian city of Dharamsala, but it did not officially recognize it. In addition, although no foreigners can own property in India, the Indian government provided land and housing to establish Tibetan farming settlements.

Furthermore, the Indian government granted the Tibetan refugees who entered through the 1970s Indian Residential Certificates for identification purposes, permission to work, domestic travel rights, Indian Identity Certificates, which allowed them to travel outside India (similar to a passport), and medical treatment. Although, according to Indian law, the Indian government has no obligation to assist refugees, the Indian government chooses to grant these early Tibetan refugees services and opportunities no other group enjoys.

With the increasing number of Tibetan refugees coming to India after 1980, however, the Tibetan refugee community began to place greater strain on Indian services. The government decided to grant substantially less assistance to the Tibetan refugees arriving after 1980. According to both the USCR and the International Campaign for Tibet, although India admitted Tibetan refugees into the country after 1980, the government has denied these Tibetans both Residential Certificates and Identity Certificates. The refusal to grant both the Residential and Identity Certificates creates serious consequences because employment, international travel, and naturalization hinge on possession of these documents. As a result, these rights are unattainable for the new arrivals. In addition, the Indian government refused to grant Tibetans new allotments of land, despite the fact that the Indian government admitted 25,000 Tibetans between 1986 to 1996, according to a 1997 U.S. Senate Committee Hearing on Foreign Relations. CTA argues that this has lead to overpopulation, unemployment, and food shortages in the Tibetan refugee community. Furthermore, press reports have described incidents of the Indian government returning to China small groups of Tibetan refugees seeking entry into India.

The Indian government's decline in assistance appears to be a result of India's attempt to improve its relations with China and domestic political opinion. Further subsidization of the Tibetan refugee community may strain India's relations with China. For instance, China could potentially view this assistance as Indian support for a Tibetan state, and subsequently, as -an affront to China's sovereign claim over Tibet. In addition, the retrenchment of assistance is an attempt to stem the overpopulation of Tibetan settlements. According to a 1998 country report on India by USCR, "Because India has no legal framework for determining refugee status, it deals with refugees on an *ad hoc* basis, which has led to refugees being used as 'pawns in regional geo-politics.'" Basing refugee policy on domestic or foreign policy contradicts the purpose of the Refugee Convention.

5

Refugee: A Creature of Circumstances

It should be appreciated that a person becomes a refugee because of circumstances which are beyond that person's control, often poignant. He/She is left with no other option but to flee from human rights violations, socio-economic and political insecurity, generalised violence, civil war or ethnic strife all these leading to fear of persecution. The import of this observation would be evident when one looks at the definition of a 'refugee'. The term 'Refugee' has a particular meaning in international law and its legal definition is laid down in the United Nations 1951 Convention relating to the Status of Refugees (to be referred to as "1951Convention") and its 1967 Protocol. Article 1 para. 2 of the 1951 Convention defines the 'refugee' as "A person who owing to well founded fear of being persecuted for reasons of race, religion, nationality, membership of a particular social group or political opinion, is outside the country of his nationality and is unable or, owing to such fear, unwilling to avail himself of the protection of that country.". Therefore, the need to give due importance to humanitarian and human rights aspects in dealing with refugees cannot be over-stressed.

Thus, it may be noted that there are well-defined and specific grounds, which have to be satisfied before a person can qualify to be a ' refugee'. These grounds are *well-founded on fear of persecution* and considerations of a number of factors which may operate individually or collectively.

DISTINCTION BETWEEN REFUGEES AND OTHER FOREIGNERS

While all persons who are not Indian citizens are 'Foreigners' including refugees, it is necessary to clearly distinguish the latter from other categories of 'foreigners'. There are considerable misgivings in the minds of many in India because of the failure to clearly understand the difference between 'refugees' and various 'other categories of foreigners'.

The consequence of this misunderstanding, particularly because of the large number of 'illegal immigrants' from Bangladesh who have spread into different parts of India, has tended to adversely influence the thinking of many in the country about the basic issues involved in the problem of 'refugees'. Unless the distinction between the 'refugees' on the one hand and all other categories of 'foreigners' on the other, is clearly brought home, our attempts to sensitise people in the various strata of our society will remain inadequate.

There are at least three well-defined groups of foreigners who are different from 'refugees'. It is important that the distinction among them is clearly understood and none of them is confused with or mistaken for a 'refugee'. These categories are:

Temporary Residents, Tourists and Travellers

Persons under this category come to India for a specific purpose and duration with the prior permission of the Government of India. However, in certain circumstances any one in this category could become eligible for being a refugee, if, during their sojourn in India, the situation in their country of origin becomes such as to endanger their lives and liberty if they were to return to their country. Many Iranians who had come to India for studies during the regime of the Shah of Iran, have stayed back in India as refugees after the fall of Shah of Iran and a revolutionary government took his place in 1978. It should be mentioned that no one can automatically claim the right for 'refugee status' under this category. It is the prerogative of the Indian government to satisfy themselves and decide each case according to merits and circumstances.

Illegal Economic Migrants

Any foreigner who might have left his or her country of origin without due authorisation from the authorities concerned, both in the country of origin as well as the country of destination, solely to improve his or her economic prospects, is *not a refugee*. After all, there is no element of persecution or coercion compelling the individual to leave the country of origin. Illegal migrants from Bangladesh are examples of this category. Such persons have to be treated as illegal and unauthorised entrants into the country and dealt with under the appropriate laws applicable to foreigners like Foreigners Act, Indian Passport Act etc. besides the IPC, Cr.PC etc.

Criminals, Spies, Infiltrators, Militants etc

None of these can ever become eligible to be refugees. They have to be dealt with under the provisions of the Indian criminal laws as well as any other special laws in force even though some of them may be in possession of valid travel documents.

Internally Displaced Persons (IDP)

Those persons who are fleeing persecution and human rights violations from one region of the country and have sought refuge in another region of the same country, fall under this category. Such persons cannot be categorised as 'refugees' as they have not crossed any international border. Moreover, they have the protection of their national government. These persons are categorised as 'internally displaced persons' (IDP). Kashmiris who have been forced to flee from Jammu and Kashmir and who have settled in other parts of India fall under this category. Incidentally, in many African countries, the IDPs are also treated as 'refugees' within the ambit of the 1951 Convention.

EVIDENCE REQUIRED TO ESTABLISH A REFUGEE CLAIM

In order for a claimant refugee to put forward a genuine claim for determination of refugee status, it is crucial to accumulate all the documents that the claimant can muster in support of the grounds of persecution or fear thereof resulting in flight from country of origin. The documentation may be in the form of an identity card of employment with some governmental agency in the country of origin, or an identity card indicating membership of a particular group. Production of the same would be evidence of a claim of involvement with particular groups and would also serve to prove the claimant's identity. Any other information that the claimant may be able to gather to prove specific persecution or fear thereof, such as names of persecutors, leaders of groups involved in committing persecution, details of areas where persecution is committed will help strengthen the case of the claimant. Similarly, the claimant must be able to establish all his statements to interviewing authorities in a consistent manner, without discrepancies. If there are obvious contradictions between the statements made by the claimant himself at different times to different persons, his claim to refugee status may be rejected. The statements made by the claimant must also not be contradictory to the general information available on the country of origin. Corroboration and confirmation of facts pertaining to persecution is an essential factor in determining refugee status. Efforts are made by authorities to gather background human rights data from a broad cross section of official and non-governmental sources in order to supplement whatever evidence may be adduced by the claimant himself. Thus, circumstantial evidence that persons similarly situated to the claimant are at risk in the country of origin, is essential.

To establish a fear of persecution, the term "fear" is not to be judged on the basis of the emotional reaction of the claimant. Instead, "fear" must be employed to mandate a forward looking assessment of risk. Therefore, persons who had already suffered persecution in their country of origin, as well as those who may be judged to face prospective risk of persecution in event of return to their country of origin, would be able to claim refugee status.

The heart of the refugee determination process is the careful consideration of the claimant's own evidence, whether provided orally or in documentary form. It is ideally required that all claimants for refugee status receive an opportunity to be heard by the authority responsible for the adjudication of their case. All the materials thus collected and collated are then tallied with independent, internationally acknowledged information available on the region from which the claimant has arrived. In possible circumstances and cases, the information thus obtained is also reconfirmed from the UNHCR office in the country of origin.

Along with making claims for refugee status, refugees may also seek redressal of immediate basic problems facing them, such as food, shelter, legal aid etc. In regard to such matters the UNHCR plays a major role by providing in suitable and deserving cases, a "Subsistence Allowance" to destitute refugees and their dependents. The UNHCR also helps in enabling the refugee to find his own accommodation or to share a tenanted accommodation with another similarly placed refugee. When a refugee seeks legal aid for himself or for his dependent, the UNHCR may provide the assistance or recommend an Advocate who is familiar with handling refugee matters, to help sort out the problem faced by the refugee. In cases where the refugee is to be deported back to his country of origin, the UNHCR officials may request the Central Government to stall deportation proceedings, pending UNHCR attempts at resettlement of the refugee in a safe country. In order to make such resettlement possible, the UNHCR takes up such cases with the Embassies of other countries for grant of travel to and stay facilities in their countries.

ACCORDING 'REFUGEE STATUS'

Even though India has been the home for a large number and variety of refugees throughout the past, India has dealt with the issues of 'refugees' on a bilateral basis. India, as explained in the earlier pages, has been observing a 'refugee regime' which generally conforms to the international instruments on the subject without, however, giving a formal shape to the practices adopted by it in the form of a separate statute. Refugees are no doubt 'foreigners'. Even though there may be a case to distinguish them from the rest of the 'foreigners', the current position in India is that they are dealt with under the existing Indian laws, both general and special, which are otherwise applicable to all foreigners. This is because there is no separate law to deal with 'refugees'. For the same reason, cases for refugee 'status' are considered on a case-by-case basis. UNHCR often plays a complementary role to the efforts of the Government, particularly in regard to verification about the individual's background and the general circumstances prevailing in the country of origin. That agency also plays an important role in the resettlement of refugees etc.

It may be restated for purposes of clarity and understanding that a refugee is defined as one who is outside the country of nationality (or even country of habitual residence) due to one of the five grounds, namely, a well-founded fear of persecution on the basis of religion, race, nationality or membership of a political or social group. In some countries, a person who flees his home country because of armed conflicts or wars or other generalised violation of human rights and who may not be targeted on account of any of the five grounds specified above, is excluded from the purview of the above definition of 'refugee'. In many countries a difference is sought to be made between persecution effected by State agents and the one effected by non-state agents as may be the case in places where 'rebel' 'terrorist' and such other groups are active. Under such circumstances it is only those who are affected by the action of the State agents who are held to fulfill the definition of 'refugee' and not the latter.

One of the principal elements to satisfy a claim to refugee status is that the claimant must be 'genuinely at risk'. Various legal "tests" have developed which concern the standard of proof that is required to satisfy what constitutes being genuinely at risk or having a genuine well founded fear of persecution. Some of these tests have been articulated by courts in a number of countries. In the case of *INS vs Cardoza Fouseca* interpretation of the "well founded fear" standard would indicate that "so long as an objective situation is established by the evidence, it need not be shown that the situation will probably result in persecution, but it is not enough that persecution is a reasonable possibility..." The above standard was considered in *R vs Secretary for the Home Department*, the case of *ex parte Sivakumaran*. The judgement suggested that the 'test' should consider whether there is an evidence of a "real & substantial danger of persecution". The Canadian Federal Court of Appeal considered the above and disapproved the House of Lords formulation in *Joseph Ayei vs Ministry of Employment & Immigration*. They considered the "reasonable chance" standard. Therefore, in sum, in considering the above 'tests' what can be gleened is a rather liberal standard which requires that if, "....there is an objective evidence to show that there is a reasonable possibility or chance of relevant prosecution in the claimant's state of origin", the claim should be adjudged well founded.

In the case of India, the decision as whether to treat a person or a group of persons as refugees or not is taken on the merits and circumstances of the cases coming before it. The Government of India (GOI) may be often seen as following a policy of bilateralism in dealing with persons seeking to be refugees. For example, Afghan refugees of Indian origin and others, who entered India through Pakistan without any travel documents, were allowed entry through the Indo-Pakistan border till 1993. Most of the refugees had entered India through the Attari border near Amritsar in Punjab. Subsequent to 1993, the Government altered its policy of permitting Afghan refugees freely into India.

In the case of a large number of them (many of them were Afghan Sikhs and Afghan Hindus) who had to flee from Afghanistan under circumstances which fulfilled one or more of the grounds specified earlier for being treated as a 'refugee', the GOI did not officially treat them as refugees. However, the UNHCR with the consent of the GOI, recognised them as refugees under its mandate and is rendering assistance to them. In such cases, even though the local Government is kept in the picture, the UNHCR becomes responsible to look after them as well as 'administer' them and also to ensure that such refugees do not in any way violate the code of conduct governing them.

In contrast, in 1989, when the Myanmar authorities started suppressing the pro-democracy movement in that country and about 3,000 nationals of that country sought refuge in India, the GOI declared that in accordance with well accepted international norms defining refugee status, no genuine refugee from Myanmar would be turned back and in fact, they were accepted as refugees by the GOI. Similar is the case of Sri Lankan Tamil refugees crossing the sea to enter the southern Indian State of Tamil Nadu. The Government of India followed a specific refugee policy regarding Sri Lankan refugees and permitted them entry despite the fact that the refugees did not have travel documents.

In cases where the Government of India recognises the claim of refugee status of a particular group of refugees, there is minimal interference if any, caused to the refugees. This is the case even though there may be no official declaration of any policy of grant of refugee status to that group. However, there are instances where refugees recognised by the Government of India and issued with valid refugee identity documents by the government, are later prosecuted for illegal entry/over stay. The National Human Rights Commission had taken up successfully the cause of a number of Sri Lankan Tamil refugees who had been likewise prosecuted.

DETENTION OF REFUGEE CHILDREN

Refugee children face many problems which deserve to be treated with due sensitivity, care and caution by the authorities concerned. Usually, access is provided to detained mothers to meet their children and tend to their needs. There are, however, cases of sufficiently grown up refugee children who may be between the ages of 15 and 18 years of age and who may be detained for non possession of valid travel documents. Such a problem mostly arises due to the fact that children are not granted separate residential permits but are included in their parent's permits. In cases involving children who do not possess separate residential permits, the UNHCR may be in a position to help sort out the problem, particularly because in cases where refugee children are separated from their families, UNHCR makes all possible attempts to reunite them. Therefore, it will be advantageous if the security agency concerned seeks the help and assistance of the UNHCR in such matters.

In the specific case of Winston Venojan, a Sri Lankan Tamil refugee, thanks to the UNHCR, the 17 year old boy, who had got separated from his parents, was reunited with them. In this case the boy was arrested on landing at New Delhi. Bail was, however, granted to him within a short time. In genuine cases of this kind, the security agency should always consider not to oppose bail. In the meanwhile, the UNHCR got clearance from the British Immigration and Nationality Department for the boy to travel to the UK.

However, the refugee could not be permitted to leave the country till the disposal of the case for the violation of some of the legal provisions under the Indian laws. Luckily this matter was speedily disposed off on the intervention of the Delhi High court. Once the court's orders were obtained, the refugee was provided with Red Cross travel documents to travel to London. The security agency can further help in such genuine case by speedy investigation and filing of charge sheet in time.

Securing that the Refugee is not Untraceable on Release from Detention

Release of a refugee from detention is often fraught with legalities. Courts are sometimes reluctant to direct release of the refugee without ensuring about securing his/her presence in a specific place. The primary concern of courts while barring the deportation of refugees is that the refugee should not become "untraceable". In some cases of this kind, courts have agreed that the refugee may be handed over into the "care of UNHCR". This would ensure that the refugee will be available whenever wanted. In addition, the UNHCR would take care of the refugee till the legal issue is disposed of. In cases where the UNHCR refuses to take custody of the said refugees, there will be no alternative but to send the refugees back to Jail.

Securing against Re-arrest on Release from Detention

The refugee on release from prison after serving his/her sentence may still not be having valid travel documents. In such circumstances, the refugee may face the risk of re-arrest while commuting from the prison to secure residential permit/refugee certificate etc., Hence the authorities are often requested to provide police escort to the refugee to enable him to reach the authorised place safely and to secure documents for valid stay in India. This measure would help speed up to regularise the stay in India, which is desirable from both the point of view of security as well as humanitarian considerations.

Timely filing of Charge Sheet by the Prosecution to Enable Pleading Guilty

The need for timely filing of charge-sheet in courts of law cannot be over emphasised, particularly in the cases of refugees. Only when the charge sheet is filed it is possible for the refugee to be aware of the charges against him and to plead guilty to the same. In some cases the refugee may require early disposal of his/her case, hence filing of charges at an early stage is crucial.

6

Tibetan Settlements in Exile

Today, after more then four decades in exile, there are now total of 12,2078 (TDS*) number of Tibetan population living worldwide. Majority of them are settled in fifty two settlements located in South Asia, Out of which thirty five in India, ten in Nepal and seven in Bhutan. There are now twenty four agricultural based settlements, sixteen agro based settlements and ten handicraft units. Besides, there are Tibetan located in scattered communities in various towns and cities of India.

TIBETAN SETTLEMENTS IN INDIA AND NEPAL

When Tibetan first came into exile, most of them were starving or wounded, sick from the low altitude and stunned by the cultural shock of coming into distant world, with the result, many died of disease, hot climate and trauma they have undergone leaving their land. In the beginning, many of them got engaged in road construction works in the hilly states of India.

Gradually, they were rehabilitated in the newly created settlements in south and central India. Tibetans were trained in cultivating local Indian crops like maize, millet, rice and mustard and soon after, agriculture became the main source of livelihood. At the same time Tibetans have started selling winter garments especially sweaters in streets of towns and cities of India. Today sweater selling business has become dominant economic activity for Tibetans in India. Although agriculture is a major primary occupation of Tibetans especially for those living in agricultural based settlements in south India.

The largest percentage share of income that is forty one percent comes from Tibetan doing trade and business which includes selling garments and doing petty business.

The salaried employment, which includes services in army, government and teaching, contributes twenty three percent of the household income, whereas agricultural and allied activities account for twenty six of the total workforce contributing a mere eight percent of the total household income.

Apart from the primary sources of income, the Tibetan households also rely on subsidiary sources of income, which include income from sponsorships, government and foreign remittances. Many of the economically deprived households are either being looked after by the government or are supported by the sponsors from abroad.

In 1990's many Tibetans immigrated abroad, especially to the United States, as a result of which their families back home have started receiving money from them. According to the official statistics, an average Tibetan household earns Rs.66800 per year, which translates into Rs. 13100 per capita per annum.

Presently Tibetan people's general standard of living can be comparable to surrounding native rural communities; in some areas the economic conditions are far better than native Indian villages. Almost all the settlements are provided with primary and secondary schools, primary health care centre and cooperative societies. There are also monasteries, nunneries and temples in the settlements. The cooperatives in the settlements play a vital role in settler's life. The cooperatives procure and advance seeds, fertilizers and pesticides, market agricultural produce collectively and provide common services such as tractors, trucks and warehousing. Cooperatives also run small business ventures like carpet weaving workshops and small incense factory. Education of Tibetan children has been the top most priority of Tibetan administration right from the beginning. Today more than 84 schools are set up in India with the help of Indian government and foreign aids. With the result, Literacy rate of Tibetans has almost reached 78 percent and the literacy rate of 99 percent is in the age group between 19 and 25.

Demography of Tibetan Population in Exile

According to the Tibetan government official statistics, there are now 12, 2078 (TDS*) number of Tibetans living in different parts of the world. The largest number of them is living in settlements in South Asia. Out of the total population, 85,000 live in India, 13,000 in Nepal and 1,500 in Bhutan. So far about 12,153* Tibetans have moved to other parts of the world. The Continent of USA and Canada has the largest number of Tibetans; the figure has reached up to 7000. The next largest concentration of Tibetan refugees in the west is in Switzerland with a population of about 2000.

New Refugees

After more than four decades of Chinese occupation of Tibet. The influx of Tibetan refugees coming into exile still continues. An average of 2000 to 2500 Tibetans come to exile in India every year. More than 44 percent of them are teenagers and young adults (age 14-25), Thirty three percent adults (26-59), More than 17 percent young children (0-13) and only 5 percent are over the age of sixty. In order to look after the needs of these refugees, Tibetan government has opened a reception centre in Kathmandu, Delhi and Dharamsala.

The young children below the age of 13 years and monks are rehabilitated easily in India by being sent to the schools run by TCV and THF and monks and nuns are sent to the monasteries in different refugee settlements. The rehabilitation of adults between the age group 18 and over is a big problem, since many of them are uneducated and unskilled. Tibetan government has set up an adult education centre for these adults where they are taught Basic English, Tibetan and Mathematics as well as arts and crafts. The CTA provides small grants to these adult refugees to start a small business. Many of them are engaged in small antique business and restaurants on the roadside.

Challenges in Exile

Tibetan refugee group of people in exile is considered as one of the most successful refugee communities in the world. They have managed to rebuild their lives in a completely alien environment achieving almost total economic self reliance. Tibetan Administration in exile has succeeded in rehabilitating the refugees in a cohesive society creating an environment where Tibetans have been able to preserve their age long rich enlightening heritage and identity.

Today, after a long period of life in exile, Tibetan Government and the Tibetan people are transitory through a very crucial period. There are many challenges and issues facing the Tibetan exiled community. The most important being the advancing age of Tibet's spiritual leader, the Dalai Lama. Tibetan government in exile headed by the Dalai Lama has left no stones unturned to resolve the issue of Tibet peacefully with the Chinese government since long, but there has been no positive response from the Chinese side, rather they have strengthened their draconian rule in Tibet imposing strict restrictions on Tibetan people their religious activities and Human Rights. Chinese government's population transfer policy aimed at wiping out entire ethnic Tibetan population is a serious concern for the Dalai Lama and his exiled government. The matter has become very serious with the completion of Beijing-Lhasa railway line last year. On the other hand Tibetan Diaspora faces a threat of disintegration as many of the new generation exiles have started moving out from the existing Tibetan settlements and their urge to move to the west makes the situation still worse. Moreover Tibetans already settled in the west are in danger of assimilating into the western culture and life style. Therefore many Tibetans believe that if Tibet issue is not resolved soon in future or during the Dalai Lama's life time, there is every chance of Tibetan identity being wiped out completely from the world. So the period of next ten to fifteen years is going to be very crucial for Tibetans inside and outside Tibet. As His Holiness has already reached 72 years, his growing age is a serious concern to all the Tibetan people. Some are of the opinion that there will be a leadership crisis in Tibetan community after the Dalai Lama, even though he has made all the preparation of future Tibet_ be it laying down a strong democratic institution in exile or setting a policy regarding the Tibetan issue with the Chinese government.

In exiled community, the major challenge we face today is the growing unemployment among the Tibetan youth. According to the Tibetan Demographic Survey, the unemployment rate among the Tibetan youth is as high as seventy five percent. On that, the number of school and college graduates increasing every year, about 1250 students passing out every year from the schools and colleges in India. The chances of these youth getting employment in our community are very low as total absorption capacity is just five percent. The major factor is the lack of employment opportunities in the settlements and the shift in the economic structure of refugees in exile.

The early refugees have adopted agriculture and allied activities as their major source of livelihood and besides agriculture, Tibetans have also started business by setting up sweater business in Indian towns and cities. But the new generation of exiles born and brought up in India which has acquired education and skills evidently are in need of better job opportunities.

The new generation of Tibetans can be accommodated either in Tibetan administration service or in other services in exiled community. Thanks to the liberalization policy of Indian government, which has benefited not only the Indian masses, but educated Tibetan youths also by getting jobs easily in the corporate world in major cities, as many Tibetan youths are presently employed in the corporate sector in jobs ranging from executive to providing customer care service. Although, it seems to solve the unemployment problem but this will have a far-reaching consequences on Tibetan community as a whole in future. Until and unless Tibetan administration in exile able to initiate sustainable rural based economy in the settlements, the problem of Tibetan migrating to other places will continue. Tibetan government in exile understands the issue and has policies to make settlement's economy sound and sustainable.

DEVELOPMENT ENTREPRENEURSHIP IN TIBETAN SETTLEMENTS

In the Tibetan settlements, a higher degree of entrepreneurship will catalyse economic growth. It will provide a robust platform for new and potentially more exciting jobs. In the long run, the promotion of small to medium sized enterprises will further the vision of the Central Tibetan Administration's desire to improve settlement viability. Settlement level research shows that there is a significant potential for enterprise development. Existing programs including the Youth Empowerment Support Program (YES) attempt to promote self employment through skill development and better access to capital.

However, the effectiveness of these programs can be improved considerably. Surveys conducted with community members indicate a relatively high preference of businesses ownership amongst the youth as compared to that of the previous generation, namely their parents. However, on average, most youth demonstrate a lack of the relevant skills, motivation, and strategies required to pursue entrepreneurship.

In the near term, Tibetan settlements would benefit from a series of interventions designed to share the benefits of entrepreneurship, develop the relevant skills required to start and run a business, and help entrepreneurs understand the nuances and options to access financial capital. In the long term, settlements will require a greater emphasis on growing and supporting existing businesses and creating self sustainability. Interventions in the near and long term require the collaboration of existing Tibetan organizations including: CTA, YES, Institute for Small Trade Learning (ISTL), Vocational Training Centre, cooperative societies and settlement leadership.

Outside organizations can and should be utilized on an as needed basis. The intervention would impact youth, especially those who are dynamic yet remain unemployed. It would give them an opportunity to establish enterprises which in turn would provide services to the settlers and others. The intervention would also help build capabilities among the various institutions that would be involved in fostering entrepreneurship. While fostering entrepreneurship within settlements can initially present legal and political challenges, a systematic, collaborative, and integrated approach involving the relevant organizations and neighbouring communities will mitigate these concerns.

Impression

At a macro level, entrepreneurship offers the possible to create sustained economic growth for countries, while offering the prospect of greater employment and prosperity. Entrepreneurs have the ability to spot opportunity in the midst of crises. Moreover entrepreneurs thrive on innovation, seeking new markets and new products regardless of economic conditions.

Several studies have proven the value of entrepreneurship in developed countries, where opportunity seeking entrepreneurs are tempted by the prospect of creating the next Standard Oil, Microsoft or Google. The risk-reward premium is clearly observed throughout the developed world. A 2008 World Bank Survey on Entrepreneurship notes that there is a high correlation between the rate of new businesses entering the market and GDP in over 100 countries. Developed countries by definition have a greater density of businesses contributing to GDP than developing countries, yet it is important to note the disparity in entrepreneurship between developed and developing countries. While at first glance it may seem that high GDP is a prerequisite for high levels of entrepreneurship, developing countries actually display a higher trend in both the number of total and new businesses generated. Moreover, some developing countries doubled their numbers from 2000 to 2008. Industrialized nations, on the other hand, displayed little variation in business creation during the same period.

Underlying principle: For the Tibetan Community in India, need and survival will function as the primary motivation for many entrepreneurs, resulting in an emergence of micro-enterprises within the settlements. However, continued interventions to develop entrepreneurs will lead to greater numbers of opportunity seeking entrepreneurs.

Present circumstances;

1. Unemployment levels in Tibetan settlements currently range between 3% and 22% with higher levels being experienced in North Eastern and Central Settlements than Southern areas.

2. A lack of compelling livelihood opportunity has been highlighted as a key factor behind migration. Parents and youth alike have indicated that the primary motivation for leaving a settlement is higher compensation. Respondents have also indicated a strong desire to remain in settlements if given the opportunity to do so.
3. Youth Preference for Entrepreneurship: While both youth and parents indicate a preference for employment with the CTA or related institutions, youth have an overwhelming preference for self employment.
4. Income Aspirations Favour Scalable Employment: Youth in the Southern and Central settlements aspire for an average monthly salary between INR 12,000 to INR 18,000 or an average annual income between INR 144,000 and INR 200,000. Salary aspirations are relatively lower for youth in the Northeast settlements, where the aspired monthly income tends to vary between INR 8,000 to INR 10,000 per month.

Given the above findings and CTA's focus on curbing migration and addressing unemployment especially amongst youth, entrepreneurship and fostering self employment seems to be way forward. Moreover, youth interest in owning their own businesses coupled with higher income aspiration levels underscore the need for entrepreneurship in settlement areas.

Intervention Design

Developing entrepreneurs and fostering entrepreneurship requires a concerted effort. The success or failure of an entrepreneurial venture depends primarily on the strength of the idea, the business plan and the operational context. Entrepreneurs also require the assistance of the community at large. Interventions planned throughout the entrepreneurship lifecycle will help develop entrepreneurs and foster entrepreneurship within and outside the settlements.

Create Awareness: The first step towards fostering entrepreneurship is creating the awareness of the concept of entrepreneurship. Our study shows that: On average, there is limited awareness of the concept of entrepreneurship in the Tibetan settlements. This is despite the existing programs like YES.

The application for and selection process of entrepreneurs is not streamlined;

Develop Skills: Once interest is observed, entrepreneurs are filled with the desire to acquire the skills and knowledge required to start their own business. Current state suggests:

There are established institutes by CTA to promote technical skills such as Institute for Small Trade Learning (ISTL) and Vocational Training Centres (VTC's). The courses and skills imparted by these institutes largely incentivize youth to work in metros and towns.

These institutes focus more on offering technical skills as compared to business skills.

Provide access to Capital: With a business plan in hand, people seek access to capital to begin their businesses. Traditional financing models include public and private capital. Public models favour guaranteed loans or grants to people starting businesses in desirable sectors. Private capital generally focuses on low interest loans with a high amount of up front collateral. Current state in the Tibetan context suggests following: CTA has provision to grant loans to entrepreneurs through YES program. These loans are provided on the merit of their business plans. Study suggests that, most of the existing entrepreneurs within the settlements have not accessed the loan through CTA/YES program. Cumbersome application process and delays are the key reason given for not accessing the loans from CTA. Awareness on the loan program is very limited both among entrepreneurs and youth in general.

Provide ongoing support: Once a business is in place, entrepreneurs experiment with various models as they strive to achieve sustainability. This can be one of the riskiest and most labour intensive periods for entrepreneurs, who often require external assistance to overcome initial challenges. Current situation in Tibetan context suggests that there is no further assistance given to the entrepreneurs in terms of strategy, business development, operational advice or organizational issues.

Make business self sustaining: As an entrepreneur gains operating experience, there is an increasing desire for self sustainability. At this point, the entrepreneur is encouraged to pay back loans and seek expansion capital from private sources. Currently no assistance mechanism is place to help entrepreneurs make their businesses sustainable.

Giving back to Society: Perhaps the most important stage of the entrepreneurship lifecycle is giveback. Successful entrepreneurs have the credibility and potential to inspire a new class of entrepreneurs. Their assistance can manifest itself in mentorship, advisory services, or in seed capital for future generations. Currently, there is no mechanism in place to recognize successful entrepreneurs and seek their help in promoting entrepreneurship in the Tibetan settlements.

The current state of entrepreneurship requires significant interventions to ensure that entrepreneurs are provided the required support to build scalable businesses. Initially the focus should be on creating awareness, developing required skills and creating systems to streamline access to capital. Further, instituting an ongoing advisory and mentoring support will help the entrepreneurs to scale up and sustain their businesses.

Towards Revitalization of Tibetan Handiwork Centre

Market Identification: For the sustained development of the Tibetan handicraft, there is a need for an on-going process to identify demand from new clients and unexplored markets.

To probe into the potential of the Tibetan handicrafts, we contacted Fabindia, the biggest retailer in the handicraft industry in India. The Chief Operating Officer (COO) of Fabindia visited the Dekyiling and Rajpur handicraft centres near Dehradun. The key highlights of the interaction are:

- The quality and finishing of the fabric particularly the multi-coloured patterns being woven in the Dekyiling handicraft centre was appreciated. Samples of bags, cushion covers, table mats and folders in various colours and sizes were requested by the COO.

- An immediate order of 250 bags (approximately INR 400,000) was given to the centre Manager.
- The COO showed her willingness to discuss the order volume further if the production at the centre can be scaled up and if other centres in India could provide similar products.
- The COO indicated a sustained relationship and shared future potential of the order to be as high as INR 5 million.

As an example, Fabindia can prove to be a tremendous opportunity for the Tibetans to showcase their products in the Indian market. Fabindia being the leader in the handicraft sector can potentially open new doors for Tibetan handicrafts. Further marketing effort in future will become easier if there is ongoing relationship with big chains Fabindia.

There is also need to be an on-going effort to locate new markets for the Tibetan handicrafts.

a. Organize road shows to leading retailers and showcase some of the samples. Some of the big retailers in India are: Fabindia, Anokhi, Industree, Good Earth, Hansiba, Tribal Routes
b. Participate in global events and build network such as the Great Indian Travel Bazaar, SATTE, Annual exhibition of CEPC
c. Associate with market facilitators-CEPC, FTCI Export Office, SOIR-IM, UHHDC
d. Participate in exhibitions and showcase the products-Dastkar Basant Bazaar, Delhi haat, Kala Ghoda festival in Mumbai, Shilp Bazaar

Design and prototype development: There is a need to develop new designs and experiment with new colours. The design intervention can be carried out in the following ways:

a. *Tie up with design institutes:* This can be done through promoting two-month internships to students that are studying design. Some of the popular design institutes in India are NID, NIFT, Symbiosis Institute of Design, Apeejay

Institute of Design, Shrishti School of design and Indian Institute of Crafts and Design. This will be a win-win situation for both parties. The internship fees charged by these designers are usually in the range of INR 10,000-15,000 a month. However, this can be negotiated in collaboration with the institutes.

b. *Utilize prototypes freely available in the market.* There are design books on carpets (especially Persian) which can be shown to the customers to help them choose the patterns.

c. *Develop Tibetan designer:* In the long run, as part of the ISTL or Vocational course, design courses can be instituted. The designing profession can be an attractive career for the youth especially young girls in the settlements.

Holistic development of artisans/weavers: The biggest challenge for the Tibetan handicraft industry today is to attract young people into the profession of weaving. The root cause of the problem is the extremely low salaries that the weavers are getting today in various settlements. Currently, on an average the Tibetans receive about 100 Rs. per working day, or approximately INR 2,500 per month.

The youth can be attracted by increasing the wages of the weavers, by providing other lucrative incentives to the artisans/ weavers and by providing trainings to the staff that helps them build new skills.

a. Provide optimum wages: According to our survey across the running handicraft centres in the Tibetan settlements, the minimum desired salary by the artisans/weavers is INR 175 per working day.

b. Provide other incentives: Rajpur Women's centre is a role model in providing incentives to attract employees. These incentives have ensured that the weavers' are more accountable and punctual, and the satisfaction level of the weavers' is higher in Rajpur than in other settlement workers. The incentives are as follows:

- Free housing
- Provident Fund (pension)

- Limited health care, and
- Education sponsorship for workers' children through Class 12

c. Organize capacity building programs and trainings: Training programs need to be organized for the office staff so as to prepare them to lead the artisans/weavers and interact confidently with the external agencies. Some of the suggested trainings are outlined below:
   - Soft skills training such as communication and personality development
   - Business and financial acumen
   - Use of technology and functional knowhow on computer
   - Export logistics.

Price determination: The current prices of the Tibetan handicrafts are calculated based on lower wages for artisans/weavers, a scenario that needs to change. While looking for new markets, the proposed central entity must look for only those markets where the goods can be sold at a higher price than the existing selling price. The Indian carpet makers are quoting a higher price in the export markets for carpets that are similar to the Tibetan carpets. There is need to identify lucrative markets and incorporate the desired designs to fetch higher price premiums. A potential scenario is described below:

- Increase in wages of working staff
- For highest quality carpet (100-knot), consider increasing the wage from current Rs. 114/sq ft to around Rs. 175/sq ft
- Evaluated increasing the sales price to Rs. 6600, which is in line with export prices captured by Indian carpet manufacturers for similar carpets.
- A compromise of six percent on the profit margins would enable the suggested, higher wages to weavers at current export markets sale price.
- Hiring a design professional could lead even superior products and higher prices captured, thus allowing profit margins to remain the same or increase.

- An increase in the size of operations (volumes) will also lead to a decrease in the overall operating costs, thus allowing the profit margin to increase.

Infrastructure development: To meet the demand from Fabindia and other retailers in future, there will be need to upscale the current production capacity of the handicraft centres. This will include improvement in the current infrastructure, availability and sourcing of raw materials and enhanced human resource. Infrastructure development will mainly comprise of enhanced quality and increased number of looms/sewing machines, computers and related softwares, printers and overall improvement in the workshop facility.

Collectivization of outputs: The central agency will need to ensure that the outputs from various centres are meeting the desired quality standards as requested by the retailers. This would require either collecting the output from various centres at one location or carrying out field visits to various sites to ensure that the quality is up to mark. Some retailers such as Fabindia specify the quality requirements and also send personnel from their organizations to check on the quality time to time. The central agency needs to also think about establishing a "Tibetan handicraft" brand in the medium to long run. This will help realize higher margins.

Overall Collision

The above interventions, thoughtfully resources and actively managed, can provide significant, substantial benefits to the Tibetan handicraft industry and the people engaged in it.

Increase in income and employment: There will be overall increase in number of working staff, especially youth and poor with enhanced income. Similar examples from partnering with Fabindia indicates following:

- Increase in Income: The artisans who have partnered w/ Fabindia in the past have seen income increase by approximately 50%. For a weaver in Hyderabad, annual income has increased from INR 10,000 a year to 10 million a year.

- Increase in employment: In case of Chanderi, an artisan group in Madhya Pradesh, Fabindia placed an initial order worth INR 5 million and increased it by INR 2.5 million every year for 5 years. The total artisans by the end of the project increased by 28%

Preservation of tradition and culture: The CTA's objective of preserving Tibetan culture and arts will also be met through this initiative. There will be increase in number of people who are skilled on traditional production processes countryside Business procedure Outsourcing in Tibetan Rural Business Process Outsourcing (RBPO) centres have the potential to create high-value; relatively high-skill jobs in Tibetan settlement areas. These 50 to 100 seat centres have the potential to provide employment to young, educated Tibetans, and match the job aspirations of many Tibetan youth. Moreover, they can help attract additional businesses such as restaurants, entertainment centres, technology services, and taxi services in and around settlements. However, there are several challenges to setting-up and running a successful RBPO business that need to be overcome through calculated planning and intervention design. These potential challenges include: Regulatory constraints associated with setting up a RBPO centre in the vicinity of the settlement and creating a smooth process for Tibetan youth to obtain the requisite work permits for gaining employment in the RBPO centre

Setting up a partnership with an institution with the requisite skills and experience in operationalizing a RBPO. (A list of potential partners is provided later in the document.)

Ensuring a consistent flow of orders and business development is imperative in creating viable sustainable development in settlements. The CTA must choose a business partner that will provide a captive model that ensures steady demand. Any internal data entry or data management required for CTA can be managed by said unit. Capability development of the Tibetan youth to match the talent requirements for a RBPO unit. Regulatory constraints need to be overcome before planning subsequent steps in the intervention the intervention design section presented later in the document describes some methodologies to overcome this challenge. While this is critical and complex challenge, it is surmountable through a coordinated effort and partnership with the Government of India and respective state governments where settlements. RBPO also requires significant investment. A RBPO centre can cost up to 5 million INR, yet can be up and running within 150 days. Public private partnerships can accelerate the timeline for viable settlements.

Among the 28 Tibetan settlements visited, three settlements, Bylakuppe, Dekyiling, and Mundgod appear well suited for a pilot intervention in the near term (in one to three years). Six others settlements also present an attractive initial opportunity in the medium term (Paonta and Puruwala in three to seven year timeframe) and long term (Bir Tibetan Society, Bir Dege, and Bir Nangchen in seven to ten years).

TIBETAN EXILES AND THE CRITERIA OF STATEHOOD

If the supposed indicia of statehood that Tibetan exiles cite are actually pseudo-indicators, did Tibet nevertheless fulfil accepted international law criteria of statehood? There are two international law theories of State recognition. A declaratory theory holds that recognition is not what directly determines whether or not a territory is a State. Instead, the territory must fulfil four criteria of statehood listed in the 1933 Montevideo Convention on the Rights and Duties of States: a permanent population, a defined territory, a government and a capacity to enter into relations with States. In practice, however, if a territory is not soon recognized by States, it lacks the capacity to enter into relations with them, and thus becomes a pseudo-State. That was the fate of old Tibet. A study of "unrecognized States" has stated "The external legitimacy accorded to proto-states through recognition can have a pivotal effect upon their eventual Statehood, elevating the status of some and encouraging the subjugation of others." It concludes that Non-recognition creates a number of obstacles for proto-states. Without external recognition, the regimes are far more likely to fail, because they have fewer resources at their disposal, fewer opportunities for trade and monetary exchange, less potential influence in governmental organizations and less legal claims to their territories and populations than their recognized peers.

Attaining statehood under the declaratory theory *ultimately* depends on recognition. Thus, the Supreme Court of Canada, ruling on whether Quebec may secede despite the strictures of the Canadian constitution, has said that "the ultimate success of such a secession would be dependent on recognition by the international community".

The constitutive theory holds that recognition by other States *creates* a new State. Even a territory that does not fulfil the four Montevideo criteria, such as the Holy See, can still be a State if it receives widespread recognition. Under this theory, old Tibet was not a State, because no established State recognized it. Although the declaratory theory prevailed until the 1990s, the recent emergence of new States has bolstered the constitutive theory. Recognition, in effect, created new States from the ex-Soviet Union and Yugoslavia. Although doubts existed about whether post-Soviet and former-Yugoslavia territories fulfilled the declaratory theory's criteria, widespread recognition determined the issue. Non-recognition in turn often reflects a realization by States that a territory has failed to fulfil the four traditional criteria of statehood.

Applying the declaratory theory produces the same result: Tibet was not a State. As to the criterion of a population, States have regarded Tibetans as both the population of Tibet and as part of China's population. As the Dalai Lama's Taiwan envoy noted, Tibetans too did not see themselves as people of a Tibetan *State*. Part of the elite of central-western Tibet, including monks, had long been "pro-China" and much of it was prepared to regard Tibetans as Chinese citizens when the re-establishment of central government authority in Tibet loomed at the beginning of the 1950s. Eastern Tibetans (Khambas and Amdowas) were not ruled from Lhasa and did not see their areas as part of Tibet and many recognized that they were Chinese citizens. The Lhasa regime did not regard the Chinese Army's entry into Kham in 1949 as an invasion of Tibet's territory, and neither did Khambas. States and the UN accepted that Tibetans under Lhasa's administration lived within China's territory. In that sense, Tibet did not have a permanent population separate from China's population.

In terms of the criterion of a defined territory, to claim statehood, a political entity must own territory free from claims by any other entity. China had long claimed the entire Tibet Plateau and no recognized State has disagreed. From the fall of the Qing Dynasty in 1911 until the end of China's civil war in 1949, the whole of China was in turmoil, yet no State disputed that Tibet was China's territory. From the official perspective of the world's States and the UN then, the Lhasa regime could only have exercised *domestic* authority in central-western Tibet on behalf of China and thus did not control a territory separate from China's defined territory.

As to the criterion of having a government, governments have two aspects: an actual exercise of authority and the right to exercise it. The Lhasa administration of 1913–1951 did not have a right to exercise *State*authority, which remained with China's central government. This principle is seen in other pseudo-States. The TRNC, for example, first separated from Cyprus through Turkey's 1974 incursion. The UN called on all States to not recognize it and declared its territory part of Cyprus, which is entitled to reclaim it. Under international law then, the Lhasa regime was a local administration that lacked legal title to be a government for statehood purposes, no matter how much administrative power it had. As a Norwegian geo-politics specialist has noted, "State sovereignty is constitutional independence, not empirical independence or strength. This holds true for old states as well as new ones."

Non-fulfilment of the final criterion, a capacity to enter into foreign relations, precludes a territory from being regarded as a State. A State requires a legal identity distinct from any other State's identity and must be subordinate only to international law. It has this identity only if no other entity carries out and accepts responsibility for its foreign relations. Tibet's foreign relations were carried out by China. Britain, the major power in the region at the time, recognized this. Although China was weak, Britain typically acceded to her demands that interactions related to Tibet be handled by China. The United Kingdom and United States knew that, for almost three centuries, the Qing had regarded Tibetans as its *chenmin* (subjects) and citizens and that they should go through Beijing to resolve Tibet-related diplomatic issues. For example, during its 1904 invasion of Tibet, Britain made a formal diplomatic protest to Beijing after Tibetans caught two British spies. When US airmen bailed out of a plane over Tibet in 1943, the ROC representative in Lhasa pre-empted the local government's move to receive and care for them and, because the United States recognized that Tibet was China's territory, it was unwilling to publicly acknowledge dealings with Lhasa over the airmen.

POSMAN: POST-EXILIC RECONSTRUCTIONS OF SACRED COMMUNITY

Although the aforementioned theological democratization is clearly documented and easy to explain, it is not the whole story. Despite the fact that exile creates a minority status and the loss of centralized sacred space, which leads to increased affinities and unification, major theological splits have occurred within each group in exile. Sometimes, when exclusivistic claims are held very strongly, there simply is no room for compromise. In post-exilic Judaism, this is the case with the Christians, while in Tibetan Buddhism this is the case with Shugden.

At first, neither the emergence of Christianity nor the destruction of the Temple created a total rift between Jews and Christians; in fact, Jews and Christians continued to worship together possibly until as late as the 4th century. However, as Christianity became more orthodox, certain tenets – namely the belief that Jesus was resurrected, was the messiah, and would return – became the only truth, thereby making it impossible for Judaism and Christianity to remain as one religion. Like the Pharisaic sect, Christianity could be easily adapted to a context devoid of the Temple or centralized sacred space. Thus the rabbis and Christianity survived, at first unified by their minority status, lack of power, and lack of outside support, but as Christianity gained the support of gentiles and grew in numbers and power, a split occurred.

The political aspect of the Christian-Jewish split can be summarized as follows: When Christianity began, Judaism was the dominant tradition in the Holy Land and framed its ideas within a political framework until the early fifth century. Christianity there was subordinate and had to work itself out against the background of a politically definitive Judaism. (Elsewhere, of course, Christianity had to work out of its subordinate position as well.) From the time of Constantine onward, matters reversed themselves. Now Christianity predominated, expressing its ideas in political and institutional terms. Judaism, by contrast, had lost its political foundations and faced the fact of working out its self-understanding in terms of a world defined by Christianity, now everywhere triumphant and in charge of politics.

Despite the obvious issue of exclusivity, here Neusner makes the point that the break is also political. Other scholars have noted regional issues, crediting its rise to ascendancy to the fact that despite its Palestinian branch, "Christianity came to maturity in the Greek world and represents the blend of Hellenistic Judaism, hellenized Christianity, and Greek ideas and Greek religion and Greek spirit." In other words, it was the Greek branch, with the syncretistic ideas and foreign support that led to the rift between Judaism and Christianity, probably more so than theology. While exclusivist theology is a factor, again we see that belief never accounts for all the factors. Again we have the question here of the dominant discourse of estrangement. Was it in fact – as it is usually maintained by scholars – the irreconcilable theologies of the two religions? Or were regional or political affinities the deciding factor? Of course, all are factors here, but the important point is that belief is not the sole, nor even necessarily the most crucial factor, though the intensity of a certain belief can create a certain amount of exclusivity.

In Tibetan Buddhism, the same pattern emerges with regard to the Shugden sect. Within the Gelugpa order, there is a protector deity known as Dorje Shugden who is responsible for maintaining the purity of the lineage. The time and circumstances of the origin of this deity are uncertain, but most likely he emerged around the time of the fifth Dalai Lama. His popularity increased around the time of the thirteenth Dalai Lama, and many Gelugpa monks have been initiated into a practice of propitiating him since that time. In fact, even the fourteenth Dalai Lama, though currently an opponent of the Shugden sect, received such an initiation and performed rituals regarding Shugden through the mid 1970s.

The condition of exile, while enabling various groups to come together in Tibetan Buddhism, has had the opposite effect on the Shugden sect. Because Dorje Shugden is primarily concerned with the purity of the Gelugpa lineage, the simple fact that exile has brought about dialogue between the orders is problematic from the perspective of a Shugden adherent. The Shugden sect is exclusivistic – it sees the Gelugpa order as pure and the other orders as corrupted. The current contact between groups along with the ability in exile to study within the confines of different orders, either in a non-denominational context or by receiving teachings from lamas of different schools, has created a Tibetan Buddhism that is less purely Gelugpa and more democratized, exactly as described above.

Therefore, in exile, it was not uncommon for Gelugpa monks to take teachings from non-Gelugpa monks and to study a variety of texts and meditation practices, not all of which are Gelugpa. As a result of these activities, coupled with the exclusivism of the Shugden sect, there have been violent outbreaks against the Gelugpa monks who have become more ecumenical, and most notably, there was a murder of the director of the Institute of Buddhist Dialectics in Dharamsala. Since Shugden has always been understood to be a wrathful deity, a group of Shugden adherents has become quite vocal about these occurrences, maintaining that they are due to the wrath of Shugden and that Shugden will continue to punish those who corrupt the pure Gelugpa lineage or those who fail to maintain their vow to propitiate him. The other possibility, naturally, is that these adherents themselves are behind the acts of violence.

The situation has come to the fore because of the Dalai Lama's own position on the issue. Once initiated into Shugden practices, there are supposedly severe ramifications for those who break their vow, and many are thus reluctant to renounce Shugden practices. Nevertheless, the Dalai Lama gave up propitiation of

Shugden in the 1970s largely because the propitiation of Shugden is at odds with the Dalai Lama's role as the head of all four lineages in exile. In fact, the Dalai Lama's stance in exile has been notably ecumenical. Moreover, the Dalai Lama's condemnations of violence apply to the violence in the name of Shugden as well.

The Dalai Lama has gradually become more and more vocal on the subject of Shugden, to the point where at this time, it is common practice for the Dalai Lama, in the midst of any set of teachings, to request that any Shugden adherents no longer attend the teachings of the Dalai Lama, and he also encourages people to come forward with any information they have regarding violence perpetrated in the name of Shugden. Of course, the Dalai Lama's stance has greatly angered the Shugden adherents. Kelsang Gyatso, leader of the Shugden sect – as it is now known – has taken offence at the Dalai Lama's statements.

He has argued that the Dalai Lama is corrupting the lineage and that moreover, he is an opponent to the freedom of religion. Kelsang Gyatso maintains that by refusing Shugden adherence admission to his teachings, the Dalai Lama is being intolerant of freedom of religion. Finally, and theologically most important, Kelsang Gyatso and his sect have elevated the status of Shugden. They claim he is a fully enlightened Buddha rather than a mere protector deity. Because of the Dalai Lama's statements and Kelsang Gyatso's attempts to receive attention from the press, this conflict has reached the ears of most Tibetans in exile.

Since a layperson cannot be initiated into Shugden practice, this controversy should be limited to the monastic context, but laypeople too are under the impression that Shugden is bad. I even met one layperson who changed his name from Kelsang to Tenzin when he found out he was named for Kelsang Gyatso (at the time of his birth, this controversy had not yet arisen). Shugden adherents have accused the schools and the government of discrimination, but none has been found to exist.

Interestingly, regional, political, and economic factors have had a significant impact on this controversy. Kelsang Gyatso, resides in the UK and has received foreign support both from Europeans and from the Chinese government. The foreign support of has created a chance for the survival among the Shudgen sect despite the lack of internal support, which is reminiscent of the gentile support for Christianity. Meanwhile, the Chinese government's involvement suggests a political angle as well. Despite the Chinese government's noted stance against religion, they support Shugden; one must speculate that their reason for doing so is to divide the Tibetans amongst themselves for political purposes. Notably, both the European Shugden adherents and the Chinese government have called into question the Dalai Lama's political authority, claiming that his remarks against the Shugden sect have demonstrated that he is against freedom of religion. UK residents expressed this in the form of a protest during the Dalai Lama's visits to Europe in the 1990s, and the Chinese government has used this position to continue their position of not negotiating with the Dalai Lama as any type of suitable authority. Once again, politics and region are as much factors in the support and survival of a splintered sect as theology. Moreover, the condition of exile exacerbates some of these factors.

Obviously, the situations of Shugden and Christianity are different in many ways, but the comparison of the two shows that not all sects become more unified in exile. Rather, a combination of factors including an exclusivist theology, a regional separation, and an increase of economic and/or political support for one group can create the opposite effect and estrange groups from one another in exile.

THE TIBETANS: STRUGGLE TO SURVIVE

Tibet is complicated by the myths and uncertainties that surround its perception by foreigners. None of us who are outsiders can dispel those difficulties at a single stroke, and even Tibetans themselves must from time to time find it hard to separate the perceived from the experienced realities of their condition: they too suffer from the lack of layered, unemotive information necessary to better explicate this complex issue.

Much of the initial work facing any westerner considering the question of Tibet is, in a sense, archaeological. For more than a century there has been in the West and elsewhere a sort of small-scale industry generating romantic or contentious notions of one kind or another about Tibet. Such notions lie like debris scattered around the area of our inquiry, so that we have to dig through an accumulation of misconceptions and half-truths before discerning even faintly the outlines of some concrete, lived experience. Even if we find such solid traces, we need still to resist the temptation to elaborate these as certain proof of the character of an entire history or civilization. The clues uncovered during any such excavation may be partial, anomalous, or atypical of the wider community whose story we seek to describe.

To some extent it could be said that the question of Tibet's political status is itself part of the debris. An entire literature has emerged that recites facts about Tibet as proof that the country was or was not independent at the time of its invasion by Chinese troops just under fifty years ago, while relatively little has been written about the basic elements of life in Tibet—the condition of the people who live there, the texture of their political and social aspirations, and the intellectual and cultural makeup of their society as it adapts to the stresses and complications of modernity. This book is part of an attempt to offer information about the condition of life in Tibet, as well as about our concerns and conceptions of that country.

One reason for turning to the society and the people who comprise it instead of focusing on the vexed subject of Tibetan independence is that it may in fact be impossible ever to give a definitive answer, in legal or historical terms, to the question of Tibet's political status. Supporters of each side in the dispute typically offer only the evidence that advances their case and ignore that which opposes it. The Chinese, on the one hand, claim that Tibetan leaders made their country a formal part of China in the thirteenth century, while the Tibetans argue that their leaders' historic links to China were merely those of religious teachers to their lay patrons. In fact the question of independence is even more complicated than the polemical accounts suggest, because the fundamental questions underpinning these discussions are rarely broached: who are the Tibetan people? And what are Tibet's boundaries?

Ethnographically speaking Tibetans are less homogeneous than one is led to believe. The Khampas from the east speak several dialects that are more or less unintelligible to the Amdowas from the northeast, and together the two ethnic subgroups outnumber Tibetans from the central and western regions. It is those central Tibetans who speak variants of the Lhasa dialect with which most Western students of Tibetan are familiar, but their dialect is initially incomprehensible to the two million or more Tibetans from Kham or Amdo.

These subgroups within the main Tibetan language family are clearly all Tibetan—they share common physical traits, a culture, and a written language which distinguishes them from others—but it is not so clear what defines them as a unified people. It is often argued, for example, that they can all be called Tibetans because of their shared commitment to the Tibetan form of Buddhism, but in fact Buddhism is a relatively recent faith among Tibetans: although it dates back as a firmly established nationwide religion to approximately the eleventh century, Tibetans consider their history to have begun over a thousand years earlier. And there are significant communities within Tibet, such as the Lhasa Muslims or the Bonpo, who are not Buddhist but who are certainly Tibetan. Neither can we define Tibetans in terms of a distinctive lifestyle: the claim that Tibetans are a nation of monks and nomads conceals the facts that many rural Tibetans have always been settled farmers, that only 2 percent of the population are now monks or nuns, and that nearly 20 percent these days live in towns. The people we call Tibetans are more diverse than is sometimes suggested and the forces that bind them more complex than we might think.

This is not to say that Tibetans do not have a common sense of identity as a single nationality—the Chinese, for example, are more fractured by regional disparities in language and history than the Tibetans—but it does suggest that this identity is not so much a provable fact of history as a situation that Tibetans have created through their determination to be considered as a single people. This determination has been heightened by the Chinese claims to their territory. To some extent, therefore, the unity of

Tibetans as a nationality is in part a political rather than a scientific fact, steeled by the arrival of a common enemy and the attack of a supremacist ideology.

Changes in the way the Tibetans view themselves have led to considerable inconsistency in defining other aspects of the situation, in particular the question of where Tibet's borders begin and end. There is no doubt about central Tibet, the heartlands around Lhasa ruled by the Dalai Lamas since the seventeenth century. But eastern Tibet had for generations been composed of a complex of principalities of differing constitutionality and with equivocal loyalties, sometimes offering allegiance to Lhasa, sometimes to China, and sometimes to neither. Amdo, formerly regarded as the northeastern area of Tibet and now mostly subsumed within the Chinese province of Qinghai, had not had any sight of Lhasa rule for some two hundred years before the Chinese invaded Lhasa in 1951. When the Chinese Communists wrested control of Qinghai from the Chinese warlord Ma Pufang in 1949, the Lhasa government made no intervention and did not claim that this area was part of Tibet, as it now does. In Kham, however, the area that lies to the south of Amdo and which is now part of Sichuan province, Lhasa had fought frequent wars with Chinese armies in the early decades of this century and, in fact, had briefly gained title to part of that area by conquering the local Chinese—but still Lhasa did not protest when the Communist armies took over that area. The figures, much quoted by exiled Tibetans and westerners, that there are now 7.5 million Chinese in Tibet have been arrived at by including large areas and cities, such as Xining, which had not for centuries been part of political Tibet. Such uncertainty about the borders of Tibet further complicates the dispute over its political status.

There is general acceptance that Tibet was in some sense part of the Chinese Empire in the thirteenth century and again in the eighteenth century, when Chinese armies were sent to protect Tibet from internal conflict and to repel invasion by the Gurkhas of Nepal and when Chinese "Ambans" or imperial commissioners were stationed in Lhasa. But it is argued by many supporters of the Tibetan case that the Chinese Empire at that time was either a Mongol (in Chinese, Yuan) empire or a Manchu (Qing) one, and that the Chinese republicans who took over Beijing in 1911 did not inherit all the rights and respects that were due to their Manchu predecessors. It is a powerful argument in terms of Asian political traditions, but generally the international system accepts the transfer of rights between dynasties.

However one resolves this debate, it is clear that, if it is once admitted that in the eighteenth and nineteenth centuries (for example) the Chinese emperors had a significant right to participate in Tibetan affairs, the claim to a full and total independence by Tibetans is not at all as definite as it is sometimes presented. Those facts that can be asserted with some confidence give, accordingly, a more complex impression. Firstly, the Chinese (or their Mongol and Manchu rulers) definitely believed themselves, rightly or wrongly, to be for considerable lengths of time in some way overlords of Tibet. Secondly, however, it is certain that these rulers and their citizens did not view their Tibetan territory as identical in status to their Chinese provinces, which were handled by a different government office from that which dealt with Tibet and Mongolia. Thirdly, it is clear that until this century, at which time the British began actively to encourage a sense of separation in Lhasa, the Tibetans, as was natural in the traditional political culture of the time, did little to disabuse the emperors of their belief in their sovereignty over Tibet. Fourthly, it is not disputed even by the Chinese that after 1912, when all Chinese officials and residents in Lhasa were expelled by the Tibetan government following the collapse of the Qing dynasty, Lhasa thenceforth exercised full control of all its own affairs, internal and external, until the Chinese army invaded its eastern borders thirty-eight years later.

This last argument is persuasive to many people, especially because the Thirteenth Dalai Lama, in a 1912 treaty with Mongolia of which the original is lost, reportedly declared Tibet to be independent. Still, it is not as conclusive as it might appear, since large parts of China were also in effect autonomous during the first half of this century— Qinghai, for example, more or less governed itself under Ma Pufang during the same period. But this could be seen as a consequence of the weakness of the then Chinese government, beset by Japanese invasion and wracked by civil war; it was not necessarily a proof in itself of separate political status. Ma Pufang apparently did not see himself or his realm as historically or culturally distinct from other political entities within China.

In the final analysis lawyers and historians may not be able to come to a conclusive answer on this question. They may concede that the nature of Tibet's status before 1912 was not of a kind that can be exactly expressed by twentieth-century notions of statehood: it was not the same as a province of China, but, except when China was too weak to exercise central control, it did not define itself in modern terms as an independent state. The Tibetans like to express this by saying that there was a chö-yon or protector-patron relationship between the two governments before 1912, meaning that Tibetans offered spiritual guidance to emperors in return for political protection. This, however, seems more a description of a personal relationship between leaders than a resolution of the question of statehood.

There is, however, one negative argument that powerfully supports the Tibetan view: no one seems so far to have found any document in which the Tibetan people or their government explicitly recognized Chinese sovereignty before the invasion of 1950. The importance of this argument lies not in its role in the legal debate, but in what it indicates in terms of the political realities on the ground. Chief among these is the question as to how Tibetans perceived and perceive themselves. The fact is that most Tibetans seem to have experienced themselves and their land as distinct from China. Few in central Tibet had seen any Chinese before the invasion and almost none of the Chinese there now have lived in Tibet for more than fifty years. Although Chinese armies traveled to Tibet four times in the eighteenth century, they were probably regarded by Tibetans as allies assisting the Tibetan government to repel threats of invasion or insurrection, not as overlords. If Tibet was at any recent time part of China, this affiliation seems to have been for the most part a traditional construct that has no exact equivalent in our time, or an abstruse diplomatic technicality arranged among the elite that seemingly was never communicated to the Tibetan people.

Certainly there were few signs of Chinese influence, let alone rule, in Tibet. All the major indicators of culture and society were entirely different from those of their Chinese neighbors—the coinage, postage, language, dress, food, and taxation of Tibet were all distinctively Tibetan, and before the Chinese invasion Tibet had developed all the political and social institutions, from an army to a civil service, that a country needs to function as a separate entity. It is these simple, experienced realities rather than any legal considerations that are of political significance, because it is largely to them, and to religious beliefs, that we must attribute the decision of hundreds of thousands of Tibetans in the 1950s and 1960s to face death in defense of their perception of Tibet as a separate country. It is in this context that we should view China's current campaign within Tibet to oblige all Tibetans to undergo "patriotic education," a program that requires everyone to attend lectures or to sign a statement saying that Tibet has been part of China since the thirteenth century. The campaign suggests that what matters to Beijing is not expert adjudication so much as popular consent: the Chinese authorities also see the Tibet issue as shaped not by the decisions of lawyers and leaders but by the views and beliefs of ordinary Tibetans.

Strangely, few people, and fewer Tibetans, have chosen to argue that, given the distinct status that the Chinese emperors accorded to Tibet compared to their provinces, Tibet must at best have been something like a colony. If this argument was pursued—and it is hard to contest—the present situation could be described as one of colonial occupation. It is one of the mysteries (some people might say tragedies) of the Tibetan case that its leaders in exile and their advisers have sought to show that Tibet has a right to absolute statehood, perhaps gambling to attract Western support, rather than to seek its people's right to decolonization, an option that might have gained them wider support in the developing world.

But these are in essence questions of strategy and definition, matters that are decided by political elites. At the fundamental, everyday level at which most of us operate, the reality is that, as far as we can tell, the majority of Tibetans do not accept their current masters as legitimate rulers. It is difficult otherwise to explain the thousands of Tibetans who since 1950 have taken part in revolt, in the guerrilla war, or in civil protests, who have been to prison or have been executed for holding such views, or who have fled as refugees. The numbers involved in these actions are too great to be discounted as all members or beneficiaries of the political elite whose power and wealth was jeopardized by the Chinese advance to Lhasa. Indeed, it was the Tibetan aristocracy who were among the first to cooperate with the Chinese in 1950, attracted by offers of wealth and status: the Uprising of 1959 seems to have been more a popular movement than an agitation by dispossessed nobles. Whether we take a political or a humanitarian view of the Tibet problem, it is probably this general perception among Tibetans of foreign occupation that is the decisive factor in assessing their situation.

This is not to say that other questions, with all their difficulties of resolution, can be discarded as mere academic abstractions—we need to grasp them in their full complexity in order to equip ourselves with at least the rudiments of intelligent discussion. But most debate in the West on Tibet focuses either on seeking a politician's Holy Grail—the pure fact that will somehow prove that Tibet is or is not part of China—or assumes that somehow the moral force of Western opinion will lead to political change in Tibet and China. But from a political point of view the answer to such issues is relatively simple: reality and "truth" are largely decided by political determination and muscle, not by legal arguments or moral rectitude. The history of struggles for decolonization in this century suggests that if the Tibetan people living in these areas choose to assert their collective identity as a people and to exercise the political will to sustain it, even the Chinese might find it hard to stand in their way.

Since the invasion, China's policies towards the Tibetans can perhaps best be described as a mix of brutality and concession. There were "hard" periods about which there can be little dispute, periods during which even the Chinese authorities now acknowledge that "serious errors" were made. But it is also important to recognize that these years of uncontested brutality were interwoven with periods during which few if any atrocities occurred. There is a tendency towards simplification in our perception of Communist regimes, which are often assumed to maintain power through force; in reality, gifts and promises are equally effective and as often used. But the complexity of Chinese rule emerges not so much from recognizing that China uses carrots as well as sticks to encourage subservience as from allowing that some of their concessions are genuinely well-intentioned. Like many colonial rulers, a significant proportion of the Chinese Communists sent to run Tibet after 1950 acted for largely altruistic reasons and believed they were offering to their new fellow-subjects practical and spiritual improvement in their lives. It is this anomaly that leads us into a bizarre hall of mirrors where Chinese officials appear simultaneously to be intent on assisting, seducing, or brutalizing their subjects.

There have been three hard periods, twenty years in total, during which Tibetans have suffered from the extremism of ultraleftist dogma in China; it is because of these periods that allegations of genocide or ethnocide have been made. The first such period was sparked by the Tibetan Uprising of 1959 and lasted until about 1962. During these years thousands of Tibetans were executed, imprisoned, or starved to death in prison camps. So far no officials have publicly acknowledged these atrocities, but we know that they took place and that the punishment was largely random because of a secret report written in 1962 by the Panchen Lama (appointed by Mao as the leader of Tibet) which was smuggled out to the West in 1996. This period also included (particularly in Kham and Amdo) the artificially induced famines that resulted from the policies of the Great Leap Forward, an attempt by Beijing to make the production of steel take precedence over agriculture and to set up communes overnight throughout China. In 1981, the Chinese leadership finally conceded that the Great Leap, which some writers now estimate led to thirty million deaths, had been a "serious mistake."[4] A report by Beijing's Economic System Research Institute found that 900,000 people died during this period in Qinghai province alone (where a quarter of the population were Tibetan), probably from starvation. Tibetan nomads were particularly affected because the plan for the communes required that all flocks be brought together in one place: the animals died en masse once they had exhausted all the available pasture. The plan did not allow them to be moved.

The second "hard" period was the Cultural Revolution defined by the Chinese as lasting from 1966 to 1976, although in Tibet it continued in effect until 1979. During these years, Mao Zedong set off a frenzied drive throughout Chinese territory to eradicate the "four olds": old thoughts, old culture, old customs, old traditions. For the non-Chinese peoples the campaign included an attempt to eradicate their culture and their distinctive identity as a people, since ultraleftist ideologists declared at that time that distinctions between nationalities and any form of religious belief were the results of the class system. The consequences for Chinese people, let alone for Tibetans, Mongolians, and other nationalities under Chinese rule, were terrible: they were forced to dress like Chinese, to profess atheism, to destroy temples, to burn books, and to condemn, humiliate, and sometimes even kill the teachers, writers, thinkers, and elders in their communities.

The period from 1987 to 1990 is still too recent for us to assess. During much of this third dark era, Lhasa was under martial law and at least one hundred people are believed to have been shot dead by police for taking part in demonstrations. Some three thousand Tibetans are estimated to have been imprisoned for joining protests during this period and a large proportion of them appear to have been tortured, often in brutal ways. It was a period of explicit repression by the security forces (in particular the People's Armed Police, a paramilitary body) and attracted international publicity, for the simple reason that it was the only one of the "hard" periods of Chinese rule to have been witnessed by foreigners. China had begun to open Tibet to tourism in 1981, so that in 1987 alone, the last year of that "open" experiment, there were forty-seven thousand foreign tourists in Tibet.

This period came to an end in May 1990, when civilian rule was to be reestablished in Lhasa after thirteen months of martial law. Unnoticed by the Western press, Chinese authorities announced that the security policy in Tibet was henceforth to shift from "passive" to "active" policing. This meant, in the obscure code used by Chinese politicians, that the practice of shooting demonstrators and of mass torture and detention would be replaced by more cautious and more restrained forms of control.

If we set aside these three "hard" periods, we are left with some twenty-seven years that cannot easily be categorized as periods of atrocity. The Chinese took over eastern Tibetan areas in 1949, those not under the rule of Lhasa, crossing into central Tibet a year later. Their army arrived in Lhasa in October 1951, by which time the Tibetan government had formally surrendered. But it was not until the Tibetan Uprising of 1959 that the Chinese authorities took over day-to-day running of the Tibetan government in Lhasa. In central Tibet those nine years from 1951 to 1959 saw no great difference for ordinary Tibetans between preinvasion and postinvasion Tibet, except that the Chinese introduced modern commodities, built some schools and nurseries, constructed small power stations, showed propaganda films, offered scholarships in Beijing, and spread new fashions.

If we find it hard to imagine how an invading army and a triumphant colonizer could behave in such a restrained way in its new acquisition, we have only to look at Hong Kong today: there also we can see a conscientious effort to avoid any visible sign of change in daily life, despite the fundamental change in status and governance that has taken place. In Tibet, too, the initial policies were in many ways driven by the same concerns. The Chinese, once they had gained a legally valid recognition of their claim to sovereignty, were extremely careful to leave the apparatus of traditional government in place, with the Dalai Lama at its head. But in actuality, the Dalai Lama and his ministers were powerless. There was a party committee for Tibet run by Chinese generals that decided what the Tibetan government could and could not do; however, except in cases of emergencies, its instructions were most likely communicated in untraceable ways through indirect channels, and would probably have been described as "advice." The Tibetan leaders would have felt themselves to have had no choice but to follow such advice, since their army was largely disbanded. But the new dispensation meant that on the surface Tibetans remained in charge; in Delhi, for example, Nehru believed that the Chinese really had achieved a peaceful transition and in 1956 persuaded the Dalai Lama, then seeking exile in India, to continue his alliance with Beijing.

The strategy of winning over potential enemies by offering concessions, such as allowing the traditional elite to retain the semblance of authority, has its own term in the vocabulary of Chinese Communism: it is called "United Front work" and there is even an agency in the highest ranks of the party, the United Front Work Department, whose sole task is to implement such concessions. In Tibet in 1950, traditional leaders had the option of very high office within the new Chinese system if they agreed to cooperate with their new rulers, as well as the perks of high office—chauffeur-driven cars, ceremonial privileges, luxurious accommodation, and high salaries. Today, for example, the Chinese authorities are said to be offering the Dalai Lama the post of vice president, once he accepts that Tibet is part of China.

Describing these swings in Chinese policy from left to right, or from suppression to co-option, is a relatively simplistic analysis and does not fully reflect the complexity of Chinese politics. The Chinese, not unlike Western colonizers who believed that they were involved in a "civilizing mission" to bring Christianity and advanced culture to backward peoples, were part of an ideologically driven movement that had a self-appointed mission to liberate the poor and oppressed. During their softer phases the Chinese accordingly made much more of an effort than the European colonizers to bring practical improvements to their newly acquired territories, and in Tibet as in China those improvements were often to the benefit of the lower levels of society. China's invasion did, in part, lead to the ending of debt and serfdom, to the land reforms of 1959, and to the reform of the quasi-feudal system in Tibet.

The policies of the final "soft" period, initiated in the early 1980s, were in many ways similar to those of the 1950s. In May 1980, Hu Yaobang, then general secretary of the party, announced that Chinese cadres were to be withdrawn from the Tibet Autonomous Region and Tibetans allowed to take over their roles in the administration. At the same time there was to be a tax amnesty for the farmers and nomads; religion and Tibetan culture were to be allowed to flourish; and investment was to be poured into the area to help in education, infrastructure, and development. It was broadly welcomed by Tibetans in Tibet, who seized upon the opportunity to acquire a high level of modern education and to take up positions as cadres in the administration. While thousands of young men and women chose to rejoin monasteries and nunneries, others became teachers in schools or colleges, or worked as writers or academics. These two areas of activity—religious vocation and Tibetan language activities—emerged as of paramount significance during this sudden phase of cultural rediscovery. Over fifteen hundred monasteries were rebuilt, mostly by local Tibetans with their own funds, allowing the community to reestablish its links to its heritage as it had been in 1959. But at the same time writers, scholars, and administrators cooperated to produce with extraordinary rapidity a significant corpus of literature in Tibetan, including creative writing as well as academic, scientific, and religious studies. This emergence of a Tibetan literature was unique, not because (as the Chinese from time to time have claimed) there had been no previous literature in Tibet but because for the first time Tibetans were producing a Tibetan culture that was at the same time both distinctive and modern.

During that period, particularly in the eastern areas of ethnographic Tibet that are now subsumed within the provinces of Qinghai, Sichuan, and Gansu, the opportunities offered by the concessional state were taken full advantage of by the coalition of reemergent Tibetan intellectuals, led by the Panchen Lama, and Chinese liberals, led by Hu Yaobang. This produced what one might call a new Tibetan intelligentsia—one could almost say, a Tibetan middle class. It was created with great speed, its members showed robustness and confidence, and they were, unlike most previous groups of educated Tibetans, fluent in Chinese and well equipped to deal with the modern world. In addition, they held positions within the administrative and cultural apparatus governing Tibet.

It is therefore perhaps not surprising that some sections of the Chinese Communist Party became nervous about the growing signs of confidence among Tibetans in the mid-1980s. In 1987, when the Dalai Lama began a campaign to seek political support in the West, the propaganda units in Tibet were ordered to publish a series of statements condemning him in language that had not been heard since the beginning of the decade. That decision led to the pro-independence demonstrations of 1987, and more or less marked the end of the last phase of concessional government in Tibet.

The situation in Tibet today requires a different understanding: it is neither a period of evident brutality nor of concession. The shoot-to-kill policy of the late 1980s has been dropped, and the number of political prisoners is (as far as we know) around seven hundred rather than three thousand. Far more Tibetans than ever before are allowed passports so they can travel abroad, and in 1992 the authorities announced a relaxation of tariffs and taxes on people setting up businesses in Tibet. The economy in the Tibet Autonomous Region has since grown by more than 10 percent each year, according to official government statistics, faster than the rate in China as a whole, and far above the world average. By the end of 1997, there had been almost no reported pro-independence demonstrations in Tibet for over twelve months, in contrast to the two hundred or more that had taken place during the previous nine years. Yet despite such indications of political calm, Tibetans currently living in Tibet say that the situation is worse than it has been since at any time since 1980, when the opening up to the outside world was first announced. How then are we to understand the apparently concessional stage that Tibet is now in?

To answer this question we have to adjust the set of concepts and presumptions that we bring to it. Generally we equate repression with certain visible incidents, such as political arrests, detention of demonstrators, or military patrols. But such signs may be typical only in the early phases of military occupations. If, for example, we were to imagine how France or Denmark might have looked to a casual tourist today had the Nazis never been defeated, we can be reasonably sure that it would not have remained as it was in 1945: there would be no need, one can imagine, for men to be patrolling in jackboots or for sentries with machine guns to be placed at each corner.

Even during the war much of France was, as we know, run by French collaborators with a civilian police force, so there was little day-to-day sign of its military masters.

Some fifty years after the onset of an occupation we would not expect much need for visible controls, since the opportunities for heroic resistance would mostly have been exhausted, and the activists probably long since eliminated or cowed. Indeed, what is striking about Tibet is that the Chinese still found it necessary until 1990 to use unsubtle methods of control, and that five decades after occupation the Chinese have not yet depleted the Tibetans' reservoirs of resistance.

Political arrests continue to take place in Tibet, armed police can still be seen in the streets whenever there is a possibility of unrest, and there are continued reports of brutal incidents in outlying areas—in December 1997, for example, a Tibetan monk escaped to Kathmandu after surviving ten days of torture in Ngari, in the far west of Tibet, where soldiers had suspected him of planning to flee the country. But in general the indicators of the political atmosphere should be sought not in visible incidents of abuse but in the signs of systemic, policy-led strategies of control—in such things as the identities and affiliations of policy makers, the language of administration, the degree of participation in the political process by people outside the elite or the administration, the breadth of cultural expression, and the syllabi of school and college history courses.

If we look at the first factor, the policy makers, we find that 66 percent of all regional-level officials in the Tibet Autonomous Region are, by one estimate, Chinese. Yet, according to government statistics, only 3 percent of the population is Chinese. Similarly, the percentage of Chinese students in technical education in the region is around 40 percent. No figures exist for ethnic participation in the economy, but it can be reasonably assumed that most capital investment and profit extraction is not in the hands of Tibetans.

These are the signs of a political structure that is organized toward the preservation of power and influence within the orbit of a subcommunity: the Chinese. In the "soft" period of the early 1980s this structure of minority dominance had been eroded by Tibetans who had taken advantage of the new concessions to launch their own cultural activity and to acquire positions in the administration. Chinese policy makers militated against this and related developments, warning about risks to the maintenance of the power of the party, so that by 1987 they had engineered, through the campaign against bourgeois pollution, the fall of Hu Yaobang, and, two years later, the crushing of the 1989 student revolt in Tiananmen Square held in Hu's memory. In China some of those reforms have been recouped, but Tibet is a different story: what we are witnessing in Tibet today is the dismantling, piece by piece, of the concessional regime initiated by Hu some twenty years ago, and the reconsolidation of power in the hands of the Chinese oligarchy. The sudden death of the Tenth Panchen Lama in 1989, the last great religious leader still living within Tibet, removed the final remaining obstacle to revisionism.

The dismantling of concessions has been a gradual process. Its most obvious manifestation was the security operation of the late 1980s, which originally took the form of what the Chinese call "passive" policing, which meant mass arrests and street executions. This was followed in 1990 by a shift to a lower police profile, keeping troops in barracks, using video technology for surveillance, a growing role for the State Security Bureau, and a major increase in the funds allocated to establishing an informer network. These changes may have appeared as a form of moderation, but they were driven by a need for efficiency: we know that in 1990 a document was circulated among high-level cadres in Lhasa pointing out that the widespread torture of prisoners was counterproductive because it increased popular determination to fight the authorities. By mid-1993 the replacement of crude repression by more subtle and efficient methods had reaped its rewards: during that summer the majority of underground resistance cells in Lhasa were penetrated by State Security, and soon after most of their members were imprisoned or forced to flee. By this time the authorities had already shifted their attention to a second front in their effort to reverse the liberal reforms of the early 1980s: the economy. Lhasa and the surrounding areas were to be opened up to entrepreneurial activity as a "special economic zone," under the banner of what was then being called Chinese market socialism. Thus Tibet became a frontier zone filled with pioneering entrepreneurs from areas such as Sichuan and Zhejiang, who began by mending bicycles in the street and who now run small shops, restaurants, and businesses in the towns of Tibet. And, although this "special economic zone" was never put into practice as such, it conveyed a simple message within China: a lot of money could be made in Lhasa very fast.

This radical change in the urban economy of Tibet did not come about unaided. In April 1992 every government office located on a main street was ordered to convert its street frontage to a row of small, garage-type shops; most of these were taken up by Chinese migrants, to the discomfort of Tibetans who perhaps saw the prospect of their newly revived culture slipping away under a wave of cheap modernism from which many of them did not even stand to profit. Later that year orders were passed removing any checkpoints on Tibet's intraprovincial borders: there were to be no restrictions on Chinese migrants into the region. By about 1995 the leadership decided that it should also offer economic incentives to the Tibetans and another policy emerged: large loans from the state banks became available at generous levels of interest to a number of Tibetan businessmen. The result has been the creation of a new appetite for wealth among urban Tibetans and a dramatic increase in the class of rich Tibetan entrepreneurs with home video systems, new houses, and all-terrain vehicles. At the same time there was a huge investment by the state (and by foreign states) in equipping Tibet with advanced telecommunications.

As far as one can tell from abroad, economic development has led to a surge in small businesses—usually karaoke bars and nightclubs, many of which are short-lived and in which much of the trade is prostitution—and has been sustaine by the reinvestment of the cheap loans on the money market in Hong Kong. The current urban boom, with its fragile economic base, could in theory lead to a more stable development of the economy but is as likely to collapse once the state finds it can no longer afford to bankroll the loans. In the meantime a new plutocracy is emerging that is distanced from the majority of its fellow Tibetans, whose opportunities for trade and employment are unlikely to increase until, as the authorities promise, infrastructural development is sufficiently advanced to entice major investors. Even then Tibetans might find themselves without increased opportunities for labor, let alone profit, because Chinese workers are likely to be brought in to work on the oil wells and copper mines planned for Tibet.

If policy in Tibet were still focused on the development of this dynamic, if dubious, economy, it could be argued that the objective of the current regime was a well-intentioned, if misguided, effort to improve the economy and social wealth. But in fact, the economic liberalism of market socialism was really being used by the hard-liners in 1992 as a mechanism to encourage migration to Tibet—a demographic device to facilitate control. And in July 1997, it was made clear that this economic reformism also included a more unorthodox political agenda. China's main representative in Tibet, the party secretary Chen Kuiyuan, made a speech in which he announced that Buddhism was "foreign" and not part of Tibetan culture. It was not that he was wrong in absolute terms—as we have seen, Buddhism arrived in Tibet only a thousand years or so ago. But the statement was clearly intended not as an academic observation but as a provocative criticism of the notion of Tibetan culture, the sustaining of which the Dalai Lama and many other leading Tibetans throughout the previous ten years had already declared to be their fundamental and overriding concern.

In November of 1997, Chen went on to identify a new form of enemy within Tibetan society, "the hidden reactionary." As examples he referred to unnamed individuals among the few great Tibetan intellectuals remaining in the universities and among the educated Tibetans who had secured relatively senior positions in the administration during the reform period of the early 1980s. These two announcements can be taken as the signal that China had opened its third front in the battle to regain control of Tibet: an attack on Tibetan culture. The police work of the early 1990s and the economic drive of the mid-1990s were now to give way to an attempt to redefine Tibetan culture.

It became clear that the unusual aggression discernible in China's religious policy in Tibet since 1995 has been part of a larger offensive. The banning of the public display of photographs of the Dalai Lama and the constant press attacks on him were a sign that he was now to be regarded as a religious fraud as well as a political outcast; this was a significant change in policy, because throughout the 1980s he had been attacked only in his political capacity. The campaign in 1995 against the child he had recognized as the reincarnation of the Panchen Lama was the most strident part of this wider cultural offensive; by obliging hundreds of Tibetan officials, scholars, lamas, and intellectuals to declare public support for the state's right to appoint the new incarnation, the authorities were persuading them to renounce any claims to the promises offered by the 1980s era.

In 1996, another major campaign, this time the drive to bring "patriotic education" to the monks and nuns in Tibet, extended the attack beyond the senior officials and lamas to the lowest levels of the monasteries and nunneries: each was to be visited by a gongzuo dui, or "work team" of party cadres who would hold daily sessions for three months on the correct view of religion, law, history, and the Dalai Lama. Each person was required to give a formal declaration of loyalty by signing a statement denouncing the Dalai Lama and recognizing Tibet as part of China. That effort is still continuing in monasteries and nunneries across central Tibet, and by October 1997 had begun in the great monastic universities of Amdo as well. In March 1998, the program was extended to schools and to the "citizens" of Tibet, so that in the foreseeable future, all Tibetans will eventually be required to declare their allegiance to the new regime.

The third, cultural, front goes beyond the strategies of policing dissent or of economic buy-offs: both are relatively straightforward mechanisms to suppress dissent. The cultural attack appears to be aimed at the long-term elimination of ideas that could in the future lead to dissent, as well as at the dismantling of the concessions offered in the reform era. It has, however, an unfortunate resonance: in language and conception it is reminiscent of the thinking of the Cultural Revolution, perhaps the most brutal of the hard periods in Chinese Communist history. At the same time it also has an aspect that did not arise during the Cultural Revolution: the fear of assimilation from the immigration of Chinese attracted to the region by economic incentives. This apprehension is fueled by frequent rumors of plans to send settlers in large numbers, as the Chinese did in earlier times in Manchuria, Mongolia, and Xinjiang. Indeed, retired Chinese soldiers based in the region have, since at least 1994, been officially encouraged to settle in Tibet. In fact, many of the new arrivals in Tibet are temporary, staying for a few years rather than residing permanently, and they are almost entirely confined to towns and cities. Their impact, however, is significant.

The "new Tibetans" are entrepreneurs, usually Chinese or Hui (Chinese Muslim), who play a prominent role in the emerging private sector of the economy, now the leading edge of China's development strategy. They not only dominate economic life but have also introduced a powerful new culture that has made rapid inroads into Tibetan life, especially in the towns. Its detractors say this alien culture is Chinese, and it is certainly true that Chinese language, art, customs, and ideas are replacing their Tibetan equivalents in many areas. But it is also true that much of the new imported lifestyle is not Chinese, but rather part of modern, global commercialism: discotheques, pop music, Michael Jackson cassettes, Adidas trainers, video recorders, a stock exchange, motorbikes, mobile phones, satellite television, and E-mail, not to mention heroin and AIDS. The onslaught that Tibetans face now with the easing of barriers to trade and travel is as much Western in origin as it is Chinese; they are confronted with many of the same choices that Nepal, Bhutan, India, and other developing nations faced as traditional societies forced to come to terms with the rough assault of modernity.

But Tibetans confront these developments with severe handicaps: except at the purely subjective level all the choices they now face—whether to regulate the inflow of modernity; what compensatory steps to take in terms of education or training; whether to adapt or to abandon Tibetan language, arts, and customs in the face of the new demands; whether to control or to encourage outside investment; whether to give preference to local, indigenous traders and initiatives—are made by their Chinese rulers on their behalf. And the signs are that the Chinese leadership in Tibet is deliberately making choices, such as encouraging the growth of prostitution and refusing to regulate immigration, that will stunt or destroy the nascent attempts of Tibetan culture, so successful in the early 1980s, to adapt itself to modernity. Thus we find that in the last two years Tibetan parents in Lhasa have started encouraging their children to study the Chinese language, because few if any jobs will be open to those children if they graduate proficient only in Tibetan. As if to emphasise the point, the University of Tibet has already closed admission to its Tibetan department.

What we are seeing is a strange, perhaps unique, hybrid, different from previous left-right swings in Chinese politics. Tibet today is a cauldron in which an experiment is taking place, where politicians attempt to achieve the intentions of totalitarians while pursuing the actions of economic reformers. The economic liberalism of market socialism was used by the hard-liners in 1992 as a mechanism to encourage migration to Tibet. The indicators of this political composite—what some Chinese refer to as "hard on the inside, soft on the outside"—are not visible to the casual observer. There are no tanks on the streets or machine gun posts on the rooftops, as there were at the beginning of this decade; there are tourist hotels, computer shops, public phone booths, and all the other signs of affluence and luxury familiar to us from our own societies. Even the growing presence of an underclass, of unemployed Tibetans, is to us a sign of normal social disparity. If we saw a political education session in a monastery or a school, it would not look untoward to us as visitors. But in fact these are the images and the indicators of what Tibet is today—an experiment in achieving targeted repression and cultural restrictions within a context of economic relaxation.

It can be argued that the perception of the Tibet issue has been confused or misrepresented by the form that popular sympathy in some Western countries has taken on the Tibet question. In the English-speaking world that interest culminated with the

Hollywood films released in the late 1990s—Jean-Jacques Annaud's Seven Years in Tibet and Martin Scorsese's Kundun, to name the best known; it had previously been symbolized in the media by the involvement of American film stars like Richard Gere and Harrison Ford in support of the Tibetans. The surge of media and public interest reflected by those films (which attempted to express the exiled Tibetans' view of the conflict) took it for granted that there is a serious basis to the aspirations of the Tibetan nationalists and to the continuance of the Sino-Tibetan conflict. Such well-meaning support is influential in shaping the popular assessment of the Tibetan question; but it is also something of a chimera. In the long term there is a risk that support for the Tibetans of this kind could potentially do damage to the cause it espouses.

There are a number of aspects of Western coverage of the issue to date which give rise to concern. One of these is that the recent increase in media coverage gives the impression that there is popular support for the issue in the West, which in turn implies that Western governments support the issue; this is not necessarily the case. The Tibet issue in the West is a classic example of one of those legislature-executive struggles that figure frequently in the history of Western-style democracies: Tibet represents one set of interests to legislators and another set of interests to foreign policy decision makers. The implications of this disjuncture have not always been fully explored and have led to some apparently unnoticed consequences. While parliaments and congresses have been pulling in one direction, the executive branches (and the business interests to which they are much closer) have pulled in another, and the Tibetans have ended up with a small burst of publicity and occasionally a parliamentary statement that has no legal standing.

The U.S. Congress, for example, declared Tibet in 1991 to be an independent country under military occupation, but the resolution has no legal significance and has apparently been ignored by lawyers and policy makers. In any case, what appears to matter now to the Chinese authorities is the position taken by governments in their implementation of foreign policy. This was not always the case: until about 1994, Beijing was in the habit of reacting quite strongly to parliamentary statements, apparently out of the belief that they must reflect, as in China, the views of their corresponding government, or that they might have some impact in shaping those views; a number of Tibetan political prisoners were released or saved from execution during that period, as a result of outside pressure as expressed by foreign parliaments and pressure groups. Experience has changed that misconception, however, and Beijing, which recently set up a research unit to study the anomalous ways of the U.S. Congress, now knows that the two units in the Western system can be treated quite separately, especially where peripheral or sentimental issues are involved. The eighteen-year sentence given in 1996, in defiance of congressional appeals, to Tibetan exile Ngawang Choephel, a graduate student from Middlebury College who was arrested for traveling in Tibet with a video camera, was presumably intended to make that clear.

Unless the Tibet issue is able to generate support more substantial than popular sympathy and media glamorization, statements by legislatures are not in themselves any longer of much concern to the leadership in Beijing, whose business is with governments and investors. It can of course be argued that in the past popular support has led to more significant institutional backing, and finally to government or financial action, but such a progression appears to happen because of a number of factors besides the extent of popular support. South Africa and Palestine, for example, became major issues, but they were of undisputed strategic significance, involved protracted military and terrorist struggles, had highly organized and sophisticated indigenous political parties representing them outside, as well as very large and active resistance movements inside the countries. None of these conditions, probably not even the last, apply at the moment in the Tibetan case.

A second weakness with the coverage of Tibet in the West is that the popular support it invokes is in fact more localized than it appears. After his escape from Tibet in 1995, the famous human rights activist Gendun Rinchen, who three years earlier had been voted Tibet's top tour guide, said that 80 percent of the tourists he escorted had little or no idea that there was any political problem in Tibet—and they were the ones interested enough in Tibet to pay to visit it. The Tibet question has remained corralled and specialized, a situation that is changed little by media coverage.

The miscalculation of the extent or significance of Western support is unfortunate, because it has communicated to Tibetans inside Tibet a false impression of international support; this has arguably encouraged them to stage demonstrations and protests in Tibet that courted publicity at great personal cost but that perhaps brought little concrete result. More importantly, it has contributed to the mood of disillusionment and frustration that now appears to be current among Tibetans who, perhaps thinking that Western support was substantive rather than marginal, expected improvements as a result of outside pressure but received few. Instead they have been left to find out that in the long run outside pressure has led to the increased sophistication of control that they now face in Tibet.

Perhaps more damaging has been the political message that Western support has communicated to the Chinese people and to those in other developing countries. The fact that foreign interest in the issue is mainly confined to westerners—and that the character of Western rhetoric about the issue is often polemical and anti-Chinese in tone, or self-evidently misinformed—has given the impression that Tibet is a Western preoccupation in part overstated to bolster the interests of the Western bloc. The unfortunate history of the Tibet issue, used by the Western powers, and by the United States in particular, in the 1950s and 1960s as part of their cold war strategy to destabilize China, has fueled the perception that criticism of Beijing's role in Tibet is a device raised by westerners to attack China in particular and developing countries in general. This has enabled Beijing to rally support from the developing world and led to the collapse of the last nine attempts at the United Nations to criticize China's human rights practices.

Another difficulty with the general presentation of the Tibetan case in the West is that the wrong elements have been condensed: the exciting things to westerners about Tibet are its exoticism and its mysticism, the colorfulness of its religion, the irrepressible charm of the Dalai Lama, the mystique of the mountains, and so on. Yet in terms of politics these factors are incidental— Kuwait, for example, was not given support against invasion because of the charm of its sheikhs. What should have been condensed in discussions of Tibet, if those involved in creating the images wished to see a political outcome, are the same issues that we consider when dealing with other disputes over colonization or occupation—who holds power, who is not given access to power, what are the political demands and program of the people involved, how close are the representatives of the various groupings to the people they represent, and so on.

The trivialization of the Tibet issue has led a number of presumptions to accumulate that may need to be reconsidered if Western discussion of Tibet is to appear meaningful. For example, the perception of the Dalai Lama as supreme pontiff of Tibetan Buddhism is a recent phenomenon, reported to be an arrangement that other religious schools reached in the 1960s partly to simplify their relations with foreigners. The role of pacifism in Tibet has been overstated: it is true Tibetans have in general chosen to follow the advice of their leader not to take up arms, but this is also a recent phenomenon and not a condition of their culture. Until 1974, thousands of Tibetans took part in a fierce guerrilla war with the Chinese, which for a period was funded by the U.S. Central Intelligence Agency. The clergy who destroyed the attempts of the Tibetan government and the previous Dalai Lama to enlarge and modernize the Tibetan army in the 1920s (and who thus destroyed any chance of Tibet ever resisting incorporation into China) were not motivated in the slightest by objections to violence, but by the fear that modernization might, by increasing links with the un-Buddhist British, lead to the diminution of the monasteries' power; indeed there were several insurgencies against the previous Dalai Lama or his regents this century led by monks in defense of that belief.

Today some ten thousand Tibetans are members of India's military forces, soldiers with a special aptitude for high-altitude warfare, posing a threat that China views with some seriousness. Neither is the level of political violence among Tibetans as low as some Western reports would suggest: at least seven bombs exploded in Tibet between 1995 and 1997, one of them laid by a monk, and a significant number of individual Tibetans are known to be actively seeking the taking up of arms; hundreds of Chinese soldiers and police have been beaten during demonstrations in Tibet, and at least one killed in cold blood, probably several more. Within the exile community itself there is a continuing streak of political intolerance, especially towards those who have made the slightest perceived criticism of the Dalai Lama, who risk beatings or threats of assassination. Neither is religion by any means above conflict: at least two of the four schools of Tibetan Buddhism are at present wracked by disputes; both cases have led to murders or threats of murder.

The mythologized depiction of Tibetans as inherently religious and pacifist is attractive, but it is also reductionist. It implies that they are passive, and that their decisions are the result of tradition not choice, and it suggests that they are neither part of the modern secular world nor suited to the competitiveness of contemporary political decision making. The political presentation of Tibet has similarly tended to focus on the suffering experienced by Tibetans under Chinese occupation. Sometimes this is presented as a general phenomenon, such as by citing the total number of those believed to have been killed, and at other times an individual case is described, such as that of a nun or monk who has been imprisoned and tortured. None of these references are invalid (although the figures used are often inaccurate), but because there is often an absence of harder analysis, they have the effect of portraying Tibetans as victims who need to be helped, rather than as agents of political change who might be supported.

It is in this area, the role of human rights in the Tibet issue, where another disjuncture between sympathy and political action can be seen. Media, parliamentary, and governmental statements have tended to focus on the question of how individuals in Tibet are treated by the current regime. But in the hard world of international politics, human rights issues are of little relevance to the process of political decision making. Although statements on human rights issues are frequently made by governments of all hues, their policies are unlikely to be significantly influenced by them—not least because almost every country has condoned human rights abuses of one kind or another within its own borders.

Governmental statements about human rights in Tibet or China are thus usually bargaining chips to create leverage for issues higher up the agenda or smoke screens designed to impress the domestic constituency while at the same time causing minimum anxiety to Beijing. A sophisticated regime like China could, if it wished, have resolved overnight most human rights criticisms by foreign governments by offering to appoint a commission of inquiry, arresting a few police chiefs for torture, or inviting UN officials to visit model prisons; that it has not done so, and that it has only recently started to respond at all to human rights criticisms, is because, among other reasons, it is in its interest, and in the interests of the Western powers as well, to keep public discussion and confrontation focused on such essentially marginal areas, thus avoiding issues of potentially irreversible conflict. The Tibetan activists inside Tibet have rarely (until recently) incorporated the issue of human rights in their protests or slogans—the language of human rights is largely a facet of exile rhetoric and Western simplification of the issue. Inside Tibet, the demands raised in wall posters have focused more on independence: rightly or wrongly, that has been to them the central issue.

No one can have been clearer about this than the Chinese leaders themselves: they have endlessly repeated the remark, usually unnoticed, that sovereignty is the main issue. When the Tibetan demonstrations in 1987 triggered a flurry of foreign criticism of China's human rights practices, the Chinese acted as if all allegations were veiled attacks on their territorial claims and demanded from each critical government assurances that its criticisms applied only to human rights practices and did not affect its acceptance that Tibet was part of China. In almost all cases the Western governments, apart from Britain, gave the required assurances to Beijing.

Thus, although China appears in the last ten years to have been battered in the Western media for its role in Tibet, in terms of the declared aspirations of its political leaders, in terms of power politics, and in terms of historical significance, it has emerged from those years of apparently stringent diplomatic attack with a wealth of political gains. Few if any countries apart from India and Nepal had specifically declared that Tibet was part of China before 1987; now most have been asked to do so and have complied. Tibet's claim to separate or at least ambiguous status was at least in part supported by the fact that few countries had specifically described it otherwise; that situation was reversed at the same time as Western criticisms of China were being popularly presented as assisting the Tibetans' situation. In other words, it can be argued that support from the West, which was anyway limited, may have damaged the political prospects of the Tibetan issue as much as it helped them.

If we have to generalize, therefore, it can be said that the Western perception of the Tibetan question has been burdened with a romantic inheritance, oversimplified information, and a blurred political presentation. It is because of such characteristics of the Western approach to Tibet, and its sometimes unfortunate consequences, that we need to seek another, more disciplined and more layered, view. That there is some resistance to this in Western discussion of the Tibet question may be due to its associations with Tibetan Buddhism, which many westerners see as antithetical to pragmatism or political thought; they have tended to invest in the religious aspects of the Tibetan situation, often as a conscious antidote to Western rationalism. The effects of this on the Tibetans have been quite concrete: since the exile of the Tibetans to India forty years ago, for example, large amounts of money and energy have been expended on the preservation of Tibetan culture outside of Tibet. A more pragmatic approach would have invested in encouraging that culture to develop rather than to remain static, equipping it in its encounter with modernity instead of helping it to become a museum exhibit. As the controversial American Tibetologist Melvyn Goldstein pointed out in 1990, Western funds have financed the production of much abstruse religious literature in Tibetan but not the writing by exiles of novels, stories, plays, or poems, so that (until the founding of the Amnyemachen Institute's translation project in India in 1992) there has been little other than advanced metaphysics for an exiled lay Tibetan to read in his or her own language. While there are thousands of Tibetan monks in exile who have received higher education in religious studies, few Tibetans in the exile community have been trained in technology or sciences. Among Western scholars of Tibet, too, the study of modern Tibet has been seriously considered only in the last eight years or so: the bulk of Tibetology was and still is focussed on classical studies. Even the contemporary study of Tibet or the writing of a modern, secular literature in Tibetan can scarcely be found anywhere outside China or Tibet itself.

The limitations of the general Western efforts to date do not mean that the Tibetan pursuit of national identity is trivial or doomed. Political change is not dictated by logical certainties, as the Soviet experience has indicated, and there is certainly nothing trivial about the Tibet experience, nor any reason why its quantitative insignificance should preclude it from having disproportionate regional impact. For example, in 1987, when Steve Lehman and I met by chance in a Lhasa backstreet during a wholly unexpected demonstration, the Tibet question was nowhere on the Chinese, let alone the international, agenda. If the Chinese government had not chosen to conceal the details of that protest, to deny that they had shot a number of Tibetans dead when we and other tourists had seen it, or to close the country off from foreign journalists ever since, the Tibetan issue might not have received much attention in the last decade. The errors of Beijing on that occasion had an effect that could hardly have been foreseen and that has had lasting repercussions. It was not so much that Tibetan discontent became known to the outside world: what was of lasting importance was that the events of that day propelled Tibetan resentment to develop into the deep and highly motivated alienation that resulted in the far greater turmoil that took place in subsequent months. Before the outbreak of protest in 1987, Tibetans had apparently been aware of the likely withdrawal of the concessions that Hu Yaobang had offered them some seven years earlier; but the response of the authorities to their demonstrations revealed the fear within the Chinese leviathan of the pinprick of Tibetan dissent. That fear, as seen in the decision to open fire on the protestors in Lhasa, was an indication that the dragon is more fragile than its fiery breath would have its subjects believe. It is in that perception that the potential for significant Tibetan impact resides.

In more technical terms, what the Chinese accomplished and are further fomenting as they move to attack Tibetan culture itself has been the stoking of a modern form of mass political consciousness among Tibetans. The politicization that several decades of explicit indoctrination had failed to inculcate is now being achieved by the same Chinese efforts that are currently directed against the rise of nationalist consciousness in Tibet.

Current Chinese policy in Tibet, replete with such examples of contradiction and extremity, has suffered ever since from a sense of fragility and insecurity, with a tendency to concentrate its attack on the apparently innocuous. Since 1995 it has banned the photographs of an amiable man in a skirt, run a state campaign ordering the denunciation of a six-year-old child, forced forty thousand monks and nuns to sign declarations concerning thirteenth-century history, and declared a thousand-year-old religious tradition to be a foreign import. Such decisions cannot be easily explained by the logic of realpolitik or national interest; we have to look elsewhere to explain the forces that drive Chinese leaders in Tibet.

It is as if China were operating, in its dealings with Tibet, in a universe sustained not so much by its army or its factories, as by its ideological constructions. After all, the central question for the leaders in Beijing may not be, perhaps has never been, their creditworthiness with international financiers or their standing with the international community, but their credibility with the people of China. They are a regime of considerable youth, scarcely fifty years old, whose power was achieved through conquest, through the incompetence and barbarity of their opponents, and through lavish, utopian promises to their followers. During their period of rule, despite some notable successes, they have committed atrocities that in many ways dwarf those of their predecessors—even Chiang Kaishek, for example, did not initiate a famine that killed a reported thirty million people. And the current regime has largely repudiated the aspirations and claims of its revolutionary progenitors—not so much because it clearly espouses capitalism and social disparity, but because it has also renounced the provision of free education, medical care, or guaranteed employment to its people.

Whatever else one might say about the Tibetans, the one thing they have in their favour is a substantial claim to legitimacy. As a nation-state, they may have failed to register their credentials, but they enjoyed all the characteristics of statehood; as a political force, they are unified to an exceptional degree in their objectives; as a movement they have a leader who enjoys unusual respect not merely in the West, where his significance is more symbolic than actual, but inside Tibet, where the political unity he commands may well be the final arbiter of Tibet's future. The strategic advantage of even partial pacifism is of great relevance not at all because of any moral virtues we may see in it, but because it can lay claim to legitimacy in a conflict where the Tibetans' opponent has little legitimacy and has depended on force.

This is not to say that there can be any predictable outcome to this dispute. The Tibetans are also capable of making strategic errors (as events have already indicated) on a large scale, just as the Chinese are. They could reject the leadership of the Dalai Lama, return to sectarian or regional conflict, decide to revive their autocratic tradition, or reach such a conciliatory compromise with the Chinese as to have no rights remaining. Or they could, for example, decide on other objectives, such as the pursuit of immediate wealth, already currently on offer to a certain class in Lhasa.

But even in these scenarios, the history of nationalist disputes suggests that such tendencies are in a sense diversions. People may be distracted for a period by the attractions of modernization or by internal conflicts, but eventually their interest in asserting their identity will reemerge, and when it does it will be equipped with increased expectations and better resources. In other words the current Chinese (and Western) strategies for deflecting Tibetan aspirations are unlikely to succeed in the long run, and may serve only to exacerbate the dispute.

When Steve Lehman, I, and other Western tourists first saw protestors take to the streets of Lhasa in October 1987, an arcane dispute emerged amongst us as to the role of foreigners. Should we witness these events silently from the sidelines, some of us asked, or should we stand in the middle of the crowd to show support and to deter the soldiers from opening fire? In the event, those who decided to stand among the crowd and wave their fists found that they were shot at, too. More significantly, perhaps, their involvement was photographed and filmed by officials so that to this day they are cited as evidence that those protests were fueled by foreign provocateurs and not an expression of Tibetan belief. Perhaps that would have happened whatever we, the outsiders, had done, but the episode was a reminder that in the final analysis the role of the foreign journalist or observer may be more limited than we like to imagine.

Though the West's response will undoubtedly be a factor in the dispute, its outcome will ultimately be decided by Tibetans and Chinese, and whether they eventually resolve their differences will depend almost entirely on their ingenuity and tenacity. The landmark decision of the Chinese in 1990 to stop killing demonstrators in Tibet may have been seen as a consequence of international criticism of Beijing, but it was also to do with the realization in China that the shooting was further antagonizing Tibetans in Tibet. In other words, the Chinese were to a considerable extent afraid of Tibetan unrest. The bottom line in this issue is thus not the legal status of Tibet, the magnitude of the army, the stature of the Dalai Lama, or the moral power of the demands: it is the risk that determined Tibetans may decide en masse to actively oppose Chinese rule.

It is ironic, therefore, that it is the Tibetans in Tibet who are least often consulted by foreign journalists and politicians, and their opinions which are most rarely documented in any detail by observers and writers. It is also why a book of this sort, as an attempt to communicate something of the experience and thinking of those people, is neither a tribute nor an elegy: it is a demand that we, the observers, focus our attention on those who are in every sense the key to the future of Tibet and the only arbiters of the seriousness or otherwise of this issue—that is, the Tibetans themselves.

7

Tibetan Refugees in Nepal

During his fresh visit to Nepal, the South Asia Forum for Human Rights (SAFHR) took a bold initiative and arranged a visit to Pokhara, situated at 200 kilometre west of Kathmandu. Pokhara means "land of lakes". It is a beautiful hilly area situated at an altitude of 827 metres from the sea and is about eight hours drive from Kathmandu. Pokhara records the highest rainfall in Nepal and has several beautiful lakes offering an eye-catching view of Himalayan peaks. The journey through the spiral roads running through the very high hills with evidence of land-slides towards Pokhara was very exciting. There was a wonderful reception from the refugees. Twenty-nine participants from eight countries working for human rights were in the list to visit the old Tashi Palkhiel Tibetan Refugee camp. Most of the Tibetan refugees were lucky enough to have escaped across the borders into Nepal to live in settlements in Kathmandu' Budhanath district and the remainder in Pokhara, Baglung, Mustang, Taplejung, Manang, Rasuwa, Solukhumbu and Lalitpur.

Virtually, Nepal is now the home of 18,000 formally registered Tibetan refugees (unofficially more than 20,000), who are known to have fled to Nepal in 1959, the year when Tibet's spiritual leader Dalai Lama fled to Dharmasala, India. Most of them are actually children and grandchildren of the refugees. In1960 the Nepalese government arranged to provide Tibetan refugees with land. They established four temporary settlements. Dhialsa in Solu Khumba Mountain, Dhorpatan in western Nepal, Jawalakhel in Kathmandu and Tashi Palkhiel in Pokhara. As the Tibetans have no right to buy property, Nepal Red Cross (NRC) purchased the land with the donations from UNHCR.

There are four Tibetan refugee camps in Pokhara and the one visited by us, Tashi Palkhiel Tibetan Refugee Camp was established in 1962 in cooperation with the Swiss development Corporation and the government of Nepal. There are about 1000 refugees in the camp with facilities of a school, old age home and a beautiful monastery. The camp in Pokhara looks like a small Tibet. The refugee houses were minute, too closely constructed by less stable materials. Food and water supply was adequate but the source was not safe for drinking. Medical care was given by only a small dispensary run mainly by a female nurse of Tibetan origin, still the Tibetan preferred not to visit the dispensary but to depend on their traditional treatment. Dysentery, diarrhoea, skin infection was not common. There is no formal training for the women who are mainly engaged in the domestic activities, child care and sales women.

Refugees are not allowed to dabble in political activities, or do business outside of their area, though some are working outside, mainly in Kathmandu having valid ID card issued before 1989. The rest who came after that time cannot assimilate and find secure employment without formal legal standing in Nepal. Tibetan refugees have no right to own property or business, cannot own houses, vehicles, land and other property in Nepal. Legal and social discrimination severely curtail their ability to secure employment. They are not permitted to acquire residential and other legal documents. The displaced Tibetan nationals have experienc harassment, extortion and deportation when they are without valid evidence. Tibetan refugees cannot travel to certain restricted regions of Nepal, and it is difficult to get travel documents for crossing international borders.

In recent years, refugees have come at a rate averaging eight person per day. The new arrivals are fed and housed at a transit camp in Kathmandu run by the administration of Dalai Lama. After their arrival, the refugees are kept in undisclosed transit camps. Many refugees spoke to the participants regarding the refugee status and valid identification. According to UNHCR's global guidelines, any refugee claimant may appeal a negative decision concerning refugee status. "We don't feel like humans here and my younger brother who is born in the camp is even in a worst situation as he has no rights at all," said Tahshi, a young Tibetan teenager in the camp.

To get to Nepal the refugees have to pass from side to side the snow-covered Himalayas, the world's highest mountain range. Many among the fleeing peoples fall prey to the cold and freeze to death. Dekhi Lama, a young Tibetan refugee remembers a 7-year old girl who died of hypothermia and difficulty of breathing at high altitudes and was buried in the snow. This is one such example. Once settled in Nepal, some Tibetan refugees decide to stay while others choose to move on to India and other parts of the world.

Though the UNHCR must inform the applicant why someone's application has been rejected, the claimants were not given any reasons for why their applications were refused. Nearly 300 newly arrived Tibetan refugees were sent back. They were handed over to the Chinese authorities by the Communist Party of Nepal (CPN) in 1995, though the Foreign Minister Prakash Chandra Lohani assured that the Tibetan refugees need fear such consequences anymore. Eight of the Tibetans, aged 14 to 18 had been forcibly removed from Honuman Dhoka jail by the Nepalese and Chinese police and officials at 7:30 am on May 31, 2003. This deportation was implemented despite strong international lobbying in support of the Tibetans over few days and high level interest. Sometimes Nepalese security guards demand bribes from the refugees caught at the border, threatening to hand them over to Chinese authorities. Sometimes the refugees were given prison sentences ranging from seven to ten months as they were not able to pay the fines. Invariably the refugees in the prison are denied access to doctors, even if they are sent by the Nepalese.

In 2000, Nepalese establishment and UNHCR agreed to change the existing one-page travel document for the Tibetan refugees to a passport style document that will be accepted by most countries. The new passport system was about to be implemented beginning in January 2001. On May 2003, the Government of Nepal turned 18 Tibetan asylum seekers including minors, over to the Chinese representatives to be forcibly repatriated to China.

The actions taken against the Tibetan refugees not only violates international norms and practices regarding the humane treatment of asylum seekers and refugees, but also puts a question mark on Nepal's long standing reputation as a peace loving country with tolerance and hospitality.

NEPAL'S SHIFTING MOVE TOWARD TO TIBETAN REFUGEES

From 1959 to 1986, but particularly in the existence before 1974, Nepal generally facilitated the work of foreign governments and humanitarian aid organizations involved in helping to resettle the first wave of Tibetan refugees. The Nepalese government viewed the settlements as an efficient long-term solution to a potentially serious refugee crisis. It therefore maintained a largely laissez-faire approach toward them. In 1975, UNHCR historian Louise Holborn lauded Nepal for "provid[ing] for the survival of thousands of Tibetan refugees" and giving them "the possibility of becoming contributing members of the societies of their host countr[y] while at the same time preserving their own identity."

Before 1986, the Nepalese government also tended to tolerate the arrival of new refugees for several reasons: It lacked the practical ability to enforce a strict border-control policy; fewer new refugees arrived during China's Cultural Revolution (approximately 1966-1979) because the Chinese government then maintained strict control over the movement of the Tibetan population; and in any event the Nepalese government did not perceive the number of newly arriving Tibetan refugees as a threat or a diplomatic liability during these years. The 1966 Agreement on Trade, Intercourse, and Related Questions Between the Tibet Autonomous Region (TAR) of China and Nepal permitted Tibetans living in the border regions of the

TAR and "religious pilgrims" to cross the Tibeto-Nepalese border without a passport or visa, provided they registered at the border. Nepal renewed this Agreement for another ten years in

1976. The Nepalese government's laissez-faire move toward Tibetan refugees began to change and tighten in 1986. In that year Nepal and China executed a new treaty that significantly restricted the ability of Tibetans to travel through or into Nepal. Soon after, in 1987 and 1989, the Chinese government suppressed a series of pro-Tibetan independence demonstrations in Lhasa. This led to a resurgence in the number of Tibetans fleeing into exile.

In 1989, pressure from the Chinese government and the growing number of new arrivals led Nepal to initiate a strict border-control policy. The Nepalese government made clear that it would henceforth refuse to accept or recognize new Tibetan refugees. At about the same time, however, UNHCR re-established an office in Kathmandu to assist Nepal with its Bhutanese refugee crisis. With the tacit approval of Nepal's Ministry of Home Affairs, UNHCR also began to facilitate the transit of newly arriving Tibetan refugees through Nepal to India. The funds for this informal and low-profile operation initially came from the United States, which provided an "infusion of $100,000 in 1991" to support the "refugee protection and processing program." The circumstances and legal status of Tibetans residing in Nepal, and the current operation of this informal "protection and processing program," are the twin subjects of this report.

Nepalese Rule

Nepal's Constitution, promulgated in 1990 after King Birenda legalized the configuration of political parties, for the most part protects only citizens. They enjoy rights to equality before the law, non-discrimination, expression and assembly, freedom of movement, freedom to engage in trade, and to own and transfer property. Non-citizens— all "persons"—enjoy a more limited set of rights. These include the rights to equal protection, religious freedom, and protection from expropriation of property. But they do not include freedom of expression, freedom of movement, and the right to acquire or own property. During the drafting of the 1990 Constitution, international NGOs urged Nepal to avoid distinctions between citizens and non-citizens for purposes of fundamental guarantees such as speech, association, and movement. But the government insisted on these distinctions, and consequently, the constitutional guarantees avail-able to refugees remain minimal. No statute or regulation of Nepal define or even refers to "refugees." The government has no official policy toward them. Tapan K. Bose, Director of the South Asia Forum for Human Rights, noted that "there is no formal process for accepting refugees.... [Refugees] have no legal status." Nepalese law classifies refugees simply as aliens.

The Immigration Act of 1992 prescribes their treatment. The Act defines "foreigners" as all persons not citizens of Nepal. It states that "[n]o foreigners shall be allowed to enter into and stay in the Kingdom of Nepal without obtaining a passport and visa," and it limits the entry of foreigners to "pre-scribed" routes. The Act also empowers immigration officers with-in the Ministry of Home Affairs to investigate infractions of these regulations and to detain, fine, and deport persons charged with their violation. UNHCR said that in recent years Nepal has been increasingly enforcing these provisions against Tibetans seeking to return to Tibet via Nepal after briefly visiting India—typically for the purposes of a pilgrimage or to visit relatives residing there.

"[T]hose returning from India are often arrested and fined under the [Immigration Act]. But they can't pay their fine." The domestic legal framework for the protection and processing of refugees in Nepal is therefore minimal. Nepalese law does not recognize refugees or provide them with rights to seek protection, asylum or legal residence. Tibet Justice Centre's interviews with officials at the Ministry of Home Affairs confirmed that the absence of a for-mal legal framework is not an oversight; it reflects a deliberate policy decision perceived to be in Nepal's geostrategic interest. At the same time, the Nepalese government does cooperate with UNHCR to handle its two major refugee populations: Tibetans and ethnic Nepalese refugees from Bhutan. The informal "gentleman's agreement" between Nepal and UNHCR for the transit of Tibetan refugees through Nepal allows UNHCR to continue to assist Tibetan refugees without requiring the Nepalese government to incur unwanted obligations toward Tibetans. Because of Nepal's strong national interest in maintaining UNHCR's overt assistance with its Bhutanese refugee population, estimated at more than 100,000, the Nepalese government also has much to gain by per-mitting UNHCR tacitly to continue to assist Tibetan refugees, an objective supported by UNHCR and many foreign aid donors.

Worldwide Rule

All persons in need, regardless of their migration status, share certain basic human rights under international law. The Universal Declaration of Human Rights (UDHR), which proclaims "a common standard of achievement for all peoples and all nations," prohibits discrimination on the grounds of national origin and provides that all persons shall enjoy the right "to seek and enjoy in other countries asylum from persecution." Nepal is also a party to three treaties that guarantee certain rights and protections to all persons, including refugees, within its borders: the International Covenant on Civil and Political Rights (ICCPR), the International Covenant on Economic, Social, and Cultural Rights (ICESCR), and the Convention on the Rights of the Child (CRC). In general, the ICCPR's provisions protect not only citizens of the state party, but "all individuals within [the state party's] territory and subject to its jurisdiction." The ICCPR guarantees freedom of thought, conscience, religion, expression, and peaceful assembly. Article 24 also extends to every child the right to acquire a nationality. The ICESCR guarantees the rights to work, an adequate standard of living, education, and the highest attainable standard of health. But the ICESCR recognizes state resource constraints and therefore provides that "[d]eveloping countries...may determine to what extent they w[ill] guarantee the economic rights recognized in the present Covenant to non-nationals." The CRC extends a similar catalogue of rights to "each child within [a state party's] jurisdiction without discrimination of any kind." The CRC recognizes the right of each child both to "preserve his or her identity, including nationality" and to acquire a nationality. This right, according to UNICEF, "renders questionable legislation that does not allow children to acquire full nationality from significant periods of residence."

Refugees and Asylum Seekers. Beyond the rights guaranteed to all persons by human rights treaties of general application, refugees and asylum seekers enjoy special protections under international law by virtue of two treaties: the 1951 Convention Relating to the Status of Refugees and the 1967 Protocol Relating to the Status of Refugees (collectively, the Refugee Conventions). The 1951 Convention defines a refugee as any person who: owing to a well-founded fear of being persecuted for reasons of race, religion, nationality, membership of a particular social group or political opinion, is out-ICCPR's language. But at a minimum, it seems clear that children born to refugee parents who enjoy no right to the nationality of the state of their parent's origin nor to that of their host state are effectively deprived of the right to acquire a nationality in violation of article 24(3). side the country of his nationality and is unable or, owing to such fear, is unwilling to avail himself of the protection of that country; or who, not having a nationality and being outside the country of his for-mer habitual residence...is unable, or owing to such fear, is unwilling to return to it. An asylum seeker is a person who seeks refugee status. Asylum seekers should enjoy the same rights as refugees until their status has been fairly determined.

The Refugee Conventions guarantee refugees a number of rights, including freedom of conscience, movement, and religion, protection from favouritism, and the right to acquire identity papers. Most critically, Article 33 of the 1951 Convention forbids the "return ('*refouler*') [of] a refugee in any manner whatsoever to the frontiers of territories where his life or freedom would be threatened on account of his race, religion, nationality, membership of a particular social group or political opinion." The principle of *non-refoulement* codified in Article 33 is the touchstone of the modern regime for the international protection of refugees. Many scholars argue that it has become a rule of customary international law, binding on all states regardless of their express treaty obligations. While Nepal has not ratified the Refugee Conventions, it serves as an observer state on UNHCR's Executive Committee and, as such, should respect UNHCR Executive Committee Conclusions. Moreover, the CRC obliges Nepal "to ensure that a child who is seeking refugee status...receive[s] appropriate humanitarian assistance," and to this end, to work proactively with UNHCR and other intergovernmental and non-governmental organizations cooperating with the United Nations.

Nepal is also a party to the Convention Against torment and Other Cruel, Inhuman, or Degrading Treatment or Punishment (CAT). Article 3 of the CAT prohibits the *refoulement* of any per-son to a "State where there are substantial grounds for believing that he would be in danger of being subjected to torture." Because reports consistently show that Chinese authorities use torture against Tibetans perceived to be dissidents, including those who attempt to flee into exile, the CAT forbids Nepal from repatriating Tibetans who may be subjected to torture. Moreover, scholars argue that Article 3 should be interpreted broadly to protect persons apprehended close to the border, not only those who have already crossed into foreign territory.

Any systematic, government-sanctioned policy of *refoulement* of Tibetan refugees therefore raises serious concerns about Nepal's compliance with its obligations under the CAT. The extent to which any of the foregoing treaty obligations—and the fundamental principle of *non-refoulement*—translate into practical guarantees in Nepal is unclear. Nepal's government, according to the U.S. State Department, has "no official refugee policy." Nepal is not a party to the Refugee Conventions, and Tibet Justice Centre's interviews with Nepalese government officials suggest strongly that Nepal does not intend to subscribe to these treaties in the near future. On the other hand, Director-General of Immigration Mainali remarked that, as a member of the United Nations, the government ordinarily will "respect UNHCR policy" on "humanitarian grounds."

Kapil Shrestha, Secretary of Nepal's Human Rights Commission, told Tibet Justice Centre that despite Nepal's accession to more than one dozen multilateral human rights treaties, "at the level of implementation, it is lagging far behind. Practically, it leaves much to be desired." The ICCPR, ICESCR, and CRC guarantee concrete rights that, in theory if not yet in practice, extend to all Tibetan refugees entering or residing in Nepal.

ORIGINS: TIBETAN REFUGEES RESIDE IN NEPAL

nowadays, approximately 20,000 Tibetans reside in Nepal. The vast majority of this population arrived before 1989 and particularly during the period between 1959, when the People's Liberation Army's (PLA) assault on Lhasa sent thousands of Tibetans into exile, and 1974, when the Nepalese government forcibly shut down the Tibetan guerilla base that had been operating for more than fifteen years in the western Kingdom of Mustang. The remainder of the Tibetan refugee population in Nepal is comprised largely of the children of this first caseload and, to a much lesser extent, Tibetans who have fled since the late 1980s. The latter group, the second caseload, almost invariably proceeds to India because the Nepalese government no longer provides sanctuary to newly arriving Tibetan refugees.

In journey from the 1959 Uprising

While some Tibetan refugees arrived in Nepal in the early 1950s, the first major influx crossed the border in 1959, following the Lhasa Uprising. At that time most did not expect to remain in Nepal for more than a few months. They established camps primarily in the Himalayan border regions of Nepal such as Mustang, a small, largely autonomous, and ethnically Tibetan kingdom in western Nepal, as well as in Nubri, and Solu Khumbu. The climate in these regions resembles that of Tibet. The refugees also felt that the proximity of the camps to the border would enable them to return home easily when the appropriate time came. Shortly, however, it became apparent to many that this time would not arrive in the near future. But few possessed the means to establish settlements with long-term economic viability. By 1961, many of the refugees faced serious food shortages and suffered from a lack of adequate shelter and healthcare.

In May 1960, Nepal requested assistance from the International Committee of the Red Cross (ICRC) and other aid organizations. Funded primarily by the United States Agency for International Development (USAID), the ICRC established emergency relief pro-grams for the refugees. With airplanes provided by the Swiss Red Cross, the ICRC parachuted supplies to refugee encampments in the remote Himalayan regions. At about the same time, Tibetan officials of the government-in-exile returned to Dharamsala, India, from a fact-finding mission to Nepal, and reported to the Dalai Lama on the dire conditions facing the refugees there. In response, the Tibetan government established the Kathmandu Tibetan Welfare Office, a branch of the Tibetan Ministry of Home Affairs. The Tibetan Welfare Office functioned as a liaison between the refugees, various aid organizations, and the Nepalese government. Also known as the Office of Tibet, it continues to serve this vital role today.

The Guerilla process at Mustang

The guerilla operation in Mustang created a second major source of Nepal's original Tibetan refugee population. From about 1959 to 1974, the Nepalese government turned a blind eye to a Tibetan military base located in the remote northwestern Kingdom of Mustang, which received covert support from the United States Central Intelligence Agency (CIA). From this base, Tibetans, primarily former residents of the province of Kham, carried out guerilla strikes against the PLA. For about ten years, the CIA funded military training for Tibetan guerillas, including in "camouflage, spy photography, guns, and radio operation," and provided them with weapons and other equipment to sustain the Mustang base. By the late 1960s, however, the U.S. government's support for this covert operation dwindled, and the CIA gradually discontinued aid to the guerillas. At about the same time, Nepal began to seek a closer relationship with China because "[n]o longer fearful, as it had been in the early 1960s, of a Chinese attack, Nepal now wished to counter New Delhi's influence in the region by furthering ties with [Beijing]."

In 1974, the Nepalese government ordered the remaining Tibetan guerillas (about 1800 men) to shut down the operation. To avoid violent conflict with the Nepalese and the endangerment of the Tibetan refugee community in Nepal, the Tibetan administration in Dharamsala agreed. The Dalai Lama then conveyed a personal, tape-recorded message to the guerilla forces requesting them to lay down their arms. The disbandment of the

Mustang guerilla forces created a second population of Tibetan refugees that required resettlement. Trained for war, however, this group, like those who fled in the after-math of the 1959 Uprising, did not possess the knowledge or means to establish new settlements with long-term economic viability. These two groups comprised the first caseload of Tibetan refugees in Nepal and established the twelve major Tibetan refugee settlements.

Establishment and growth of the Settlements

In the early 1960s, the Nepalese government arranged to provide the first caseload of Tibetan refugees with land. It established four "temporary" settlements: (1) Chialsa, in the Solu Khumbu mountain range east of Kathmandu; (2) Tashi Palkhiel, on the outskirts of Pokhara; (3) Dhorpatan, in western Nepal; and (4) Jawalakhel, on the southern edge of Kathmandu. The Nepal Red Cross (NRC), founded in 1963, purchased the land for these settlements with funds donated by UNHCR. Apart from their inability to afford the land at that time, Tibetan refugees did not enjoy the legal right to purchase it. They required an intermediary to hold the land in trust for their use. The NRC served this critical function. It also enabled the Nepalese government to disavow any direct support for the refugees in order to avoid jeopardizing its tenuous relationship with China. The result, as the NRC's present executive director remarked, was that the NRC aided the refugees "with the [tacit] *sup-port* of the government," but "not exactly *for* the government." By 1969, seven Tibetan settlements had been established in Nepal.

As it became clear the their exile would not be short-term, the Tibetan government required to bring the refugees scattered through-out Nepal together in the newly established settlements. Shanmo Palchung, an elder Tibetan at the Tashi Ling Settlement in Pokhara, recalled that in 1964 Tibetan officials asked him to gather the refugees temporarily settled at encampments near the border and bring them to Pokhara. He arrived in Pokhara that year with 377 Tibetan refugees from throughout Nepal and then petitioned the NRC to purchase land for them from the Nepalese government. The Nepal Red Cross "gave [us] land for living and agriculture," he said, "but it was bad [and undeveloped] land"; and in the first year, sixty refugees, living without shelter, died from exposure to the heat and monsoon rains. The Nepalese government soon recognized that it must take steps to make the refugee settlements self-sufficient.

In 1964, Nepal asked the Swiss government—acting through the Swiss Red Cross and the Swiss Association for Technical Assistance—to help to resettle the refugees and administer the settlements. On November 22, 1964, the two governments entered into an agreement stipulating the main goals of the settlements: long-term economic self-sufficiency and gradual integration into Nepalese society. Thereafter, the Swiss groups provided the residents of the settlements with basic humanitarian aid, technical assistance, and vocational training. Other organizations, including USAID, the Protestant United Mission, the Nepal International Tibetan Refugee Relief Committee, the Norwegian Refugee Council, and United Nations affiliates, such as the U.N. Children's Fund (UNICEF) and the World Health Organization (WHO), contributed additional aid in the form of medical care, primary school education, construction of housing, and food rations. At about the same time, the Tibetan government-in-exile recognized a need to establish its own permanent representatives to administer the settlements. For each settlement, it appointed a "Welfare Officer." These individuals cooperated with the Tibetan government's principal representative in Kathmandu to administer the settlements and look after the needs of their residents.

UNHCR offered monetary assistance to the ICRC and other aid organizations from the outset. Its role expanded significantly, how-ever, in 1964. At that time, the High Commissioner, at the request of the Nepalese government, sent an envoy, J.D.R. Kelly, to appraise the situation. Kelly reported that Tibetan refugees remained in dire need of humanitarian assistance. In August 1964, the Nepalese government authorized UNHCR to open an office in Kathmandu to serve as a liaison between the Tibetan community and the government. In 1965, the government asked UNHCR to begin to assist with the resettlement of those Tibetans not already residing in one of the initial camps. UNHCR remained actively involved throughout the 1960s and the early 1970s. Its role shifted over time.

Initially, UNHCR focused on providing urgently needed emergency relief; in later years it began to search for more permanent solutions. In 1973, however, UNHCR discontinued its assistance program for Tibetan refugees and closed its Kathmandu office. It concluded that Nepal was well on its way to achieving a durable solution to the problem through local integration. In the early years, Tibetans worked to make sure the long-term avail-ability of basic necessities for the settlements. With the assistance of non-governmental organizations, they built roads, homes, schools, and medical facilities. Thereafter, each settlement began to establish industries with which to sustain itself. These included, for example, agriculture, handicraft production, and carpentry. But the refugees achieved their greatest financial success in the carpet industry. Swiss aid workers first encouraged the development of this trade at the Jawalakhel, Chialsa, and Tashi Palkhiel settlements. In 1966, the factories were converted into private companies managed, though not owned, by the Tibetan refugees themselves. By the early 1980s, the Tibetan carpet industry had "evolved into the primary source of income for the entire Tibetan community in Nepal." By the late 1980s, it had become the largest handicraft industry and the second-largest earner of foreign currency in Nepal. Some Tibetans also recognized private shops, hotels, and restaurants, particularly during the first two decades of their exile. Until the late 1970s, Tibetans in Nepal, by contrast to those in India, "did not need any legal document or down payment to open their stores." The mass exodus of Tibetans in the late 1960s and early 1970s also coincided with Nepal's economic expansion and the development of its tourist industry. This, too, created some opportunities for Tibetan entrepreneurs. Restrictions on their rights to own property, travel, register businesses, and work, however, prevented them from securing a strong foothold in the tourist industry.

Today, more than one dozen Tibetan settlements exist in Nepal, including Jawalakhel, Boudha, Swayambunath, and Jorpatia, in the vicinity of Kathmandu; Jampaling, Paljorling, Tashi Ling, and

Tashi Palkhiel, in the Pokhara region; and Dhorpatan, Chialsa, Chairok, Shabrus, and Lumbini, in the northern regions of Nepal. The majority of these were established either in the early to mid-1960s or in 1974, when the Nepalese government terminated the Mustang guerilla operation. Six of the settlements rely on handicraft industries, four sustain themselves by agriculture, and the remainder are "self-reliant," meaning their residents work individually in various jobs.

Nepal, with the aid of foreign governments and confidential donors, thus succeeded in resolving the immediate humanitarian crisis provoked by the mass exodus of Tibetans in the aftermath of China's annexation of Tibet and the 1959 Lhasa Uprising. But the prospect of a long-term and durable solution that led UNHCR to close its Kathmandu office in 1973 has proven elusive. Because of the isolation of the settlements and their residents from mainstream Nepalese society, local integration of the Tibetan refugee population has been minimal. Tibetans who were resettled in the 1960s and 1970s are permitted to remain in Nepal, but their legal status is ambiguous and their financial situation precarious. Without the rights to own property and businesses, to travel, and to work freely in industries and vocations outside the settlements, Tibetans residing in the settlements remain economically and socially alienated from Nepalese society. With the notable exception of some Tibetans in the carpet industry, which has been in decline in recent years, relatively few of the refugees in the settlements have been able to improve their standard of living far beyond subsistence. The precarious status of the settlement residents highlights the need for a more durable solution that either permits the refugees to acquire Nepalese citizenship or affords them a more expansive set of rights consistent with those ordinarily afforded to permanent resident aliens under international law.

THE POSITION OF TIBETANS RESIDE IN NEPAL

By 1989, the Nepalese government ceased completely to permit newly arriving Tibetan refugees to remain in Nepal. This created two classes of Tibetans in Nepal: (1) residents who entered Nepal before 1989 and their children, the subject of this section of the report; and (2) new arrivals with no right to remain in Nepal, the subject of the following section. Nepal's new policy reflected in part the heightened force placed on Nepal by the Chinese government in the late 1980s. China's economic development of Tibet during the 1980s brought a massive influx of Chinese settlers, including cadres, engineers, traders, and small-business owners. By 1987, Chinese migration and reinvigorated political repression in Tibet caused political tensions to rise. Expressions of sup-port for the Dalai Lama and his "Five-Point Peace Plan" precipitated large demonstrations, which China crushed with military force. These culminated in the Tibetan protest of March 4, 1989, just three months before the Tiananmen Square Massacre of June 4, 1989. Shortly there-after, Beijing declared martial law in Lhasa. The heightened repression in Tibet during this period caused a dramatic increase in the number of Tibetans fleeing persecution. Because China perceived these Tibetans as dissidents and traitors, it sought to prevent their flight to India via Nepal as part of its campaign to "quell the counter-revolutionary rebellion." China asked Nepal to cooperate.

In the late 1980s, Nepal maintain a delicate political relation-ship with China. To promote its economy and solidify domestic political stability, it sought to improve that relationship. At about the same time, Nepal's relationship with India began to deteriorate. In 1988, Nepal purchased weapons from China without informing India, an action perceived by India as a deliberate diplomatic slight. On March 23, 1989, in retaliation for this breach of etiquette—and for Nepal's refusal to allow resident Indians to work there without a permit—India imposed a trade embargo on Nepal. It permitted only essential supplies to enter the country. Nepal responded by strengthening its ties to China. This drift toward a pro-China foreign policy cause Nepal to heighten its border security with Tibet and to cease to permit Tibetans to enter and settle in Nepal. It also led the Nepalese government to increase restrictions on the political and cultural activities of Tibetans already residing in Nepal. In November 1989, the Chinese Premier visited Nepal. Then-Prime Minister Marich Man Singh emphasized that Nepal has "always recognized that Tibet is an integral part of

China, and Nepal has always believed in the principle of non-interference in the internal affairs of another country." The following month, the Nepalese government cancelled a Tibetan cultural festival and refused to permit Tibetans in Kathmandu to celebrate the Dalai Lama's receipt of the Nobel Peace Prize.

Today, according to official estimates, about 20,000 Tibetans reside in Nepal. While the government does not permit new arrivals to settle in Nepal, it allows persons who arrived in or before 1989, and their children, to remain. The government does not deem these Tibetans to be "refugees," even though it has periodically issued some of them RCs that describe their nationality as "Tibetan refugee." But in response to Tibet Justice Centre's question about the number of permanent Tibetan refugees residing in Nepal, Home Secretary Regmi replied: "They are *not* permanent residents; no one [of the Tibetans] is a permanent resident." UNHCR, by contrast, made clear that it: still consider[s] [legally resident Tibetans] "refugees," but they do not need assistance. They are somehow self-sufficient. We look after them in discrete ways; for example, the kids of these refugees, when they reach the age of [eighteen], they need to have an identity document and receive a card like the one that has been issued to their parents.

Most such Tibetans live in the Kathmandu valley, generally in the Boudha and Swayambunath regions on the outskirts of the city or at the Jawalakhel settlement. The majority of the others reside in Tibetan settlements located in or around Pokhara, Nepal's second-largest city. The remainder live in isolated settlements such as Namgyaling, in Mustang, or Chialsa, near Paphlu. Notwithstanding their long-term residence in Nepal, most Tibetans remain isolated from mainstream Nepalese society. Few can become Nepalese citizens. Their status remains uncertain and insecure because no law or regulation defines it. Home Secretary Regmi described this legal limbo, remark that the Tibetans "are not permanent residents....We provide a refugee identity card to them. They are [thus] easily identified. Once the Tibet problems are resolved, we will repatriate them to Tibet." Many resident Tibetans, however, particularly the children of the original settlers, lack these identity cards or "RCs." Without them, Tibetans enjoy little security from harassment by officials and possess no proof of their right to remain in Nepal. Even with an RC, Tibetans cannot claim the protection of fundamental rights, such as freedom of speech and assembly. Nepal's Constitution guarantees these rights only to citizens. Nor can legally resident Tibetans own property, incorporate a business, travel freely within the country or internationally, or participate freely in political and cultural activities. Tibetans in Nepal are stateless—residents with no defined legal status and severely limited political and economic rights, and nowhere else to go. In general, no country claims Tibetans in exile as nationals. While China periodically informs them that they may return to "the Motherland," it conditions this right of return on untenable restrictions on their civil and political rights.

Nationality

While Nepal's Citizenship Act makes many Tibetan residents theoretically eligible for citizenship, the government does not view citizenship as a viable option for Tibetans. Section 6 of the Citizenship Act permits an adult to apply for citizenship if he or she:

(a) has the ability to speak and write the national language of Nepal

(b) has renounced citizenship of any other state

(c) is a member of any profession in Nepal

(d) has resided in Nepal for at least 15 years

(e) is a citizen of a country that permits naturalized citizen-ship to citizens of Nepal

(f) is of good moral character.

Candidates for citizenship must also reveal that they have made or can make a substantial contribution to science, philosophy, art, literature, world peace, the welfare of humanity, Nepalese industry, or economic improvement generally.

Nepalese law therefore does not technically bar Tibetans from acquiring citizenship. But government officials candidly conceded that Nepal does not want Tibetans to become citizens. Home Secretary Regmi and Undersecretary Dhakal said—apparently mistakenly—that the law categorically does not permit refugees to acquire citizenship. Expressing a fear that naturalization would encourage Tibetans to assimilate and thereby threaten the Nepalese cultural identity, Secretary Regmi remarked that repatriation rather than naturalization would be the most desirable solution for Nepal's Tibetan residents. Other officials argued that Tibetans never relinquished their prior citizenship as required by the Citizenship Act. In any event the bottom line, as former Home Minister Ser Bhadadur Duepa remarked to the Nepalese National Assembly in 1993, is that "there is simply no policy of giving the [Tibetan] refugees Nepalese citizenship."

A few Tibetans manage to obtain citizenship. Tibetan women who marry Nepalese men, for example, automatically become citizens, but the converse is not the case, i.e., Tibetan men cannot obtain citizenship by marrying Nepalese women. While the CRC obliges Nepal to respect the rights of every child "to acquire a nationality" and "to preserve his or her identity, including nationality," children born to Tibetan refugees in Nepal generally do not have a right to acquire Nepalese citizenship; rather, they inherit the precarious status of their parents. Only children of mixed marriages whose fathers are Nepalese can become Nepalese citizens.

Some Tibetans seek to acquire citizenship papers so that they can purchase a business. But because the naturalization process is cumbersome, most Tibetans who need to own property or incorporate a business find it easier to either purchase false citizenship papers or secure the cooperation of a Nepalese citizen in whose name title will be held. Karma Samten, a refugee who resides at the Paljorling Settlement, said that citizenship papers cost about U.S. $2000 on the black market. But purchasing citizenship papers illegally is risky. Tsering Yanki, a refugee at Jawalakhel, explained that "[t]hese days it is possible to make citizenship [papers for] Nepal, but it is not real; it is a duplicate, and very risky. If the police catch you, you go to jail." But to obtain citizenship through the legal process, she continued, is even more difficult. Tsondu Tharchin, for example, a resident of Tashi Palkhiel, said that he applied for citizenship in about 1995 by submitting an application to the Pokhara office of the Ministry of Home Affairs, but "[t]hey showed me something in the Constitution and said, 'You're a refugee, you can't get citizenship.'" Tibet Justice Centre did not interview any Tibetan who had successfully acquired Nepalese citizenship through the naturalization process established by the Nepal Citizenship Act.

Most Tibetans, though, never attempt to become citizens. The reasons for this are twofold: First, most recognize that few, if any, legal avenues to citizenship exist; and second, some Tibetans feel that to acquire Nepalese citizenship would be to compromise or dilute the integrity of the Tibetan national identity. The latter reason seems to be more of a concern among older Tibetans. By contrast, several Tibetan interviewees under the age of thirty expressed a desire to acquire citizenship. Karma Samten, for example, a resident of the Paljorling Settlement, explained: "If I had Nepali citizenship, I would have more rights....I would be able to buy land, do business, and have better options." Kunga Gyatso, another resident of Paljorling, similarly remarked that, with citizenship, "you can own a building or buy property or [do] anything." For some second-generation Tibetans, the benefits of citizenship thus appear to outweigh the concerns expressed by older Tibetans about maintaining the integrity of the Tibetan national identity.

But most Tibetans interviewed by Tibet Justice Centre did not desire Nepalese citizenship. Shakya Honnkte Parkeanghuk, a resident of Tashi Palkhiel, captured this sentiment plainly: "I do not want to become a citizen of Nepal. I want to return to a free Tibet." In part, this widespread view originates in a now-defunct policy of the Tibetan government-in-exile, adopted in the aftermath of the 1959 exodus of the Dalai Lama and the thousands of Tibetans who followed him into exile. At that time, the Tibetan government-in-exile believed that exile would be short-term, and that the purpose of exile should not be to seek a new and better life in foreign lands, but to struggle to regain their country by any means available. The Tibetan government-in-exile thus adopted a policy discouraging naturalization. This policy is no longer in effect. By the early 1990s, the Tibetan government-in-exile had come to recognize that naturalization, far from eroding the Tibetan national identity, provides greater opportunities, particularly to Tibetan children, to achieve higher education, to express their political views freely, and to more effectively advance the Tibetan cause in the international arena. But the bias against naturalization nonetheless remains among many older Tibetans. "Until recently," Tibetan Youth Congress President Kelsang Phunstok explained, "the perception was that you should remain refugees; citizenship was seen as a betrayal." Younger Tibetans, too, while more pragmatic in their views, remained concerned that to exchange refugee status for Nepalese citizenship—even were it legally feasible—would be to betray their Tibetan identity. "I don't want to obtain [Nepalese] citizenship," insisted Jamyang Dorjee, a thirty-year-old resident of Tashi Ling. "I am Tibetan. How can I become Nepalese?" Most Tibetans interviewed hoped to return to a free Tibet.

In reality, however, residual stateless and without legal rights leaves Tibetan refugees in a dangerously precarious situation that threatens their long-term survival. Phuntsok, a fifty-seven-year-old refugee at Paljorling, acknowledged that for members of the Tibetan exile community today, seeking citizenship in their host country may be the most viable, perhaps the only, alternative to statelessness. "No Tibetans want to be citizens of another country," he said, "but circumstances sometimes compel them to do so." At this stage, the resilience of the Tibetan exile community depends on the willingness of governments, UNHCR, and the international community to begin to take steps to address the precarious status of the Tibetan refugee populations in Nepal and India by, among other things, advocating and supporting meaningful local integration and third-country resettlement.

Third-country resettlement of Tibetan refugees already has proven successful on a small scale. In the early 1960s, the Swiss Red Cross facilitated the resettlement of about 1500 Tibetans to Switzerland. Many achieved higher levels of education and thrived economically, and about 2000 Tibetans now reside permanently in Switzerland. Based on this initial positive experience, the Dalai Lama approached the Canadian and U.S. governments during the last years of Lyndon Johnson's administration. At that time (approximately 1969 or 1970), Canada agreed to accept about 500 Tibetans. But for reasons that remain unclear, the United States did not then respond to the Dalai Lama's request. In 1990, however, the U.S. Congress, with the support of Senator Ted Kennedy, and Congressmen Barney Frank, Charlie Rose, Ben Gilman, Tom Lantos, and John Porter, passed the Immigration Act of 1990, section 134 of which authorized the issuance of "1,000 immigrant visas to 'displaced' Tibetans living in India and Nepal." Third-country resettlement has therefore proved to be a viable and historically successful option. Much more could be done in this regard to provide Tibetan refugees with a durable solution, assisting them to achieve greater stability and control over their lives.

Identity Cards (RCs)

Because Nepal does not grant Tibetans legal status, refugee identity cards (RCs) are critical for Tibetans residing in Nepal. RCs provide a modicum of security from harassment by authorities and, potentially, even expulsion to India. Director-General of Immigration Mainali said that RCs entitle Tibetans to "refugee status," which allows such Tibetans to remain in Nepal with certain minimal rights, such as the (theoretical) ability to acquire a travel document. "Without an identity card," Home Undersecretary Dhakal remarked, "they [Tibetans in Nepal] are not refugees." Again, however, it is important to emphasize that "refugee" is not a term of art in Nepal; it does not define a legal category of persons or provide persons so identified with any status consistent with the Refugee Conventions. Accounts vary, but it appears that the Nepalese government first provided documentation to Tibetan refugees in the mid-1970s. In 1974, the government registered the former Mustang guerillas for administrative and security purposes. In 1995, UNHCR urged the government to issue RCs to all legally resident Tibetans (those who arrived in or before 1989) above the age of eighteen, and the government agreed. But later that year it suspended the program, apparently since of a change in government. Subsequently, the central district officers (CDOs), lower-level functionaries in the Ministry of Home Affairs, sought to provide RCs to most Tibetans in the settlements in the Kathmandu valley. But officials evidently did not return to the Pokhara settlements after 1995. For this rea-son, particularly in Pokhara, Tibetans who had not been present in 1995, or who subsequently reached the age of eighteen, continue to lack RCs. Many legal Tibetan residents in Nepal therefore lack an RC even though the Nepalese government's policy is to provide RCs to all Tibetans who arrived before 1989 and their adult children.

The Department of Immigration requires that RCs be renewed annually. Nepalese officials generally visit the settlements once each year to extend the validity of RCs already issued, but except as noted above, new RCs have not been issued. Tibetans not present at the time of these visits must go to their local central district office to renew their RCs. Dekyi Wangmo, a resident of Tashi Palkhiel, described the some-what erratic nature of the renewal process: It is difficult to renew the Nepali refugee identity cards. Sometimes, officials come here, but sometimes we have to go into town and wait for three to four days. To renew the card, we have to show our existing identity, and the [central district] office also maintains a registration list. It would be much better if the RCs were valid for a longer period of time than just one year.

Renewal is particularly hard for Tibetans not present on the official registration day and for those who reside outside the settlements because it is the settlement officers who generally confirm the status of the refugees and pay the fees on their behalf. Some Tibetans also reported that, outside of the settlements, immigration officials may delay the renewal process and extort bribes in exchange for the required renewal stamp. Dhondup Tsering explained:

When the Nepalese officials come to the settlement, it takes them ten hours to renew everyone's ID. If people miss the opportunity to have their IDs renewed here, then they have to go to an office in town. In town, they have to pay 25 Rs for their renewal, plus usually a bribe on the side....Otherwise, the officials will say to come back the next day.

UNHCR explained that "obtaining an identity card is a cumber-some process," and "the [Nepalese] government makes more of a headache for itself." But UNHCR also emphasized that ensuring the efficient registration of legally resident Tibetans would be in the government's best interests. The registration process could enable the government accurately to distinguish pre-1989 residents from new arrivals.

Without an RC, Tibetans cannot obtain documents to purchase a motorbike, apply for a driver's license, travel freely within Nepal (to non-restricted areas), or acquire a refugee travel document, which permits limited foreign travel. Karma Choezin, a resident of Tashi Palkhiel, complained that "sometimes when we go by tourist bus to Kathmandu, we need the identification card. Otherwise, they [the Nepalese authorities] would take us off the bus." Travel across the boundary to India may also be difficult. Jigme Wangdu said that "[c]hildren [with no RC] who go across the border are asked, 'Where are you going?' If they don't have an RC, there are problems." This is a serious concern because many children of Tibetans residing in Nepal travel to India to obtain an education in the schools run by the Tibetan government-in-exile. Individuals without an RC may also face obstacles to attending Nepalese schools and securing employment. Additionally, refugees said that Nepalese officials periodically come to the settlements to check whether Tibetans there possess RCs. The police sometimes suspect that Tibetans without RCs are new arrivals remaining at the settlements illegally; at other times, the situation reportedly provides the officials with a means to extract minor bribes.

The Special Case of Children. Tibetan community leaders and NGO representatives from the Pokhara area pointed to the lack of documentation for adult children of resident Tibetans as one of the chief problems facing the Tibetan community in Nepal. The vast majority of Tibetans residing legally in Nepal without RCs are young men and women. Without RCs, their futures are bleaker than those of their parents. Unable to seek higher education or employment or to travel freely within Nepal, they are fast becoming the Tibetan community's greatest concern.

The children of Tibetan residents are entitled to receive RCs at the age of eighteen. But in practice, most young adults find them-selves unable to obtain RCs. Moreover, children born after

1999 in the Kathmandu settlements (and after 1995 in the Pokhara settlements) are not listed on their parents' RCs. They therefore possess no official evidence of their legal right to remain in Nepal. This creates serious problems because, as one Tibetan remarked, "[t]he children of Tibetans who are legal residents have no status. They can go to school, but need identification at the secondary level. The only way out for them is to purchase false documents and pretend; this is the only way to avoid being stateless." Many interviewees expressed grave concern about their children's lack of legal status. Budharpo Yichung of Tashi Palkhiel said that he frequently worries about his children's future: My children do not have refugee identification cards. This is the main problem. Children are now above eighteen years old, and they still do not have an ID card. If they don't have an ID card, they have no identity. They just stay here, and they have never been to another place.

Some older Tibetans also lack certification. Settlement Officer Jigme Wangdu estimated that between forty and fifty individuals in the Tashi Palkhiel Settlement never received an RC because they were away from the settlement on the date the government distributed them. At Jawalakhel, where the government reportedly issued RCs again in 1999, Settlement Officer Thinley Gyatso said that about twenty individuals do not possess RCs for the same reason; and between forty and fifty young people, who had been under the age of eighteen at the time of distribution, also lack RCs.

The Tibetan government-in-exile, UNHCR, and the United States government have all made attempts to call the Nepalese government's attention to this problem. Settlement officers informed Tibet Justice Centre that despite repeated requests, they have been unable to obtain the RCs for the children of settlement residents. Individual refugees like Karma Sonam Tsering, a legal resident not present at Tashi Palkhiel at the time the Nepalese government last distributed RCs in 1995, said he submitted personal requests to the Department of Immigration on several occasions without success. UNHCR Representative Dupoizat emphasized that UNHCR continually urges the CDOs (branches of the Home Ministry) to issue RCs to Tibetans who come of age, but "we are not very satisfied with how it's going, and some people fall through the cracks." According to former U.S. Assistant Secretary of State Taft, last time she visited Nepal in 2000, the Nepalese government had committed to issuing RCs to all Tibetans entitled to one. At the time of Tibet Justice Centre's research, the government had yet to follow through on this commitment. Notwithstanding the foregoing problems, the Nepalese government does not appear to be unwilling to issue RCs. Bureaucratic inefficiencies, rather than any desire to withhold status from Tibetans residing legally in Nepal, appears to be the principal reason for delay. Jawalakhel Settlement Officer Thinley Gyatso said that while he engaged in several promising discussions with the central district officers (CDOs) for Kathmandu about having RCs issued for Tibetans who have reached the age of eighteen, he feared that the upheaval caused by the June 2001 massacre of the Nepalese royal family would delay the process once again. Tibetan representatives of the Pokhara settlements emphasized that the United States, acting through the Kathmandu Embassy or the State Department's Special Coordinator for Tibet—currently, U.S. Under Secretary for Global Affairs Paula Dobriansky—could remedy this situation by requesting that the Nepalese government implement its own policy: to issue RCs to all legally resident Tibetans and their children.

A COMPARISON BETWEEN BHUTANESE AND TIBETAN REFUGEES

This comparison is not exhaustive because the time dimension of these two groups of refugees is different. However, it demonstrates that there are more differences between these two refugee groups than there are similarities. In fact, except that both these groups were forced to leave their homeland and have been known as refugees such as Tibetan or Bhutanese, they differ in most other attributes. More importantly, even though the number of Bhutanese refugees is several times greater than that of Tibetans, their issue is little known outside South Asia. The physical complexion complexion /com·plex·ion/ (kom-plek´shun) the colour and appearance of the skin of the face. The natural colour, texture, and appearance of the skin, especially of the face., the sheltering locations and occupational characteristics of both these refugees are far distinct. The economic success of Tibetan refugees is their most notable feature. These refugees are far better off than one would think of any refugee. For them the free world had reason to express their concern on Tibetan refugee issue because their cause was related to the action of the communist world. Encouraging and supporting them to invest on carpet business and promotion of carpets made by Tibetan refugees in the western world cannot be explain as the actions of these refugees alone. On the contrary, the cause for BONO refugees in the 1990s and at present has been muted in the world arena amidst Afghan refugees Afghan refugees (known as *Muhajir Afghans* in South Asia) are people who fled Afghanistan after the Soviet invasion in 1979 and during the civil war that followed. Since the early 1980s to the late 1990s, there were approximately 3 million Afghan refugees staying in, Bosnian case, let alone similar cases in African countries primarily Eritrea, Sudan, Somalia and Sierra Leone Sierra Leone , officially Republic of Sierra Leone, republic (2005 est. pop. 6,018,000), 27,699 sq mi (71,740 sq km), W Africa..

The political contexts of these refugees are also different. The Tibetan case has more to do with the political and ideological identity of People's Republic People's Republic country, land, state-the territory occupied by a nation; "he returned to the land of his birth"; "he visited several European countries" is that national social identity is based on the symbolism of majority ethnicity (Bose 1998). But despite BONO constituting demographically largest group in the country, they have been turned to be victim of nation building and identity making of the group; which is not a majority in the country. Being turned into refugee for diverse political and contextual factors and from two different countries, it is understandable that these two groups of refugees differ many of their social and economic attributes. Interestingly, the official approach of the host government has also been different for these two groups of refugees. During the time of Tibetan refugees for reasons of their relative small size, international politics (communist block versus free world) and the favourable demography of the country, Nepal's approach to Tibetan refugee was to integrate them into economic life of Nepal. On the contrary, in the 1990s, with the troublesome growth of both population and poverty in the country, Nepal is forced to take a policy of repatriating BONO refugees despite their cultural and ethnic similarities with Nepal and public sympathy for their cause.

TRANSIT OF TIBETAN REFUGEES THROUGH NEPAL

In recent years, between 2500 and more than 3000 Tibetans have runaway from Tibet via Nepal annually. In 1989, Nepal ceased to permit newly arriving Tibetans to remain or seek refuge in Nepal. By informal arrangement with the Office of the U.N. High Commissioner for Refugees (UNHCR), however, Nepal has acceded to an agreement whereby it facilitates the transit of new arrivals through Nepal, typically to Tibetan exile communities in India. This should operate as follows: Newly arriving Tibetans apprehended at the Sino-Nepalese border by Nepalese authorities will be denied entry to Nepal. Those apprehended within Nepal, however, will be turned over to the Nepalese Department of Immigration, which ordinarily then transfers them to UNHCR's custody. UNHCR cooperates with the Tibetan Welfare Office to make a preliminary determination that these Tibetans are "of concern to the High Commissioner," a broad, non-specific designation used by UNHCR to refer generally to asylum seekers, refugees, internally displaced persons, and others. UNHCR does not conduct refugee status determinations for Tibetans. Newly arriving Tibetans remain temporarily at the Kathmandu Tibetan Refugee Reception Centre, which provides them with food, shelter, and medical attention. By tacit agreement, they generally must depart for India within two weeks. After UNHCR processes new arrivals and determines them to be "of concern," it ordinarily recommends to the Department of Immigration that they be issued an "exit permit," which solely provides Tibetans with the right to travel from the Reception Centre to the Indo-Nepalese border. It provides no right of re-entry, legal status, or protection of any kind. Indian border authorities typically take these permits, together with a small "fee," when Tibetan refugees cross into India.

Operation of the Gentleman's Agreement in Practice. The "terms" of the gentleman's agreement are rarely followed. In practice, most

Tibetans arrive at the Reception Centre in Kathmandu independently, usually by one of two routes: via the Friendship Highway, which extends from Lhasa to Kathmandu, or via the Nangpa-la pass in the Solu Khumbu region of the Himalayas in northern Nepal. Tibetans often employ freelance guides to assist them in journeying safely to Kathmandu. Both the Friendship Highway and Nangpa-la routes are fraught with danger, including natural perils such as a lack of adequate food and shelter, particularly in the winter months, and the risk of apprehension by Chinese or Nepalese authorities. Contrary to the gentleman's agreement, Nepalese police increasingly appear to be forcing Tibetans apprehended within several days walking distance of the border to return to Tibet, often at great risk to their lives and safety. China treats these Tibetans as political dissidents. Reports of detention, torture, and other maltreatment by Chinese authorities are commonplace. Even without reference to the gentleman's agreement, the act of returning refugees to a state where their lives or freedom may be threatened violates the bedrock principle of international refugee law prohibiting *refoulement*.

The "Parties" to the Gentleman's Agreement. The gentleman's agreement requires the active cooperation of UNHCR, the Nepalese government, the Tibetan government-in-exile, and the United States Embassy in Kathmandu. UNHCR plays several vital roles. It provides a modicum of legitimacy that the Nepalese government deems crucial to its cooperation in implementing the agreement. UNHCR channels funds received from donor governments, particularly the United States, to support the day-to-day operation of the agreement. And until recently, it conducted missions to the border regions of Nepal in order to inform the Nepalese police of the terms of the agreement and international human rights law, and to monitor compliance. For reasons that remain somewhat unclear, the Nepalese government ceased to permit these missions as early as 1998, and

Tibet Justice Centre's research suggests that the consequences have included: an increase in instances of *refoulement* and other abuses, and an increasing lack of knowledge on the part of the police about their obligations under the agreement. The government of Nepal has acceded to the gentleman's agreement for two principal reasons: It requires UNHCR's assistance with its Bhutanese refugee crisis, and cooperation in the gentleman's agreement appears to be something of a *quid pro quo* for that assistance. It also remains under pressure from the United States, the European Union, and other foreign-aid donors to assist Tibetan refugees in need. Countervailing pressure from the Chinese government to repatriate Tibetans and tighten border control, however, has led to increasing incidents of non-compliance. The Tibetan government-in-exile, operating through the Tibetan Welfare Office in Kathmandu performs most of the practical work required to maintain the gentleman's agreement, including providing food, shelter, and medical care to new arrivals, assisting in their processing, cooperating with UNHCR to ensure that Tibetans reach the Reception Centre, and arranging for their departure to India. While the Nepalese government does not officially recognize the Tibetan Welfare Office because this would be perceived by China as an intolerable political statement, it relies on the assistance of the Tibetan Welfare Office to implement the gentleman's agreement. The United States Embassy in Kathmandu, finally, cooperates with UNHCR and the Nepalese government to ensure compliance with the gentleman's agreement. It participates in meetings with the Ministry of Home Affairs and works actively to advance the interest of the United States in ensuring the safe transit of Tibetan refugees through Nepal. The United States also provides much of the funding, channelled through UNHCR and the Tibetan Welfare Office, that supports the operation of the gentleman's agreement.

Allegations of Abuse and Refoulement by Nepalese Police. The gentle-man's agreement cannot operate effectively unless the Nepalese police understand and comply with it. Tibet Justice Centre's research suggests that because UNHCR no longer carries out border missions, and because pressure from China appears to have caused the Nepalese government to cease to comply conscientiously with the gentleman's agreement, Tibetans arriving in Nepal increasingly face dangers of *refoulement* and, at times, police abuses. The police in Solu Khumbu reported receiving a directive from the Ministry of Home Affairs in Kathmandu instructing them to return apprehended Tibetans to the border, in violation of the fundamental principle of *non-refoulement*. In practice, this appears to have translated into a trend whereby the police will "encourage" Tibetans to return to China—at times, at gunpoint— and follow them back toward the border for several hours or even days. Because Nepalese police face dangers from the Maoist insurgency, and because, according to Tibet Justice Centre's interviews, they have not been receiving the stipends to which they are entitled for their cooperation, the police are reluctant to accompany Tibetans to the Kathmandu Reception Centre as required by the agreement. In some cases police reportedly resort to theft or extortion of money from new arrivals to supplement their salaries. In rarer instances there have been reported incidents of more severe abuses, including detentions, shootings, and rape. Resumption of UNHCR's border missions and greater efforts by the government to educate the police about the gentleman's agreement are vital steps to prevent such abuses in the future.

NEPAL'S OFFICIAL POSITION AND ACTIVITIES OF TIBETANS IN NEPAL

Nepalese law does not recognize Tibetan refugees' rights as articulated in the United Nations conventions that form the basis of international refugee law. In recent years China has persuaded the Nepalese government with the notion that Tibetans who flee across the Himalayas are either illegal economic migrants, or criminals.

While Tibetan refugees possessing the RC are allowed to remain in Nepal, RC-holders have no right to an official employment permit, to own businesses or property, or access to colleges and universities on the same basis as Nepalese citizens. For international travel (not including India), RC-holding Tibetans must go through a complex process to obtain a Nepalese government issued travel document.

Although Tibetan refugees livelihood in Nepal lack many basic legal rights that impact their social, economic and cultural life, there is a popular conception among Nepalese citizens that the Tibetan refugee community in Nepal is wealthy and their presence in Nepal has led to difficulties with the Chinese and criticism from western countries. In reality, many Tibetans lack employment opportunities and higher education, forcing many to do manual agricultural work in remote areas in exchange for food. Tibetans living in Nepal typically reside in crowded and poor housing conditions in clustered Tibetan settlements. Increasingly the Nepalese government has denied or curtailed Tibetans' rights to hold cultural, religious, and school events in public and has consistently prohibited peaceful political demonstrations.

Chinese Pressure in Nepal

In August 2004, Nepal's Crown Prince Paras Bir Bikram Shah Dev met China's President Hu Jintao in the Great Hall of the People in Beijing.

During the meeting, Hu said that since the countries recognized diplomatic ties 49 years ago, relations have been growing steadily, and that he particularly appreciated the King of Nepal and the royal family for their "special and important role" in developing the relationship.

He stated that China is "willing to push the good-neighbourly partnership between the two countries to a new level." Crown Prince Paras reiterated Nepal's support for the "one-China" policy, and invited Hu to visit Nepal. Crown Prince Paras' visit resulted in the signing of agreements with Beijing for several new projects – China agreed to provide nearly 450 million Nepalese rupees ($6.4 million) to Nepal to support ongoing projects as well as start new ones. These included laying optical fibre cable from Kathmandu to the border region of Khasa in Tibet for better connectivity; surroundings up an Ayurvedic drugs research centre in Nepal; and building two roads.

These developments followed new trading accords in 2003. On December 3, 2003, China and Nepal opened two new trading posts along the Tibet-Nepal border; one in the Makalu region of east Nepal and the other in west-central part of Nepal. A Chinese development package was also promised to Nepal that will provide over $10 million dollars in aid, some of which will be used for on the ground experts to complete a road linking Nepal and Tibet at Rasuwa in Nepal and Kyirong in Tibet. The trade volume between Nepal and China reached 20 billion Nepalese rupees ($274 million) during Nepal's fiscal year 2003-4, according to Xinhua (September 28, 2004). Kathmandu now has a multi-storey Chinatown shopping centre that opened in March 2003 and sells a wide range of Chinese-made goods, including TV sets, electronics, computer parts, and textiles.

Tibetan Community in Nepal

Nepal states that it will not tolerate "anti-China" activity on its soil, and applies this policy with varying rigor. On the third day of Tibetan New Year, February 23, 2004, local authorities denied Tibetans permission to hold a gathering at the Boudha stupa, an important religious site and centre of the Tibetan community in Kathmandu, with the display of a portrait of the Dalai Lama. A community prayer gathering was held at the nearby Samtenling Monastery compound instead. Nepalese police tolerated a limited commemoration of the Tibetan National Uprising Day on March 10, 2004, at Samtenling Monastery with traditional prayers for those who lost their lives, as permission to hold the event at the Boudha stupa was denied. A spontaneous outburst of slogan-shouting by Tibetan youth as they walked around the Boudha stupa was also tolerated by police.

On July 6, 2004, the 69th birthday of His Holiness the Dalai Lama was observed in the Boudhanath neighborhood on the football grounds of Srongtsen Brikuti Boarding School. Prior permission had been sought from the Chief District Officer (CDO) and the Ministry of Home of the Nepalese government was also informed. Permission was granted by the CDO with strict orders that Tibetans not engage in any "anti-China" behavior. Representatives of several diplomatic missions in Kathmandu attended the events. On December 10, 2004 Tibetans were allowable to mark International Human Rights Day and the anniversary of the awarding of the Nobel Peace Prize to the Dalai Lama. The occasion was celebrated with a traditional Tibetan prayer meeting at Samtenling Monastery, although permission to display the portrait of the Dalai Lama at the Boudha stupa was again denied.

Journey the Himalayas

To reach Nepal, Tibetans embark on a hazardous journey that, depending on their point of departure and weather conditions, can take from a minimum of two to three weeks, to a month or more. The dangers lie not only in the harsh geographical conditions of the trade routes that Tibetans commonly use to cross the border on foot, but also in the risk of being captured by Chinese or Nepalese border guards. In order to minimize the chances of capture, most Tibetan refugees traveling without papers make the journey in winter, as the Chinese People's Armed Police (PAP) troops patrolling the Tibetan side of the border are believed to be less active during these months. The PAP is responsible for China's internal security, the protection of state installations and prisons, and is the primary security presence in the mountain passes. This report includes new images of a People's Liberation Army post about a day's walk from the Nangpa pass, maintained in order to observe Tibetans leaving and entering Tibet from Nepal.

Approximately 80% of new arrival Tibetan refugees complete the journey in the winter months of 2004 (January to April and October to December), when the mountains are deep in snow and glacial areas are frozen. In order to disguise their intentions from the local authorities, Tibetans *en route* often carry little or no food or clothing. Hypothermia, snow blindness, frost-bite, as well as injuries from slipping on ice or falling, are common. Injury can lead to abandonment by the hired guide, who is often the key to evading border security. In the summer months, snow can turn to slush and fog can obscure trails and deadly crevasses. Since 2003 the PAP has tightened border security and access to remote mountain routes. Tibetans caught attempting to escape to or return from Nepal or India are sent to the Snowland New Reception Centre, a special prison opened for this purpose outside Shigatse in 2003.10 Tibetans can be sentenced to many months in prison if caught returning to Tibet, and are commonly held at Nyari prison in Shigatse as well as this new detention centre.

Border security on the Nepal side has also greater than before due to the presence of a "unified command" of the Royal Nepal Army (RNA) formed by army soldiers, armed police and regular police. It is common for Chinese and Nepalese security to cooperate in initiatives to ensure the borders are secured. ICT has received reports of communication and cooperation between Nepalese border police and their counter-parts on the Chinese side of the border regarding refoulement of Tibetan refugees.

The Routes

There are well-established historical and cultural ties between Tibet and Nepal. Nomads, pilgrims, traders and businessmen, both Tibetan and Nepalese, have crossed the border in both directions since the eighth century. Many of these ancient trading routes, such as the Nangpa la – nearly 19,000 ft. above sea-level-are still used by Tibetan traders leading their yak caravans from Tibet into Nepal. Towering over the spectacular Solu Khumbu region in Nepal to the west of Mount Everest, the Nangpa pass, at an altitude of 5,700 meters, is crossed by an average 2,000 Tibetan refugees a year. The ancient route, some 100 km west of Everest connects the southern Tibetan town of Tingri (at an altitude of 4,250 meters) to the Nepalese Himalayan foothill towns of Namche Bazaar, Lukla, and Jiri, one of the first Nepalese towns along the border route from Tibet into Nepal via the Solu Khumbu range. Under ideal climatic conditions the trek from Tingri to the Nangpa mountain pass usually takes two or three days but can take five and even ten days. Another two days is the average time to cross the frozen Nangpa pass, and no less than two to three weeks to reach Kathmandu on foot. Dram (Chinese: Zhangmu, Nepalese: Khasa) is the gateway to Tibet for many Indian and Nepalese truck drivers who wait in town for days to receive custom clearances before continuing their drive. Tibetan refugees seeking to enter Nepal from this point must cross the Friendship Bridge. From the Kodari border post on the Nepalese side, the road to Kathmandu is approximately 114 kilometers through the border towns of Tatopani and Barabise, taking a week to ten days walking or six to seven hours by bus.

Tibetan refugees also enter Nepal through the distant Himalayan regions of Mustang and Humla. Some Tibetans cross through the Tibetan town of Puran (Chinese: Burang) along the

Humla Karnali River, close to Mount Kailash (Tibetan: Khang Rinpoche), one of the most sacred mountains in Tibet, worshipped not only by Buddhists, but also by Hindus, and followers of the pre-Buddhist Bon religion of Tibet.

TIBETANS IN NEPAL: POLICY AND COMPLETION

Under the Gentleman's Agreement, Nepal allows UNHCR to facilitate the transit of approximately 2,500 Tibetan refugees per year who flee Tibet. Under this unwritten agreement between Nepal and the UNHCR, Nepalese police are supposed to ensure that Tibetans escaping into exile reach Kathmandu, where the Department of Immigration passes them into the custody of the UNHCR. Over the past few years, while staying at the Reception Centre in Kathmandu, Tibetan refugees are processed by UNHCR in cooperation with the Tibetan Refugee Welfare Office (TRWO) in order to determine that these Tibetans are "of concern to the High Commissioner." Here they are offered food, shelter, assistance, and medical attention.

In practice, however, the terms of the Gentleman's accord are loosely followed and most of the Tibetan refugees who enter Nepal do so clandestinely, reaching the TRRC independently or with the help of local guides. They thus risk apprehension and abuse by local Nepalese police, which may force them to return to Tibet in violation of the fundamental international legal principle of non-refoulement. The most well documented violation of the agreement to date was the government-sanctioned refoulement of a newly arrived group of 18 Tibetan refugees, including ten minors, who, on May 31, 2003 were taken from a prison in Kathmandu and handed over to Chinese authorities at Kodari, the Nepalese town on the China-Nepal border.

Tibetan refugees who entered Nepal before December 31, 1989, and their children, are permitted to remain in Nepal, in accordance with the Gentlemen's Agreement. These Tibetans are eligible to receive a Refugee Identity Card (RC). According to the UNHCR, there are at present some 4,617 eligible Tibetans who have yet to receive an RC, and most applications have been pending for several years due to the systemic failure of the Nepalese government to process them. In 2004, the UNHCR, TRWO and supportive embassies in Kathmandu continued to urge for their issuance. Although RCs do not provide Tibetans the same civil and legal rights as Nepalese citizens or a defined legal status, they do confer certain civil rights and freedom of movement within Nepal and, most significantly, security against forcible repatriation.

Tibetan refugees who entered Nepal after the 1989 cut-off date are processed by the UNHCR in Kathmandu to determine their status as "of concern" to that office, provided emergency shelter, food and medical assistance at the TRRC by the TRWO through its partnership with the UNHCR and, as expeditiously as possible, moved onward to India. According to the *UNHCR Global Report for 20044*, there were 20,000 "persons of concern" of Tibetan origin in Nepal, and UNHCR provided assistance to 700 recent arrivals. The UNHCR "continues to urge the Government of Nepal... to protect and assist newly arrived Tibetans in transit in Nepal" and notes that "the lack of a legislative framework in Nepal continues to affect UNHCR's approach to protection". Generally, the UNHCR provides assistance to Tibetan refugees in Nepal, is responsible for the maintenance of the TRRC, covers transport costs for Tibetans in transit,, and advises Tibetans on some legal matters. The report concludes that "the escalating insecurity created additional burdens on UNHCR's operations, in terms of staff and refugee security, relief delivery and movements of populations of risk within and beyond Nepal's borders".

8

The Government of Tibet in Exile

From July 20 to 23, 1994, Beijing staged the Third Forum on Work in Tibet which recommended the total destruction of an entire civilization flourishing on the Tibetan Plateau for thousands of years. This cultural "empire" once encompassed far-flung areas like Buryatia, Tuva and Kalmykia in Russia; Mongolia; Laddakh, Lahaul-Spiti, Sikkim, and Arunachal Pradesh in India; Mustang, Dolpo and Solo Khumbu in Nepal; Bhutan and parts of western China. The policy formulated in 1994 in Beijing-and these days pursued with Cultural Revolutionary zeal in Tibet-will mean the annihilation of the spiritual homeland of this shared culture. Implementation of the Third Work Forum is thus having a crippling impact on the traditional culture of millions of non-Tibetans as the well-spring of their cultural inspiration is forcibly drained and there is nothing to replenish the continuous growth and development of this distinct and highly evolved civilization.

Losing Hearts and Minds

The decisions made at the Third Forum rest on two fundamental conclusions which Beijing drew. It realized it was losing out in two vital fields-ideology and propaganda. For a state whose existence is justified by its ideological superiority and the power of its propaganda to shape the thinking of the masses, the implications of this for the future was at best uncertain, at worst dangerous. Beijing concluded it was losing the ideological war because, despite the unrelenting assault on Tibetan Buddhism, Tibetans were as devoted to their traditional beliefs as ever. Beijing has succeeded in physically enslaving the country but it has not won over the hearts, minds and loyalty of the Tibetan populace.

Communist ideology, enforced by the military might of China, had failed to dent the heart of Buddhism. Added to this was the communist authorities' total bafflement at the non-violent policy underpinning the Middle Way Approach advocated by His Holiness the Dalai Lama to resolve the issue of Tibet's future status. For a regime which is based on Mao's dictum that political power grows out of the barrel of a gun, this supposedly eccentric philosophy which says victory lies in capturing the hearts and minds of people by the power of ideas rather than killing by the power of the gun comes as a bolt from the blue. Much of Beijing's knee-jerk reaction to, and its bafflement at, His Holiness the Dalai Lama's new policy of rapprochement lies at the heart of its new hardline policy.

Beijing considered it was losing the propaganda war because, for one reason or the other, the world's media and its pop culture considered-at least for the moment-Tibet and Tibetan Buddhism their very own cuddly pandas. Despite its financial might China found it extremely difficult to exterminate this image of Tibet and get its voice heard on the Tibetan issue in the court of the international media. In order to address these weaknesses the Third Forum concentrated on two issues. One was to focus on Tibet's economic development in the hope that this would keep Tibetan demonstrations off the streets. This was tantamount to bribing the Tibetans with promises of riches to come if they toed the party line. The other concern was to win the coming and new generations of Tibetans over to the Chinese viewpoint.

Beijing has given up on the present generation of Tibetans as a lost cause. If the coming generations of Tibetans were also lost to the 'Dalai Clique' this, the Chinese concluded, would have dangerous consequences for Chinese rule in Tibet. The 15-year-old Gyalwa Karmapa's dramatic escape from Tibet in January 2000 was a warning to the Beijing authorities of the erosion of loyalty to China. The Karmapa's flight, and the earlier escape of Agya

Rinpoche, the abbot of Kumbum Monastery, came as a huge embarrassment for China, because retaining these high lamas gave China a degree of legitimacy for its rule in Tibet. This is the reason why Beijing is enforcing with greater strictness its 1993 instruction of recalling young Tibetans studying in schools and monasteries run by Dharmasala in India. This is also the rationale for Beijing closing down schools in Tibet which are privately run by Tibetans.

For these reasons Tibet today is in the throes of a second Cultural Revolution as the Chinese authorities step up their long-term strategy to exterminate Tibet's distinct cultural and ethnic identity. The authorities are pursuing a four-pronged strategy to achieve their final objective. They have stepped up repression while employing their huge propaganda machine to paint a rosy picture of Tibet. They have quickened the pace of economic development to dampen Tibetan nationalism and are simultaneously moving more Chinese settlers onto the Tibetan Plateau to change Tibet's demographic composition and to ease social unrest because of mounting unemployment back in China. The Third Work Forum on Tibet was convened by the top Chinese leadership and was presided over by President Jiang Zemin. The authorities have now enshrined this Work Forum as the most "important strategic policy to rejuvenate Tibet" and have hailed its directives as the new manifesto for party work on the plateau. The significance of the Third Work Forum lies in the fact that it overturned the more liberal policies laid out for Tibet's "development" by the First and Second Work Forums held in 1980 and 1984.

The first two work forums were initiated by the late Hu Yaobang, then Secretary General of the Chinese Communist Party. This liberal and somewhat maverick leader is credited with masterminding a series of measures to improve the social, economic and political conditions in Tibet. The brief spell of liberalization markedly improved the living conditions of the majority of Tibetans and contributed to a more relaxed intellectual and social climate.

The Third Work Forum reversed these policies and reinstated hardline measures under which Tibet is still reeling today. The Tibetans in Tibet perceive the current repressive policies as a second Cultural Revolution. The question is why did China choose to jettison its earlier more liberal policies and adopt a manifesto which is leading to the systematic destruction of Tibet's distinct culture. The answer lies in domestic and international events which forced China to formulate a series of hardline policies on Tibet which eventually crystallized into the Third Work Forum for Tibet. The world which confronted China in the late 1980s and early 1990s was a frightening one.

Starting from 1987, Tibet was rocked by a string of protest demonstrations, which called for Tibetan independence. One of the largest demonstrations which erupted on March 5, 1989 in Lhasa, forced the authorities to impose martial law on the city. These demonstrations are now seen to have been an inspiration behind the outburst of Chinese students' pro-democracy uprisings. The authorities saw the series of Tiananmen Square demonstrations as a sign of their Central Government losing control, and in an attempt to regain supremacy, the authorities slaughtered-perhaps hundreds if not thousands of students on June 4, 1989. These demonstrations were a chilling replay to the authorities of the May 4, 1919 student demonstrations in Beijing which signalled a political and cultural awakening across the erstwhile Middle Kingdom.

Bejing's fears of losing control were exacerbated by external events which saw the unraveling of the communist world. The Solidarity Movement in Poland, the fall of the Berlin Wall, and the implosion of the Soviet Union fed Beijing's paranoia over threats to the Chinese Communist Party hold on power. Official China's fears were further inflamed by the rapidly changing attitude of the broad masses as they turned back from communism to traditional beliefs like Confucionism, Buddhism, Islam, Christianity and indigenous folk cults. In the eyes of ordinary citizens communism was becoming totally discredited and this, more than anything else, was the biggest nightmare for China's leadership. The leadership's justification for staying in power was being disavowed by the masses. For a one-party dictatorship this historically indicates the first step along the slippery road to dissolution and removal of power.

For these reasons the Chinese leadership then reverted to its earlier view that traditional beliefs were its real enemy. In competing with Buddhism, Confucionism, Islam, Christianity and other isms, communism was losing out in terms of its ability to retain the loyalty and allegiance of the masses. The leadership revived the old aphorisms once served up to the Tibetan people to justify their policies to destroy Tibetan Buddhism during the Cultural Revolution. Bewildered Tibetans were then told that just as there cannot be two suns in the sky, so there cannot be both Buddhism and socialism in Tibet. Inevitably Buddhism then had to give way to socialism. And again, today, religion is being blatantly sublimated to Chinese state power.

These were the fears of the Chinese leaders when they met in Beijing in 1994 to hammer out their new Tibet initiatives. For the Chinese authorities Tibet is an especially sensitive issue because of their conviction that hostile Western forces are using the issue of Tibet to "westernize" China and to lead to its territorial fragmentation. The third generation Chinese leaders came to the conclusion that stability in Tibet was vital to the stability of China as a whole. Earlier, Tibet was merely of peripheral concern to the vital interests of China's sprawling communist empire. Now, with the Third Work Forum, the authorities were saying, "We must clearly understand that we must do our work in Tibet not only for the sake our of own region's stability and development, not only for the interests of our people, but also for the sake of the whole nation's stability and development."

In Tibet, China faced peculiar problems because of the inherent strength of Tibetan Buddhism and the depth of devotion of the populace to His Holiness the Dalai Lama. The sustained burst of religious revival that followed in the wake of the brief spell of liberalization in Tibet confirmed the leadership's worst fears that decades of concerted assault on Tibetan culture and religion had not extinguished the people's traditional beliefs and values. From merely nuisance value, the Chinese leadership now viewed Tibetan Buddhism as a very real and imminent threat to the stability of Chinese rule in Tibet. At the same time the Chinese leadership's attitude towards His Holiness the Dalai Lama changed. From being an uncertain ally in the peace process in Tibet, the current Chinese leadership now saw him as a full-blown "enemy". A top-level conclave held in Beijing on March 10, 1993 concluded that, "There are different factions within the Dalai Clique; they are, however, unanimous in their political nature and position. They differ from each other in ideological viewpoints and ways of expressing them. Different strategies must be adopted to use their differences, to deal with them differently in order to divide and destroy them." Repeated statements by high-level officials describe the struggle against "splittism", the official term for Tibetan independence, as a "life-and-death struggle". At the 1994 annual meeting of the "TAR" Communist Party Committee to brief members on the policy thrust of the Third Work Forum on Tibet, Raidi, deputy Secretary of the Committee said, "Up to now, his (the Dalai Lama's) standpoint on Tibet's independence has never changed, and we must reveal his double-faced true colour. The focal point in our region in the struggle against splittism is to oppose the Dalai Clique. As the saying goes, to kill a serpent, one must first cut off its head."

In short, the Third Work Forum decided that Beijing was in a position to solve the Tibet issue without the Dalai Lama's involvement. It abandoned the earlier liberal policy of including His Holiness the Dalai Lama in any future settlement of Tibet's status. His Holiness the Dalai Lama was clearly singled out as the cause of China's "Tibet problem".

The Third Work Forum also abandoned the policy of granting concessions to Tibet because of the plateau's "special characteristics". This policy had been the cornerstone of recommendations made by the First and Second Tibet Work Forums.

To carry out its new hardline policies in Tibet, Beijing appointed Chen Kuiyuan as the "TAR" Party Secretary in 1992. Chen Kuiyuan's appointment is significant because he had a track record for being a tough and ruthless administrator. He had already served as the First Secretary of the Chinese Communist Party in Inner Mongolia and is credited with repressing the rebellious Mongols, many of whom refer to him as "the butcher". Chen

Kuiyuan was especially recommended to the post by Hu Jintao, the current Vice-President of China, who was then the First Secretary of the Chinese Communist Party in Tibet.

Tackling Tibetan Nationalism

The Third Work Forum policies chalked out for Tibet contained four key elements. China stepped up the scale of repression in Tibet. External propaganda work was escalated. The pace of economic development in Tibet-and its corollary of encouraging more Chinese settlers and businessmen to take advantage of the economic boom on the "roof of the world"-was also increased. In short, Beijing had decided to tackle Tibetan nationalism head-on and observers are still assessing the consequences on both Chinese rule in Tibet and on the populace.

Beijing remains convinced that these key components of its current policy will stabilize Chinese rule over Tibet and solve once and for all, the vexed problem of its negative image over the way Tibet has been handled. One main target of the current policy of repression is Tibetan Buddhism. Chinese leaders are increasingly alarmed by the proliferation of monasteries and temples which the period of liberalization spawned throughout Tibet: they are seen as the bastions of Tibetan nationalism. The authorities have set up "Democratic Management Committees" to control monasteries and nunneries and created "Work Inspection Teams" to supervise the "education" of monks and nuns.

A major thrust is underway to break the bond of loyalty between the clergy in Tibet and His Holiness the Dalai Lama in India. Campaigns like "Strike Hard" and "Patriotic Re-education", unleashed in 1996, are aimed at crippling the rise of Tibetan Buddhism which the authorities suspect is weaning the loyalty of the Tibetan people away from the communist party and towards His Holiness the Dalai Lama. One salient feature of the "Strike Hard" campaign is how differently it is interpreted in China and Tibet. China's "Strike Hard" campaign was started to weed out corruption. Tibet's version is used as a political tool to eliminate those whom the authorities label "splittists". In Tibet, rather than striking at corruption, the authorities turn a blind eye to this social disease in the hope that it will erode the traditional morality of Tibetans and undermine Tibetan Buddhism.

In fact, at a secret meeting held in December 1999 in Chengdu, capital of Sichuan province, Chen Kuiyuan, the hardline Party Secretary of "TAR" recommended to the Central Chinese Government that an all-out effort must be made to eradicate Tibetan Buddhism and culture from the face of the earth so that no memory of them will be left in the minds of coming generations of Tibetans-except as museum pieces.

Chen Kuiyuan stated that the main cause of instability is the existence of the Dalai Lama and his Government-in-Exile in Dharamsala and these must be "uprooted". He recommended that Tibet, Tibetan people and Tibetan Buddhism-in other words the very name of Tibet-must be destroyed and the "Tibet Autonomous Region" be merged with provinces like Sichuan. While treating Tibetans to boot-heel subjugation at home, internationally China was on an overdrive propaganda blitz. At a brainstorming conclave held on March 10, 1993, Zeng Jian-hui, Vice-Minister of the Propaganda Ministry, told participants, "The propaganda work on the question of Tibet is one of the focal points of the entire external propaganda work...With regard to attacks by the West and the Dalai Clique and their frequent activities, our external propaganda should launch offensive. We should expand our spheres of influence; in particular, we should infiltrate our propaganda into the mainstream life of the West.

"Firstly we should continue to send Tibetan scholars and Tibetan singing and dancing troupes abroad to lecture and perform. Secondly, relevant embassies and consulates should aim at the public opinion and the activities of the Dalai Clique in the countries where they are stationed and utilize speeches, picture exhibitions, special articles and other forms to carry out propaganda work, so as to win over officials and people of those countries... We should reinforce the work of utilizing the power of foreign propaganda. A few years ago, in the light of the situation of that time, we made arrangements for foreign journalists to visit Tibet."

The September 3, 2000 edition of *People's Daily* carried a story headlined "Tibet Welcomes Foreign Journalists for Objective

Reporting". It stated that "A senior Tibetan official said Sunday that Tibet welcomes foreign journalists to come for objective and just reporting, but not those who take distorted views. Raidi, Deputy Secretary of the Tibet Autonomous Regional Committee of the Communist Party of China and Chairman of the Standing Committee of the Tibetan Autonomous Regional People's Congress, made the remarks at a meeting here with a press delegation of Thailand." In this context, it is interesting to note that N. Ram, the editor of India's *Frontline* magazine, devoted 36 pages of the September 15, 2000 issue to promote the Chinese line and recommended that the Indian Government expel the Central Tibetan Administration from Indian soil for being the main stumbling block to normal relations between India and China. It is difficult to assess to what extent the views contained in his stupendous reporting marathon are his own.

These editorial outbursts are in line with policy decisions outlined in the early nineties. During a two-day secret conclave in March 1993 in Chengdu, Vice-Minister Zeng Jian-hui, told participants, "All foreigners that we entertain and send to Tibet must have a relatively objective opinion of Tibet. We should use people from abroad to carry out the propaganda on Tibet for us, which is more powerful than if we do it."

Along with its external public relations strategy, China is presently carrying out a potentially much more dangerous policy of speeding up the pace of Tibet's economic development and its related drive to bring more Chinese settlers onto the Tibetan Plateau. Beijing's Western China Development Programme, which incorporates Tibet in its ambit, is devised to shift the focus of China's economic activities from Coastal China to the interior-both to narrow the imbalance in the level of economic development between the two regions and to ease population pressure on the coastal areas which attract millions of migrant workers. The focus of Beijing's Western China Economic Development Programme in Tibet is to exploit the plateau's still untapped minerals and other natural resources and to upgrade Tibet's infrastructure-like roads and telecommunications-to facilitate transportation of these resources to China. The other purpose of the heightened level of economic activity is to divert the Tibetans' attention from their political fate to focus on their livelihood-thus undermining Tibetan nationalism.

The Chinese authorities aim to manipulate the situation in Tibet still further by bringing in more Chinese settlers who would then demographically cement Chinese rule once and for all. These current hardline policies and their implementation in Tibet are impacting the stalled Sino-Tibetan Dialogue and will vitally affect the ability of Tibetans to survive as a distinct people and culture.

Beijing's Flawed Perceptions

The basic flaws in China's new policy in its search to resolve the problem of Tibet is thinking the solution can exclude the involvement of His Holiness the Dalai Lama. The other is in attempting to solve the problem over the heads of Tibet's citizens.

These two fundamental mistakes will exacerbate China's Tibet problem, not solve it. The reason lies in the history of Tibet and in the sentiments of the people. The institution of the Dalai Lamas of Tibet is more than 600 years old, if we start from the birth of the first Dalai Lama in 1391. In the course of its growth and development, the very institution itself came to symbolize fundamental beliefs and the political destiny of the nation. The bond between the Dalai Lamas and the Tibetan people is fundamental and unbreakable; any attempt, however sustained, will never succeed in driving a wedge between the two.

Consequently, China's current policy of forcing Tibetans-especially monks and nuns-to denounce His Holiness the Dalai Lama and pledge loyalty to the Chinese Communist Party will prove counterproductive. In view of this the Third Work Forum's basic assumption that in the case of Tibet time is on the side of China, and that Beijing can stall the problem of Tibet till the demise of the present Dalai Lama whereupon the issue of Tibet will solve itself, is fatally flawed-based as it is on a mistaken perception of the role played by the institution of the Dalai Lamas in the development of Tibetan history.

This assumption, if not reviewed, revised and abandoned, will prove catastrophic for the Chinese leadership and for those who chose to turn their whimsical personal analysis into state policy. The reason is simple. The Chinese Communist Party was founded in the 1920s and came to power in 1949. Within this short span of time the masses have lost faith in communist ideology, and members of the party these days pay mere lip service to the ideological justifications of the party. Conversely, the institution of the Dalai Lamas as a political force is more than 300 years old. These days the Dalai Lama is recognized by Tibetans throughout the world as the heart of Tibetan nationalism. How can a party which has lost its soul outlast an institution which symbolizes the very soul of a people? For these reasons it is imperative for China to review and re-assess its current hardline stance towards Tibet. China must re-start its stalled peace process over Tibet and consider His Holiness the Dalai Lama as a vital and active partner in the procedures. If China does this it will have won a powerful ally and companion along the road to peace, stability and continued prosperity.

PRESERVATION OF TIBETAN CULTURE IN EXILE

An excellent new book has appeared to fill out the incomplete information on modern Tibet. It is a history of the Chinese invasion and the Chinese attempts at total domination of Tibet: The Dragon in the Land of the Snows: A History of Modern Tibet Since 1947 (1). The author, Tsering Shakya, was born in Tibet and later attended London University where he is now a research fellow. This book is well balanced, providing recognition for Chinese efforts that were aimed at helping the Tibetans (within the confines of the policy to absorb the nation into China) as well as those that were destructive. The early and dramatic part of the story—the Communist take-over in China and the subsequent invasion of Tibet in 1949 leading to the exile of the Dalai Lama in 1959—has been portrayed in the popular film *Kundun* and in the book My Land and My People by the Dalai Lama (1962). It is now possible, through this new work by Shakya, to get a closer look at the events leading up to the "Lhasa Uprising" that instigated the Dalai Lama's escape and the subsequent intensification of repression by the Chinese.

What happened in Tibet after these proceedings has not been depicted in the historical literature until now. A number of books have appeared in the past that were based on personal experiences and observations, such as Return To Tibet (2) by Heinrich Harrer (based on a 1982 visit) and Sky Burial (3) by Blake Kerr (based on visits in 1987 and 1991).

The later books revealed some of the terrors imposed by the Chinese, especially during the Cultural Revolution of the 1960's and early 1970's, and then in Tibetan revolts that took place in the late 1980's. But this new book is a carefully researched and documented text that reveals the overall social, political, economic, and religious situation in Tibet during the period 1959–1989, ending with the massive anti-Chinese demonstrations in Lhasa in which many Tibetans were killed and hundreds more were arrested. Earlier that same year, the Tiananmen Square incident took place, which dominated the media attention, leaving the Tibetan situation of less importance to most of the world. Still, the Western world took some notice of the worsening situation in Tibet and recognized the Dalai Lama in the least political fashion possible, by awarding him the Nobel Peace Prize in 1989.

Information is also provided in this book about the state of affairs the Tibetan refugees have faced in India. During the first three years of exile, the Indians grudgingly allowed the Tibetans in, not wanting to worsen relations with China by doing anything to support the refugees (especially the Dalai Lama, as their leader). At times, Tibetan refugees were refused entrance to India and had to camp at the border, where many succumbed to the weather, until pleadings by the Dalai Lama led to their release (4). It was only after the India-China war over the border between India and Tibet that India—having lost the war—became a willing host to the Tibetan refugees. The Indian government came to realize that foreign assistance for its struggle with China (from the U.S., who had been supportive, though not openly, of Tibetan claims against the Communists) was easier to get if the Indians were seen as aiding the Tibetans. As a result of this effort, India allowed more freedom for the Dalai Lama to operate in Dharamsala; the government then set aside some unused land, most of it in a climatically harsh portion of southern India (Karnataka State), far away from the border, as a refugee centre. Tsering Shakya relays:

The Indian policy towards the Dalai Lama and the Tibetans underwent a dramatic change as India came to realize the potential benefit of the presence of Tibetans in their country. They began to adopt a more supportive policy and encouraged the Tibetans to organize themselves, eventually leading to the Dalai Lama's setting up of a *de facto* 'government in exile' based in Himachal Pradesh in Dharamsala. The Indian Government began to allocate substantial aid for the rehabilitation of refugees and, as Indian public sympathy naturally moved towards the Tibetans, the different state governments began to allocate land for the resettlement of Tibetan refugees.

At first, many of the Tibetans were used as labourers to build roads in the Himalayan region. Later, each of the monastic groups received a few dozen acres of land to use for surroundings up living quarters and some cultivation of food, an amount which seemed adequate for the few hundred refugees at each of the sites. The Government of India also provided a small annual stipend for each refugee to help in gaining the minimal requirements of food, clothing, and shelter.

It is first encountered a Tibetan while he was monk visiting the West in 1975. He had come as a representative of the exile community to try and educate Westerners about Tibetan culture. In small meetings with limited attendance, mostly by people who had studied yoga and other aspects of Indian culture, he and a few other Tibetans described Buddhism, but not what had happened in Tibet. During the next few years, It was able to study with Tibetan monks and Tibetan doctors and learn about the culture; but little was said about Tibet or the situation in India, other than that Dharamsala had become the new residence of the Dalai Lama and the new Tibetan medical school. Interest in Tibet grew throughout the Western world; a student of ITM attended the Kalachakra Ceremony conducted by the Dalai Lama and 26 other lamas in Switzerland in 1985, where it was reported that 5,000 people from 37 countries attended. In 1982, Heinrich Harrer (best known for his book Seven Years in Tibet, later made into a popular film) visited the Dalai Lama who explained that "Tibet has a great cultural heritage to preserve, and it is that which gives meaning to the people's lives and gives them courage to face their existence. That is why it is important for us to concern ourselves with Tibetan culture and religion; even in exile we have done everything possible to preserve them. I have travelled a great deal over the past 24 years: I have been to North America, Europe, Australia, and Japan. We have set up a great many new Buddhist centres and, by participating in major exhibitions, have acquainted the world with our culture."

The conditions there were appalling and reflected the damage done by the Cultural Revolution during the 1970's, more than ten years before my arrival. Despite a liberalization of the Chinese policy towards Tibet allowed by Deng Xiaoping during the early 1980's (that made it possible for me and several thousand other tourists to enter the country), Tibet was a very troubled nation. The monasteries, which had been the centre of Tibetan culture, were in ruins; the Potala had been retained as a historical site only, and a small portion of it was available for viewing by visitors. A handful of monks were living at the major religious sites to maintain what was left of them (compared to earlier populations of several thousands). At what remained of Drepung Monastery at the edge of the city, I was shown the central prayer hall which had been painted with beautiful Buddhist images. The lower half of the images were worn away; I was told that the Chinese army, after closing down the monastery and destroying most of the buildings, had converted this hall to a grain storage depot. It has been reported that of 6,000 monasteries that were destroyed; less than a dozen have been partly or fully reconstructed.

During his return visit to Lhasa, Heinrich Harrer visited Drepung Monastery, where he had been able to spend time prior to the Chinese invasion. He asked plaintively: What had become of the beautifully carved wooden tables, or the silver jugs and teacups chased with good-luck ornaments? What had become of the heavy brocade-framed thangkas, what of the abbots and ministers who had such an air of power and severity in their magnificent garments? I was keeping my eyes open for the three novices who were allegedly to be found there, the first since the occupation. But, all I saw were small clusters of tourists, sightseeing like myself. Men and women from all over the world, all talking excitedly and at the same time: 'Frightful, this destruction, how beautiful these stones are....' Not even a shadow of doubt or misgiving crossing their faces. Had they no idea of what had stood here in the past?

Central Lhasa outside the Potala Palace had been transformed into an ugly city of grey cement block buildings. These apartment buildings dominated the scene, where one could still see just a few of the brightly-coloured traditional-style Tibetan homes. The structures had been rapidly built to house huge numbers of Chinese who were forced to live in this remote area that was of no interest to them. Harrer commented: "Lhasa, whose name means 'place of the gods,' no longer bears any relation to that lovely name; looking at the ugly hutments and tin roofs, at the new buildings and their alien architecture, as they choke the few old quarters of the city, it is hard to believe that the gods would choose this spot for their seat on earth." By the time I had arrived in Lhasa, six years later, thousands more Chinese had poured into Lhasa, all requiring quick housing solutions.

Starting in 1984, some Chinese came there voluntarily to Tibet, especially Lhasa, to find work among the thousands of other Chinese, receiving financial incentives from the Beijing government, and escaping the "one family, one child" policy that was enforced in China but largely ignored in Tibet at that time. A greater Chinese presence was desired by the Party and that was eventually accomplished. From a population of just a handful of Chinese in 1949, there were 30,000 Chinese living in Lhasa by 1959 and an estimated 200,000 by the end of 1999, now making up more than 60% of the city's population. These high figures for the current Chinese immigrant population do not include the huge army presence (which resides in separate barracks at the edge of the city) nor an increasing number of unregistered Chinese migrant workers seeking employment wherever they can find it. In other words, Tibet has been converted to a Chinese Province by moving in more Chinese than Tibetans in the major population centres.

There are about 8 million Chinese now living in the lands that once were Tibet, versus 6 million Tibetans.

During my visit I could see that the Tibetans were clearly unhappy about their situation and, from time to time, they got into scuffles with the Chinese (which, in later years, rose to the level of protest demonstrations and riots; two of the best known ones taking place in 1987 and 1989). There was little food, with the commune system destroying the natural productivity of both the land and the people. The Chinese tended to be more wealthy than the Tibetans, despite the economic ideology of Communism that should assure equality, so the best food often went to the Chinese dinner table. The Chinese leaders I spoke with regarded the Tibetans as lazy, not realizing that they were talking about a hard working people who were being forced to do things that were entirely unnatural for them. One of the stories relayed in The Dragon in the Land of Snows has the Chinese taking away the traditional plow the Tibetans used effectively to till their fields, replacing it with another that the Chinese deemed more efficient. Eventually, the old way was restored when it was realized that it actually worked better, at least in the hands of the Tibetans. Most of the fruits of Tibetan labour were taken away by the Chinese, reducing the incentive for any hard work.

There was a small tolerance for religious observation at this time which one could see by the presence of a few elderly persons making the traditional circumambulation of the Potala and the flying of some prayer flags (which had all been torn down during the Cultural Revolution), but the overt practice of religion had largely been eliminated. A few years earlier, during a brief attempt to normalize relations between China and Tibet, the Chinese Communist Party had allowed a few delegations from exiled Tibetans representing the Dalai Lama (including a brother and sister on separate visits) to tour portions of Tibet. Huge crowds came to greet them, nearly causing a riot in Lhasa (merely from the crush of well-wishers trying to get to the visiting tour bus). The Chinese were amazed and embarrassed to see that the decades of imposing the Communist way of life had obviously failed to diminish the Tibetan interest in their native leaders and culture.

Future visits of the exile group that had already been planned were cancelled. Negotiations between the Chinese and the Dalai Lama (via intermediaries) eventually broke down completely.

Further attempts at opening Tibet and relaxing strict Communist rule were undertaken by order of Deng Xiaoping during the year of my visit. This is the story as relayed by Tsering Shakya in his new book (pages 402–404): In 1986, the [Chinese Communist] Party allowed the celebration of the Monlam ceremony [the major Buddhist celebration in Tibet] for the first time since it was banned in 1967. This had a major social and psychological impact among Tibetan people, not only in the TAR [Tibet Autonomous Region] but throughout the ethnic Tibetan areas [such as Amdo and Kham, which had been absorbed into Sichuan and Qinghai Provinces]. When the news was released that the authorities would allow the monks to hold the ceremony, thousands of pilgrims flocked to Lhasa from every corner of the country. More than anything that the Party had done over the past five years, the decision to allow the Monlam ceremony convinced the Tibetans that the Chinese were prepared to allow the Tibetans to define what type of reforms they wanted.

The Tibetans took full advantage of Wu Jinghua's [newly elected First Party Secretary in Tibet] liberal policy towards religion. For the first time they began publicly to display photos of the Dalai Lama and to defy Chinese laws restricting the rebuilding of monasteries and temples [that had been destroyed during the Cultural Revolution]. The state law forbade anyone under eighteen years of age to become a monk [in the past, children as young as 12 years old were sent to monasteries to become monks], but no one paid any attention to the restriction and hundreds of young boys were sent to the monasteries. In some remote areas like Dagyab, there were more students entering the monasteries than local schools [that had been set up by the Chinese for modern education]. The Chinese authorities wanted to restrict the numbers of monasteries and temples rebuilt, and the local people were supposed to seek permission from the Religious Affairs Bureau for such projects, but since the people were able to raise funds privately, there was very little the Chinese could do to prevent increasing construction. The new phase of reform also served to heighten the Tibetans' political awareness and awaken deep-seated grievances. This pushed the reforms in a direction over which the Chinese authorities had no control.

The Communists had hoped to promote a limited but controlled revival or Tibetan culture and religion [in order to better manage the "Tibet problem"]. But people were simply not prepared to accept officially defined limits to the new freedom of religion. The Communists had always known that there was an inherent danger in arousing the Tibetans' latent aspirations, which were naturally linked to the question of religion. While the Chinese had granted some privileges to the former secular elite, namely the aristocracy, they hesitated in promoting many of the Tibetan lamas and Rinpoches and tried to draw a clear distinction between what they regarded as the legitimate expression of religion and its illegal use. It was stressed that the authorities would not tolerate the use of religion to undermine the 'unity of the motherland' or to impede economic development [for example, by having many people spend their lives pursuing religious activities instead of laboring to reach the Communist goals]. Religious institutions approved by the Chinese, such as the Buddhist Association, commanded little or no respect from the Tibetans; neither did officially promoted Rinpoches such as Phagpa Gelek Mangyal, the head lama of the Chamdo region. The Communists were cynical about such high-ranking lamas and Rinpoches, who were used to convey the Party's message of economic progress and modernization. While in public the Party promoted Phagpa Gelek Namgyal as a prominent religious leader, it was commonly known in Lhasa that an internal Communist Party document had described him as a 'hooligan' and that he was held in contempt. The officially promoted Rinpoches and lamas were consequently not seen by the Tibetans as natural leaders.

By the middle of 1986 the Chinese were encountering difficulties in limiting the growing number of monks and related religious institutions. As we shall see later, this was to present a major challenge to the authorities. The revival of religion as the centre of Tibetan life was seen by the Chinese as a step backwards both in terms of ideology and of the modernization of the region. This view was also shared by many Tibetans [who grew up under the Chinese system and adopted the Chinese view] who say the revival of monasticism as an obstacle to modernization. More importantly, the awakening of religious feelings brought to the fore the question of the Dalai Lama's return. It was evident that there was universal devotion and loyalty to the exiled leader. The Chinese tried to separate the Dalai Lama's spiritual and political authority, but in the minds of the Tibetans, the two were fused. There was no doubt that the Tibetans saw the Dalai Lama quite simply as their saviour, *Kyabgon*.

One of the main contradictions that emerged during Wu Jinghua's period was that while the Party was prepared to make limited concessions to local conditions, it was not willing either to endorse social pluralism or to accept the emergence of social institutions [e.g., monasteries] independent of the Party. The demand for change stemmed mostly from religious institutions and the central question was whether the Chinese authorities would be able to contain the growing demand for greater religious freedom in Tibet, which it had hoped to satisfy by the readoption of the United Front [i.e., the principle of having a united effort of China and the minorities, especially Tibet, rather than simple imposition of Chinese rule over the minorities] and the extension of patronage to religious figures. However, it was apparent that the Chinese authorities would do their utmost to resist any demands that advocated independence. This was reflected in the imprisonment of Geshe Lobsant Wangchuck, a scholarly monk who had openly argued that Tibet not only had the right to independence but that she had never been a part of China. In February 1983, when wall posters appeared in Lhasa advocating Tibetan independence, the Chinese authorities quickly arrested a number of monks from Drepung monastery. In August a monk named Palden Gyatso was found guilty of spreading 'counter revolutionary propaganda' and was sentenced to eight years imprisonment. The Tibetans were painfully aware of the limits of Chinese tolerance and knew that they would have to work within the restrictions imposed by the Chinese.

In 1987, the Dalai Lama visited the U.S. and made an address to Congress. He described the aspirations of the Tibetan people and made a proposal for resolution that was entirely unacceptable to the Chinese. This engendered a harsh criticism by Beijing against the U.S. government for allowing the Dalai Lama to have this forum.

Shakya relays: Had it not been for the subsequent developments in Lhasa, the events in Washington would have passed as a minor diplomatic discord between Beijing and Washington. The Chinese would simply have ignored the Dalai Lama's proposal. But on September 27, at 10 A.M., 21 monks from Drepung monastery marched to Lhasa and staged the first pro-independence demonstration since the fact-finding delegations of 1981. The monks circled around the Barkor (the centre of Lhasa), carrying the Tibetan national flag, and shouted demands for Tibetan independence. The demonstrations were immediately suppressed by the Chinese police, and most of the monks were beaten and arrested.

Several demonstrators were shot and killed; the demonstrations and the violent police reaction, were observed for the first time by some of the Western visitors. These visitors learned that many of the Tibetans that were taken prisoner were severely tortured; the events stimulated one of those visitors, Blake Kerr (Sky Burial), a young medical doctor, to investigate Chinese medical activities in Tibet.

THE DALAI LAMA AND HIS FOLLOWERS FLED INTO EXILE IN 1959

The previous Panchen Lama, in his famous "70,000 Character Petition" to Chairman Mao Zedong, wrote that out of 2,500 monasteries in the Tibet Autonomous Region, only 70 (3%) were left in 1962, three years before the Cultural Revolution began. According to the Panchen Lama's survey, ninety-three percent of the 100,000 clerics had been forced out of the monasteries. The situation was reportedly even worse in Eastern Tibet, with 98-99% of the Tibetan Buddhist monasteries shut down. This account is consistent with two other Chinese sources.

Despite such destruction, Tibetans have held firmly to their spiritual beliefs. When a small period of political openess appeared during the initial phases of China's new liberalization policies in the early 1980s, Tibetans began to voluntarily finance the rebuilding of their destroyed monasteries. Today they have revived many, but the quality of religious practice is limited to rituals and is often quite minimal, due to arbitrary and restrictive measures still imposed on religious practices. This brief discussion cannot address in any depth related issues, such as the imprisonment and torture of 121622 lay people, monks and nuns for taking part in political activities, including for refusal to denounce the Dalai Lama and recognize the Chinese-appointed Panchen Lama. However, April 25, 1999, marks the tenth anniversary of the birth of the Tibetan Panchen Lama, which will be observed worldwide by Tibetans and Tibet support groups, including those in Boston, as marking the disappearance of possibly the youngest political prisoner in the world.

As many tourists who have been to Tibet since liberalization know, it is a common experience to be followed by Tibetan children asking for the "Dalai Lama's photo" even though the photograph is officially banned. If, as the Chinese have argued, the monastic system had been so oppressive and the Dalai Lama the head slave owner, this popular revival of Buddhist institutions and desire for the return of the Dalai Lama would be hard to understand. If the pre-1951 order had been so horrible in the eyes of the Tibetans, the Cultural Revolution ought to have been an opportune moment for them to "liberate" themselves from religion and the Dalai Lama. But as both these examples prove, Tibetans take great pride in their religion, which dates back 2500 years. In contrast, Communism is a modern foreign ideology brought in from China, with little hold on Tibetans' hearts and minds.

Communism failed in Tibet and has never been able to compete with Buddhism's rich spiritual message. However, this is not to say that religion is the right basis for political rule; all religions have both good and bad effects on society and the concept of a religious political order is a very complex one. Rather, it suggests that the Tibetan way of life and values are quite distinct from and in many ways foreign to that of the contemporary Chinese. Religion matters to Tibetans in a way most Chinese find hard to understand.

Modernizing "Feudal" Tibet

To lessen the strong influence of religion in Tibet, the Chinese government attempted to replace traditional monastery schooling with modern, secular schools. Currently, the Chinese government claims that it has established more than 3,000 schools in the TAR, special Tibetan schools in inner China, and institutions of higher education, like the School of Agriculture and Animal Husbandry, and Tibet University. Some Chinese officials argue that these progressive measures have helped Tibetans both improve their lives and move toward the modern world.

Yet, when closely analyzed, the results show a peculiar pattern of discrimination and a far less progressive policy.

Contrary to official statements, the majority of schools in Tibet are constructed and funded by local Tibetans. In addition, as of 1995, Tibet continues to be the least literate region in China, with a higher than sixty percent illiteracy and semi-literacy rate-whereas China's illiteracy rate has fallen to under seven percent.

One of the most contentious issues between Chinese and Tibetans is the medium of instruction used in schools. Article 4 of the Chinese Constitution and Article 37 of the Minority Nationality Act of 1984 clearly indicate that the language of each nationality should be adopted both as a medium of instruction in schools and for official use in the government wherever minorities are dominant. In Inner Mongolia, another Autonomous Region like Tibet, there are schools and colleges where the medium of instruction is Mongolian. However, in the TAR, Chinese is the language of instruction in schools above the secondary level, despite the fact that "ninety-five percent of the Tibetan population do not speak or understand the Chinese language." From the Tibetan perspective, Chinese education policy, rather then modernizing, represents one more tool to eradicate Tibetan civilization and identity.

As one might imagine, the use of Chinese as the language of instruction in schools has had highly discriminatory effects on

Tibetan students. Higher levels of education in the TAR are in fact dominated by ethnic Chinese. In the School of Agriculture and Animal Husbandry, supposedly established for Tibetans and located in the TAR, 446 (71%) of the total 630 students are Chinese and only 184 (29%) are Tibetan. In the Tibet Nationalities Institute in Xianyang, 938 students out of the total 1,165 students are Chinese and only 227 are Tibetan. The Chinese government maintains that only 4% of the population in the TAR is Chinese. If 4% of the population takes more than 70% seats in the educational institutions, then these figures beg the question of who is really being educated in Tibet.

The historical boundary of the Tibetan Kingdom

The major exception to this pattern is Tibet University in Lhasa where the majority of students are Tibetan (1,018) and Han Chinese are in the minority (208).31 Still, on closer examination of the data, even at Tibet University one finds that Han Chinese are the majority in science and technical courses, with Tibetans constituting only 26% of the students in these areas. In contrast, Tibetans are heavily concentrated in the humanities, representing 70% of the students enrolled in those courses. Sadly, one of the core parts of the humanities program, the Tibetan language department, has been closed for the past three years, and the local government is pressuring teachers to teach Tibetan history using the Chinese language.

The situation worsens at the highest level of education. For the last forty years fewer than ten Tibetans have graduated or are graduating from Beijing University. When questioned about this statistic, the Chinese respond that Tibetans are unable to compete intellectually with the Chinese. But, if that were the case, why, in just the last ten years, have there been at least ten exiled Tibetans who have graduated or are about to graduate from Harvard University? Exiled Tibetans constitute only 5% of the Tibetan population or 130,000 in total (far less than the 150,000 Chinese students in the US in any given year).

Each year hundreds of Tibetan children ranging in age from six to eighteen years cross the Himalayas seeking secular or monastic education in India. The real land of opportunity for Tibetan education is now outside of Tibet.

Chinese "Investment" in Tibet

Many claim that if nothing else, Chinese involvement in Tibet has brought with it greater economic development and modernization. Chinese spokespeople always note that the government is pouring money into Tibet. It is true that roads and factories are constructed and that almost ninety percent of the TAR Government budget is subsidized by the central government in Beijing. However, the bulk of the subsidies are spent on two fronts: 1) Urbanization developing cities to encourage Chinese migrants from inner China to settle in Tibet, a phenomenon discussed later, and 2) Bureaucracy funding the burgeoning administrative and institutional structure to control the volatile situation in Tibet. "From 1952 to 1984, the cost of direct administration was more than 15 percent of the total subsidies expended" and is still increasing. The agriculture and animal husbandry sector, which constitutes 90% of the Tibetan population, receives a meager 15% of the total subsidies. Therefore most Tibetans living in rural and nomadic areas have not progressed much for the last forty years.

In 1994 at its "Third Work Forum" on Tibet, Chinese leaders announced 62 development projects targeting industrial growth in the TAR. Certainly this level of investment seems impressive, and in fact, the accounting can be confusing. The government usually fails to make clear how Tibetan natural resources are exploited as part of this infusion of money. 126 different minerals, such as chromium, lead, sulfur, copper, borax, iron, petrol, gold and uranium to name a few, are found in Tibet. These are not included in the gross product and, consequently, are also not listed as a source of income. Also "because of high altitude and location, Tibet acts as a principal watershed for Asia." Major rivers like the Yangtse, Brahmaputra, and others originate in Tibet. Net hydrological flows in Tibet comprise roughly 6% of Asia's runoff and about 28% of China's (excluding Tibet), and 34% of India's total river water resources. Tibet's rivers have enormous potential for hydroelectric generation. As a result, despite the huge reserves of natural resources it contributes, Tibet remains on the accounting ledgers as the poorest region in China, a paradox best described by two Chinese economists in the aptly titled book, The Poverty of Plenty.

Economic Advances?

A Lhasa woman recently told me that although ten years ago Katmandu in Nepal felt like a big city, it now looks like a small village compared to modern Lhasa. In this sense, Tibet has developed economically, and urbanization has taken off in several parts of the Tibet. Although some Tibetans seem to have benefited from the growth (a few Tibetans own fleets of Land Cruisers and luxurious houses), in fact the major benefits of these alleged improved economic conditions in the cities seem not be reaching most Tibetans.

Economic development in urban Tibet is real, but again I have to pose the question: for whose sake has this development taken place and under whose terms? According to a census, outside of the traditional Tibetan "Bharkor" market, there are more than 3,500 to 4,000 shops and restaurants in Lhasa, but Tibetans own only 400-450 of them, leaving the remaining 85% under non-Tibetan (usually Han Chinese) ownership. One reason for the Chinese-dominated commerce is that Chinese migrants entering Tibet use their clan and local village networks to support their own ethnic group; another factor is the use of guanxi (connections) among Chinese officials to exploit economic opportunities. In the process, Tibetans have been economically marginalized and deprived of their own fair share. When asked why this has happened, Chinese react that they are more skilled and hence they dominate the market. However, even age-old businesses, which require traditional Tibetan skills like wood-carving, sewing aprons and traditional dress, and selling Khatas (silk scarves) in front of Jokhang temple have been taken over by Chinese migrants. This takeover is justified by saying that the Chinese are more hard-working than Tibetans. Another area where hard-work is not necessarily the baseline criteria, but where economic and cultural encroachment has offended Tibetans, is the growth of prostitution in Lhasa. Recent figures indicate that there are approximately 8,890 prostitutes in Lhasa 9% of the female population double the number in London, where the population nears eight million. Although prostitution is outlawed in China, it is quite common to find brothels in front of army barracks and government offices in Lhasa, where officials look the other way. Since Lhasa is a holy city for Tibetans, this type of immoral encroachment by the Chinese is particularly resented.

Urbanization

As stated earlier, one of the primary targets of subsidies is urbanization. Like other towns, the city of Lhasa has expanded, and the population has increased from 30,000 in 1950s to 200,000 in 1998. Though these figures seem impressive, it is again necessary to look at the finer details of the statistics to see both who these new people are and who is benefiting from the urbanization. It is estimated that as much as 60-70% of the population in Lhasa now is Chinese. Not only do they dominate private businesses as shown earlier, but they also occupy most government-related employment. "Approximately 95 percent of official Chinese immigrants are employed" in the state-owned enterprises. Most Tibetans feel marginalized by such an encroaching demographic reversal that limits their educational, cultural, and economic opportunities. Even Tibetans who might support or sympathize with the Communist ideology resent this process of marginalization.

The continued migration of Han Chinese into Tibet has intensified the sense of separate identity among Tibetans, creating an increasingly overt feeling of "us vs. them." In almost all the Tibetan areas, conceptual and physical separation of the two groups has created two separate worlds. In their everyday lives in most of the inner towns and cities of Tibet, Tibetans work and live in physically segregated areas. Consequently, while the number of Chinese moving to inner urban Tibet has dramatically increased, the conceptual and physical separations between the two populations foster a strong desire in Tibetans to resist ethnic assimilation.

Despite economic development and urbanization in Tibet, most Tibetans have not felt themselves to be the beneficiaries of this modernization. Rather, Tibetans have felt increasingly marginalized in their own territory and see themselves as mere observers of an economic development benefiting others. This has made the ethnic "us vs. them" sentiment all the more concrete, since it is usually the Han Chinese who reap the profits of change.

This is not to reduce the issue of Tibet to a mere theory of economic deprivation as the Chinese government seems to believe, i.e. if economic discrepancies in Tibet are taken care of, the issue of Tibet will wither away. On the contrary, it can be convincingly argued that economic discrepancies can be a catalyst to exacerbate ethno-national tensions, but they are not its primary cause. Catalans in Spain are economically better off than the Spanish, but their sense of nationalism and call for separate identity is strong. Similarly, Slovenia separated from Yugoslavia even though Slovenes were economically more advanced, and the most radical group calling for secession in Quebec is the successful young urban professional, bilingual Quebecois. It is a common sight that every day tens and hundreds of Kosovars are volunteering to join the Kosovo Liberation Army. Many of them are leaving the relatively comfortable life of Western countries to sacrifice their lives to fight against the Serbs in the Balkans. Therefore, it is an established fact that an "X" factor beyond comfort and economy, such as a respect for a distinct identity and nationality, binds people together and calls for recognition. In the case of Tibet, Tibetans are distinct from Chinese in terms of language, religion, culture, history, ethnicity, civilization, and geography. Respect and recognition of these distinctions will therefore remain at the core of the resolution of the Sino-Tibetan conflict. The "Tibetan issue" will not disappear for a long time to come; therefore, open-minded Tibetans and Chinese must sit down together and find a peaceful solution. The alternative is inevitable violence, a tragic disaster for both Tibetans and Chinese.

The Future

As this article shows, Given the deep bitterness of many Tibetans, the potential for violence and outbreaks of ethnic clashes throughout Tibet should be taken seriously. The frustration level both in exile and inside Tibet is real. Last year, the Tibetan Youth Congress held hunger strikes even to the point of death for sixty-seven days in Delhi (one of the longest hunger strikes held in the world). Out of frustration and as a sacrifice, an exiled Tibetan named Thupten Ngodup immolated himself. Inside Tibet, in 1997, there were seven bomb blasts in the TAR region alone.Similarly, in May 1998, an attempted prison escape by Tibetans in a prison near Lhasa escalated into a riot that left eleven people dead. The crime rate in Lhasa is high and might also take on an ethnic dimension. Crime mixed with nationalism might lead to an all out ethnic war like the ones in East Turkestan in China or Kosovo in the Balkans. Time is running out!

Let me end with the same question that I began with: is there any way that the spirit, if not the total substance, of the mutual respect and recognition during the Golden Age of the Tang dynasty in China and the Yarlung dynasty in Tibet can be revived again? I believe so.

The answer to this question might be found in the very story of the Chinese Princess Wang Chen and the Tibetan King Songtsen Gampo in 641 AD. The Chinese princess brought to Tibet the Jowo Sakyamuni statue, which is now enshrined in Lhasa's Jokhang temple. Ironically, the Jokhang temple has become the Tiananmen Square of Tibet, one of Tibet's most sensitive and volatile landmarks. Since the Chinese occupation of Tibet, Jokhang has served as the center of political activities for ordinary Tibetans and for monks and nuns demonstrating against Chinese rule. Chinese policemen and plainclothes intelligence personnel roam around the temple and surveillance cameras monitor the movements of people in the nearby market. Nomad, peasant, and exile Tibetan pilgrims flocking to the temple to pay their respects to Jowo Sakyamuni must pass through these security devices caught in an ironic web of politics that has transformed this holiest of holy sites into a symbol of the police state.

Have these cameras and policemen deterred Tibetans from adhering to their religious practices and beliefs? It seems not. Pilgrims continue to come to the temple by the thousands and visit the top floor where a statue of the Tibetan King Songtsen Gampo stands. To Tibetans, the King represents the manifestation of the Buddha of Compassion. To the left of him stand the statues of the senior Nepali Princess Bikrikuti and the junior Chinese Princess Wang Chen, believed to be the emanation of the Goddess Tara. Showing the highest form of reverence, pilgrims from Tibet and exiled pilgrims from abroad fall to the ground, prostate themselves in front of these statues, and offer them Khatas (white scarves).

Prostration is the highest form of respect for Tibetans, and, physically, it is more difficult to perform than the traditional Chinese kowtow. The prostration by Tibetans to the Chinese princess, reflects how sincere Tibetans have been in paying respect where it is due. Therefore, if Tibetans inside and outside are complaining about the situation in Tibet, their judgment should be trusted.

The great respect and love pilgrims in Tibet and in exile have shown toward the statue of Princess Wang Chen for more than a millennium is proof that there is no inherent hatred among Tibetans towards the Chinese per se. The intense resentment felt by Tibetans results from policies issued and enforced by the Chinese Communist government. If left to rule and live in their own way, Tibetans can live peacefully with the Chinese and show them respect. The barrier to peace in Tibet is not the pilgrims flocking to Jokhang temple to pay their respects, but the lack of reciprocity by the Chinese made worse by the presence of the surveillance cameras and policemen monitoring this holy site.

View of the Tibetan Government-in-Exile

In 1959, the 14th Dalai Lama fled Tibet and established a government in exile at Dharamsala in northern India. This group claims sovereignty over various ethnically or historically Tibetan areas now governed by China. Aside from the Tibet Autonomous Region, an area that was administered directly by the Dalai Lama's government until 1951, the group also claims Amdo (Qinghai) and eastern Kham (western Sichuan). About 45 percent of ethnic Tibetans under Chinese rule live in the Tibet Autonomous Region, according to the 2000 census. Prior to 1949, much of Amdo and eastern Kham were governed by local rulers and even warlords. A proclamation issued by 13th Dalai Lama in 1913 states, "During the time of Genghis Khan and Altan Khan of the Mongols, the Ming dynasty of the Chinese, and the Qing Dynasty of the Manchus, Tibet and China cooperated on the basis of benefactor and priest relationship." The relationship did not imply "subordination of one to the other." He condemned the Chinese authorities for attempting to colonize Tibetan territory in 1910–12. "We are a small, religious, and independent nation," the proclamation states.

The view of the current Dalai Lama is as follows:

During the 5th Dalai Lama's time [1617–1682], I think it was quite evident that we were a separate sovereign nation with no problems. The 6th Dalai Lama [1683–1706] was spiritually pre-eminent, but politically, he was weak and uninterested. He could not follow the 5th Dalai Lama's path. This was a great failure. So, then the Chinese influence increased. During this time, the Tibetans showed quite a deal of respect to the Chinese. But even during these times, the Tibetans never regarded Tibet as a part of China. All the documents were very clear that China, Mongolia and Tibet were all separate countries. Because the Chinese emperor was powerful and influential, the small nations accepted the Chinese power or influence. You cannot use the previous invasion as evidence that Tibet belongs to China. In the Tibetan mind, regardless of who was in power, whether it was the Manchus, the Mongols or the Chinese, the east of Tibet was simply referred to as China. In the Tibetan mind, India and China were treated the same; two separate countries. The International Commission of Jurists concluded that from 1913 to 1950 Tibet demonstrated the conditions of statehood as generally accepted under international law. In the opinion of the commission, the government of Tibet conducted its own domestic and foreign affairs free from any outside authority, and countries with whom Tibet had foreign relations are shown by official documents to have treated Tibet in practice as an independent State.

The United Nations General Assembly passed resolutions urging respect for the rights of Tibetans in 1959, 1961 and 1965. The 1961 resolution calls for that "principle of self-determination of peoples and nations" applies to the Tibetan people. The Tibetan Government in Exile views current PRC rule in Tibet as colonial and illegitimate, motivated solely by the natural resources and strategic value of Tibet, and in gross violation of both Tibet's historical status as an independent country and the right of Tibetan people to self-determination. It also points to PRC's autocratic policies, divide-and-rule policies, and what it contends are assimilationist policies, and regard those as an example of ongoing imperialism aimed at destroying Tibet's distinct ethnic makeup, culture, and identity, thereby cementing it as an indivisible part of China. That said, the Dalai Lama has recently stated that he wishes only for Tibetan autonomy, and not separation from China, under certain democratic conditions, like freedom of speech and expression and genuine self-rule.

Tibetan passports

In 2003, an old Tibetan passport was rediscovered in Nepal by Tibet independence supporters. Issued by the 13th Dalai Lama to Tibet's finance minister (Tsepon Shakabpa) for foreign travel, the passport was a single piece of pink paper, complete with photograph, and had visas issued by many countries, including Britain. It has a message in typed English and hand-written Tibetan, similar to the message by the nominal issuing officers of today's passports. There is no Chinese on the passport, but two stamps could be official Chinese seals, or they could be Chinese entry stamps. However, acceptance of a passport does not indicate recognition of independence, as for example the Republic of China passport is accepted by almost all the countries of the world, even though very few of them recognize the ROC as independent.

A spokesman for the Chinese Embassy said it was not clear if the passport was genuine since experts had not examined it.

Third-party views

During the Tang Dynasty of China, Tibet and China frequently warred. Parts of Tibet were temporarily captured by the Chinese and became territories of the Tang dynasty (618–907 AD). Around 650, the Chinese even captured Lhasa. In 763, Tibet reversed this situation and briefly took the Chinese capital of Chang'an during the Chinese Tang civil war.

Most scholars outside the PRC say that during the Ming Dynasty (1368–1644), Tibet was de facto independent while Ming nominal suzerainty remained. According to historian Zahiruddin Ahmad, since the 18th century, when the Qing Government was setting up its local government structure and promulgated laws for the governing, Beijing had, in the words of a foreign missionary, "absolute dominion over Tibet". Other western scholars agree that since the mid-18th century China had control over Tibet Luciano Petech, a scholar of Himalayan history, writes:

In 1751 the organization of the protectorate took its final shape, which it maintained, except for some modifications in 1792, till its end in 1912. The ambans were given rights of control and supervision and since 1792 also a direct participation in the Tibetan government.

Tibetologist Melvyn C. Goldstein writes that Britain and Russia formally acknowledged Chinese authority over Tibet in treaties of 1906 and 1907; and that the British invasion of Tibet stirred China into getting more directly involved in Tibetan affairs and working to integrate Tibet with "the rest of China."

Barnett observes that there is no document before 1950 in which Tibet explicitly recognizes Chinese sovereignty, and considers Tibet subordination to China (in the periods when China had most authority) comparable to that of a colony.

F. Spencer Chapman questions the validity of China's purported authority in deposing the Dalai Lama twice in the early 20th century, noting that, at the same time China "deposed" the 13th Dalai Lama, it made claims not only over Tibet, but also over Nepal and Bhutan.

The "Patron-Priest" relationship held between the Chinese court and the Tibetan lamas has been subjected to varying interpretation. The 13th Dalai Lama, for example, knelt, but did not kowtow, before the Empress Dowager and the young Emperor while he delivered his petition in Beijing. Chinese sources emphasize the submission of kneeling; Tibetan sources emphasize the lack of the kowtow. Titles and commands given to Tibetans by the Chinese, likewise, are variously interpreted. The Chinese gave the 13th Dalai Lama the title of "Loyally Submissive Vice-Regent", and ordered to follow China's commands and communicate with the Emperor only through the Chinese Amban in Lhasa; but opinions vary as to whether these titles and commands reflected actual political power, or symbolic gestures ignored by Tibetans. The kneeling before the Emperor followed the 17th-century precedent in the case of the 5th Dalai Lama.

Thomas Heberer, professor of political science and East Asian studies at the University of Duisburg-Essen, Germany, wrote: "No country in the world has ever recognized the independence of Tibet or declared that Tibet is an 'occupied country'. For all countries in the world, Tibet is Chinese territory." However, in 1991, United States President Bush signed a State Department Authorization Act that explicitly called Tibet "an occupied country", and identified the Dalai Lama and the Tibetan Government in Exile as "Tibet's true representatives".

Other tibetologists write that no country publicly accepts Tibet as an independent state, although there are several instances of government officials appealing to their superiors to do so. Treaties signed by Britain and Russia in the early years of the 20th century, and others signed by Nepal and India in the 1950s, recognized Tibet's political subordination to China. The Americans presented their view on 15 May 1943:

For its part, the Government of the United States has borne in mind the fact that...the Chinese constitution lists Tibet among areas constituting the territory of the Republic of China. This Government has at no time raised a question regarding either of these claims.

The 1994 U.S. State Department report to Congress declares:

Historically the U.S. has acknowledged Chinese sovereignty over Tibet. Since at least 1966, U.S. policy has explicitly recognized the Tibet Autonomous Region...as part of the People's Republic of China. This long-standing policy is consistent with the view of the entire international community, including all China's neighbors:

no country recognizes Tibet as a sovereign state. Because we do not recognize Tibet as an independent state, the U.S. does not conduct diplomatic relations with the self-styled 'Tibetan government-in-exile'.

The US government recognizes Tibet as part of China, but the US Congress has at times expressed a different perspective, calling Tibet an occupied country.

The latest US official statement on Tibet being part of China came from President Obama to Chinese President Hu Jintao during his State visit to Beijing in November 2009.

In 2008, European Union leader Jose Manuel Barroso stated that the EU recognized Tibet as integral part of China:

I have confirmed that the EU is attached to the territorial integrity and unity of China, and that naturally applies to Tibet

In October, 2008, the British government clarified their official position on Tibet's status:

Our ability to get our points across has sometimes been clouded by the position the UK took at the start of the 20th century on the status of Tibet, a position based on the geopolitics of the time. Our recognition of China's "special position" in Tibet developed from the outdated concept of suzerainty. Some have used this to cast doubt on the aims we are pursuing and to claim that we are denying Chinese sovereignty over a large part of its own territory. We have made clear to the Chinese Government, and publicly, that we do not support Tibetan independence. Like every other EU member state, and the United States, we regard Tibet as part of the People's Republic of China.

Until 2008 the British Government's position remained the same, that China held suzerainty over Tibet, which might imply full or less-than-full sovereignty. It was the only state still to hold this view. David Miliband, then the British Foreign Secretary, described the old position as an anachronism originating in the geopolitics of the early 20th century. Britain re-repackaged its view on 29 October 2008, when it recognised Chinese sovereignty over Tibet unambiguously by issuing a statement on its website. The Economist stated that although the British Foreign Office's website does not use the word sovereignty, officials at the Foreign Office said "it means that, as far as Britain is concerned, 'Tibet is part of China. Full stop.'"

The British Government sees their new stance as an updating of their position, while some others have viewed it as a major shift in the British position. Tibetologist Robert Barnett thinks that the decision has wider implications. India's claim to a part of its northeast territories, for example, is largely based on the same agreements — notes exchanged during the Simla convention of 1914, which set the boundary between India and Tibet — that the British appear to have just discarded. It has been speculated that Britain's shift was made in exchange for China making greater contributions to the International Monetary Fund.

However, as related by a pro-Tibet-independent website Britain has not changed its position at all, and had deprived Tibet's right to independence in 1959 at the United Nations. Secretary Milliband's statement was merely a "re-assemblage of its former position on Tibet".

Britain has not suddenly taken a unilateral action to decide upon now recognising Tibet as being part of communist China. It is reasserting its position within a collective European framework, and even then Miliband employs a term ('regard'), no doubt chosen with minute attention to diplomatic meaning by his Foreign Offices advisers, that implies a previously held position, whilst leaving space for interpretation and manoeuvre, as opposed to 'recognize' which defines a more legal and final acceptance. Tibetologist Melvyn C. Goldstein also says that a 1943 British official letter "reconfirmed that Britain considered Tibet as part of China."

Actually, Britain has explicitly "recognized" Chinese "sovereignty" over Tibet. In 1999 when Chinese President Jiang Zemin visited Britain, the spokesman for British Prime Minister Tony Blair stated clearly and unambiguously that, "They [i.e. the Chinese] are well aware of our position on Tibet. We do recognize their sovereignty over it."

On 1 April 2009, the French Government reaffirmed its position on the Tibet issue:

France fully appreciates the importance and sensitivity of the Tibet issue and reaffirms her adherence to the One China Policy and her position that Tibet is an integral part of Chinese territory, in conformity with the decision taken by General de Gaulle which has not changed and will not change. With this in mind and with due regard for the principle of non-interference, France objects to all support for Tibet's independence in any form whatsoever.

This lack of legal recognition of independence has forced even some strong supporters of the refugees to admit that:

...even today international legal experts sympathetic to the Dalai Lama's cause find it difficult to argue that Tibet ever technically established its independence of the Chinese Empire, imperial, or republican.

On the other hand, in 1959 and 1960, the International Commission of Jurists evaluated in its studies the status of Tibet in international law:

The Commission feels that although, due to its peculiar history and local conditions, the international position of Tibet is difficult to appraise it is clear that Tibet has been to all intents and purposes an independent country and has enjoyed a large degree of sovereignty. Tibet demonstrated from 1913 to 1950 the conditions of statehood as generally accepted under international law.

The Permanent Peoples' Tribunal, gathered in Strasbourg to examine testimonies and arguments in November 1992, concluded that the Tibetans meet the legal criteria, generally accepted, of "a people" having the right of self-determination and "are therefore entitled to exercise the right to self- determination." The Tribunal concluded also that "the presence of the Chinese administration on Tibetan territory must be considered as foreign domination of the Tibetan people." The Tribunal also concluded that "the Tibetan people have from 1950 been, continuously, deprived of their right to self-determination."

In January 1993, in London, a conference gathered 30 eminent international lawyers from many countries to consider issues of the right of self-determination of the Tibetan people. At the issue of their work, the participants concluded in a written statement that: Under international law the Tibetan people are entitled to the right to self-determination, that this right belongs to the Tibetan people and that it is not for the state apparatus of the PRC, or any other nation or state, to deny the Tibetan people's right to self-determination.

Since the military action of 1949-50, Tibet has been under the alien occupation and domination of the PRC and has been administered with the characteristics of an oppressive colonial administration. In the particular case of Tibet and having regard to its long history of separate existence, the Tibetan people's claim to self-determination, including independence, is compatible with the principles of national unity and territorial integrity of states.

Another view supported by a number of international groups, including the Free Tibet Campaign, is that Tibet should be granted total independence from China. Passage of Tibetan Refugees throughout Nepal

According to different estimates, between 2500 and more than 3000 Tibetans cross the border into Nepal each year, typically in transportation to Tibetan exile communities in India. Because of pressure from China, Nepal no longer recognizes newly arriving Tibetans as refugees or permits them to remain in Nepal. Shree Kant Regmi, Secretary of the Ministry of Home Affairs, emphasized that to "recognize" Tibetan refugees or extend them political asylum would implicitly validate the claim that China commits human rights violations in Tibet:

It is the established policy of the [Nepalese] government that Tibet is the integral part of China, and [China] is our good neighbor. We have very good neighbouring relations with China. We don't think there are human rights violations [in Tibet]....If we allow asylum to Tibetan refugees, that is another way to say that [the Chinese government] is violating human rights in Tibet; and I say that there [are] no human rights violations in Tibet. Michel Dupoizat, UNHCR Representative in Kathmandu, similarly remarked that for Nepal to acknowledge Tibetans as "refugees" would be an intolerable "political" statement in the view of the Chinese government. For this reason, Tibetans entering Nepal without legal documentation after 1989 are in theory deemed illegal aliens subject to detention and deportation under section nine of the Immigration Act.

Despite the formal state of and, even more tacitly, with the Tibetan government-in-exile's office in Kathmandu. This agreement remains "in force" to date. In theory, it governs the procedures for the transit *through* Nepal of newly arriving Nepalese refugees; it does not contemplate or permit the resettlement of Tibetan refugees in Nepal. "There is no formal arrangement," said Director-General of Immigration Mainali, "but only an explicit policy with an under-standing with the [Nepalese] government and UNHCR."

TO THE TIBETAN GOVERNMENT-IN-EXILE

The Tibetan government-in-exile should be acknowledged and commanded for its efforts to provide for the security and welfare of the Tibetan community in exile, to preserve the Tibetan identity and cultural heritage of its people, and for its continuing work to ensure the safety of Tibetans fleeing persecution.

- Concerning newly arriving Tibetans, emphasize to the Nepalese government that it is the Tibetan government-in-exile's policy to facilitate the transit of Tibetan refugees through Nepal, not to facilitate their illegal resettlement in Nepal.
- Clarify to the Tibetan community in exile that the Tibetan government-in-exile does not seek to discourage Tibetans in exile from obtaining citizenship in other countries.
- Encourage collaboration between Tibetan organizations and Nepalese non-governmental organizations to address issues of mutual concern and to promote closer relations between the Tibetan and Nepalese peoples.

To Non-Governmental Organizations (NGOs):

- Urge the Nepalese government immediately to cease the practice of *refoulement* of Tibetan refugees; to halt the imprisonment of Tibetans seeking voluntarily to return to Tibet through Nepal; to ratify the Refugee Conventions; and to guarantee Tibetan residents their civil and political rights, including meaningful access to citizenship.

- Collaborate with the Tibetan Welfare Office and Tibetan NGOs to address issues of mutual concern.
- Offer technical assistance and personnel resources to UNHCR, the Nepalese government, and the Tibetan Welfare Office to assist them to, *inter alia,* register resident Tibetans, assist with border missions, and monitor compliance with the gentleman's agreement.
- Work with foreign governments to promote and facilitate the resettlement of Tibetan refugees in third countries.

Methodology

This report documents the conclusions of a fact-finding mission carried out by Tibet Justice Centre in cooperation with Yale Law School's Allard K. Lowenstein International Human Rights Law Clinic. Following preparatory legal and factual research in Spring 2001, Tibet Justice Centre conducted field research in Nepal from May 18 to June 14, 2001.

The mission had two principal objectives: *first,* to ascertain the legal status, rights, and treatment of Tibetans residing—whether permanently or temporarily—in Nepal; and *second,* to investigate Nepal's compliance with the "gentleman's agreement," an informal arrangement in place since 1990 that permits newly arriving Tibetan refugees to transit through Nepal. In the course of this research, Tibet Justice Centre also documented and gathered information about related issues including freedom of cultural expression for Tibetans in Nepal; the issuance of refugee identity cards and inter-national travel documents to Tibetans residing legally in Nepal; allegations of Nepalese police abuses against newly arriving Tibetan refugees; the effect of the Maoist insurgency on Nepal's ability to comply with the gentleman's agreement; and the relationship between the Nepalese people and the substantial Tibetan refugee population—estimated at roughly 20,000—that resides in Nepal.

To gather information on these issues, Tibet Justice Centre conducted interviews with Nepalese government officials, the Nepal country representative of the United Nations High Commissioner for Refugees (UNHCR) in Kathmandu and other

UNHCR staff, representatives of non-governmental organizations (NGOs), both within and outside of the Tibetan community, journalists, police, Nepalese citizens, Tibetans residing (with and without formal legal status) in Nepal, and newly arrived Tibetan refugees in transit to Tibetan exile settlements, monasteries, and schools in India.

Tibet Justice Centre's research included thirty-four interviews with newly arrived refugees at the Tibetan Refugee Reception Centre in Swayambunath, Kathmandu; thirty-eight interviews with residents at the Tibetan settlements of Jawalakhel, Tashi Ling, Paljorling, and Tashi Palkhiel; interviews with Sherpas and Nepalese police in Thame and Khunde, villages in northeastern Nepal situated along the route traversed by many Tibetans after crossing the Tibeto-Nepalese border at the Nangpa-la pass; interviews with Nepalese government officials including (a) Shree Kant Regmi, Secretary, Ministry of Home Affairs; (b) Chakra Prasad Bastola, Minister, Ministry of Foreign Affairs; (c) Udaya Nepali Shrestha, Secretary, Ministry of Law and Justice; (d) Ganesh Dhakal, Undersecretary, Ministry of Home Affairs; (e) Umesh Prasad Mainali, Director-General, Department of Immigration; and (f) Kapil Shrestha, Secretary, Nepal Human Rights Commission.

As this report goes to press, some of the individuals interviewed by Tibet Justice Centre no longer hold the official positions that they occupied during the period of research.

But news reports and evidence gathered subsequent to the mission suggest that the findings presented in this report continue accurately to reflect Nepal's policies and practices toward Tibetan refugees.

Tibet Justice Centre worked principally in Kathmandu and sur-rounding areas, but also conducted research at Tibetan settlements in Pokhara and in Solu Khumbu, the northeastern region of Nepal through which many newly arriving Tibetan refugees pass in the course of their escape from Tibet.

At the Reception Centre, Tibet Justice Centre elicited information about the flight of refugees from Tibet; the difficulties they encountered on their journey; and their interactions with

Chinese and Nepalese authorities, local Nepalese citizens, and UNHCR staff. The interviews did not inquire into the reasons for Tibetan refugees' flight except insofar as this clarified questions concerning the border control and flight issues central to the objectives of Tibet Justice Centre's research.

At the settlements, interviews focused primarily on the rights and status of Tibetans resettled permanently in Nepal as a result of their arrival before 1989. Many of these individuals have resided in Nepal since the 1960s and 70s, at which time the Nepalese government resettled the first wave of Tibetan refugees, most of whom arrived in the after-math of the 1959 Lhasa Uprising. The vast majority of the other permanent residents at the settlements are their children.

9

Chinese Rule in Tibetan Administrative and Religious Systems

These administrative and religious systems were substantially overthrown by the arrival of Chinese forces in the 1950s. Initially there was little change but an uprising in eastern Tibet in 1956 led to a tightening of Chinese rule and, eventually, to the flight into exile of the Dalai Lama in 1959. In Amdo the people refer to 1958 as the date when the Chinese 'came' to the region, when they crushed final resistance and began to exercise a close control over the pastoralists' economic and religious affairs. Over a number of years they were organised into groups for collective herding, all the livestock and its produce being taken into state ownership. The older generations who lived through this period talk of the closure of the monasteries, the persecution of the monks, many of whom were either imprisoned or forced to take wives, the battles during which hundreds of Tibetans perished and the hunger they endured during the collective period. The Cultural Revolution, which began in 1966, saw the most consistent persecution of former leaders and the elevation of those deemed to be from the poorest families into superior positions. One old woman told me that this had been a good time for her, but the vast majority of my informants shuddered at the deprivations they had endured.

After the death of Mao in 1976 a period of reforms swept through China, reaching the Tibetan plateau in the early 1980s.

The 'Household Responsibility System' was a policy introduced to try to promote economic development, which had singularly failed to occur under the collective system (Goldstein 1994: 98-99). The animals were returned to the private ownership of nomad families, being distributed according to family size, and along with this went infrastructure developments and land reforms. After a few years all restrictions on the sale and disposal of animals were removed and the nomads became almost fully autonomous again in their pastoral activities. At around the same time most of the monasteries were allowed to re-open and monks and senior *lamas* were released from gaol. The redistribution of livestock has done much to balance out what were previously great disparities in wealth. Formerly many families had no livestock and had to work as servants for the rich, although the class system, which saw aristocratic families elevated to a higher social status in central Tibet, did not extend into Amdo. Initially every family was given enough animals for subsistence, although imbalances are now reappearing.

For administrative purposes the authorities have divided the population into *xiang*, units of one to two thousand people. These have largely been mapped onto the previously existing *dewa*, in terms of both population and territory. There has, however, been some reorganisation of nomadic groups. In Machu county, where there are ten *xiang*, Ngulra, the largest *dewa*, has been divided into two *xiang* and two smaller *dewa* have been combined into one. A defunct horse-breeding station has also evolved into a new *xiang* of nomadic families, named Matang. The Tibetans still use the old names and regard Ngulra as a single *dewa*, but also recognise Matang as a new *dewa*. The *xiang* are governed, as far as the authorities are concerned, by representatives who join the Communist party. These are responsible for transmitting orders issued by the governmental authorities at county level, collecting taxes, organising livestock vaccinations, and so on. As far as the pastoralists are concerned, however, organisation within the *dewa* is undertaken by a council made up of the *gowa* of the *repkor* (*ru skor*), the smaller groups into which each *dewa* is organised. The *repkor* consist of thirty or forty tents, that is around two hundred people, and they often have an identity which pre-dates the Chinese occupation. Their *gowa* are selected in the *repkor* meeting, normally holding office for a number of years. It is two or three of these who are put forward as *xiang* leaders to the authorities (and they have to join the Communist party in order to take up their appointments) but within the *dewa* they are not regarded as having any particular authority. The council, as a whole, takes the place of the *gowa* formerly sent by the monastery or supplied by a hereditary ruling family. Their tasks involve making arrangements for the visit of senior *lamas*, dealing with government authorities and dealing with the 'problems' that arise in the *dewa*, by which they mean cases of theft and conflict. Chinese rule has, thus, resulted in a certain (unintended) democratisation of *dewa* organisation. The position is rather more complex in Golok, where the tribes formerly made up a larger confederacy. Here I found that local control over the leadership of the *xiang* is much less strong and there is no reference to *repkor* (as also noted by Levine, n.d.). My informants insisted that the new leaders are government appointees, rather than their own *gowa*, here known as *xhombo* (*dpon po*). Given the previously strong leadership of the larger tribal groups here the *repkor* were, in any event, probably of less significance, while members of the old ruling families were systematically persecuted and imprisoned during the Cultural Revolution. Now the *xhombo* just do the work of mediators, they told me, but former tribal loyalties are still strong and emerge at times of conflict. Moreover, the *xhombo* still play a crucial role as respected and effective mediators.

Significant material changes introduced by the government have been the establishment of new towns and the construction of a network of roads, a programme which has received new impetus with Jiang Zemin's 'Develop the West' campaign initiated in 1999. These have resulted in major material improvements in nomadic life, as they bring trading points and markets for food and household goods within easy reach of most families. Most nomadic movements can now be conducted by truck, which has significantly eased this laborious process. Schools, health care, post offices and telephones are readily available in the towns and the headman of the group I stayed with in Machu described his plans to improve the educational possibilities for the children by asking the local authorities for assistance with accommodation in town. Many educated Tibetans are able to get salaried employment there, within government offices or the police force, as teachers, medical assistants and so on. Indeed, many of the local government officials are now Tibetans, although the higher level regional administrators are still predominantly Han Chinese. In many ways, therefore, the pastoralists have come to accept the norms of modernity: they value education and respect those who obtain positions as teachers or in government. They have adopted new standards of dress, cleanliness and material wealth and are taking advantage of new economic opportunities.

The authorities exercise strict control in many areas of nomad life, however. As well as levying animal taxes, they oblige the nomads to vaccinate their animals, a process that the pastoralists regard with suspicion and resentment, not least because they have to pay for vaccines they regard as useless.

They also enforce a population control policy, requiring women to undergo sterilisation after their third child. My informants were never very clear about what sanctions the authorities would impose for non-compliance: 'they force the women to have the operation', they said, giving the impression that physical coercion was employed at times. The imposition of heavy fines on a family was also mentioned. This policy is deeply resented and some families evade these rules by giving a child to a relative with a smaller family, but most of the women of child-bearing age that I knew about had the operation, or were resigned to having it when the time came.

Most controversially, the authorities are implementing a policy of fencing the pastureland, as part of the official regulation of pastoral practices, designed to promote ecological sustainability through private land ownership (Goldstein 1996: 12). Land is now officially held by individual families on 50-year leases (Banks et al. 2001), but the authorities have also made it a requirement that the nomads should erect fences between their individual plots, instead of letting their livestock graze together with others in their encampment, as they would prefer. This is much resented by the pastoralists who complain that they can no longer 'go anywhere' with their animals. Boundaries mean possession of land and scope for disputes between neighbouring groups and have been implicated in recent instances of violent conflict . Some groups are able to evade these requirements by erecting temporary fences which make it look as if the pastureland has been divided. However most are resigned to the fact that sooner or later permanent fences will have to be erected. The view of my educated informants in Machu is that this is part of the government's attempts to pin down and control the mobile and elusive pastoralists. These are cases in which the government's actions are consciously resisted, although the scope for evasion is very limited. New sets of norms have, therefore, been introduced, some of which are resisted, others accepted. Very new structures of power and control have also been established, but without entirely undermining older forms of authority.

MODERN ADMINISTRATIVE SYSTEM

Relations between dewa

While the former *dewa* have been substantially recreated as *xiang* under the modern administrative system, the new boundaries and fencing policies have not allowed the pastoralists to revert fully to their formerly flexible land tenure arrangements. A whole *repkor* used to move as a single body, its pasture being used as common property. Only the winter camping grounds were occupied by the same families on a recurrent basis, building winter shelters of a semi-permanent nature and harvesting a crop of oats as winter fodder. Yeh argues that there has been a significant increase in conflict amongst the Amdo nomads since the area's incorporation into the PRC, which can be traced to these territorial policies. They contradict old forms of socio-territorial identity, she says, precipitating boundary conflicts and giving rise to new forms of domination and resistance. There is much force in this but, as I have discussed elsewhere, the conflict she describes can largely be regarded as a continuation of former practices (Pirie 2005). The new territorial arrangements have occasioned new conflicts but the forms of retributive violence according to which they are played out represent a historic tradition, based on social norms which have persisted into the period of modern state control.

The Amdo Tibetans talk frequently and readily about both actual and potential violence and the men display self-consciously masculine qualities in their daily lives: most carry knives and the lead weighted ropes that they use to round up the animals are also potentially lethal weapons. They talk as if their neighbours are always just about to attack or steal from them and everyone could tell me stories of fighting and killings that had occurred within their families or villages within the last few years. One of the Ngulra *gowa*, for example, described a fight that had occurred between two men, one from Ngulra and one from the neighbouring *dewa* of Chocomama. The Chocomama man had been killed and men from his *dewa* came almost immediately to take revenge on two men of the killer's *repkor*. The *gowa* told me that they had come right into the encampment to attack the people and this had made the men of Ngulra 'angry' and determined, as a body, to retaliate. A number of men explained to me that they 'have' to get angry if a member of their family has been killed and they must take revenge on a member of the murderer's family. In the event of a serious theft of livestock it is also expected that men of the victim's tent will get angry. Although they may be restrained from initiating a fight, if they happen to meet a member of the thief's family, they would 'have' to fight him.

When a conflict occurs within one *dewa*, or two neighbouring *repkor* who normally maintain good relations, procedures for resolving it are relatively informal. Mediation is carried out by the *gowa* and there is considerable social pressure on the disputants to agree to a settlement. When 30 sheep were stolen from the tent in which I stayed, for example, the elder son, Jamku, went, with some friends, to identify the thief, on the basis of divination clues given by a monk. When they found him, in another *dewa*, Jamku declared his intention to fight immediately, but his friends restrained him. On their return to the tent members of his family and relatives persuaded him to let the *gowa* intervene and to arrange a compensation payment. The whole matter was settled in this way over the course of a few weeks with an agreement to return the animals and make an additional apology payment. This recalls the informal processes of mediation, and 'community consensus' in favour of peace which took place in the 1930s and 40s (Ekvall 1968).

If Jamku had initiated a fight, however, the violence could have escalated to include his friends, family and, ultimately, the whole *dewa*. Once retaliatory killings have begun, such a feud can only be resolved through more elaborate procedures of mediation.

Injuries must be compensated for by payment for the value of the damage and death with blood money, *mnyö rtong* (*mi stong*). Acceptance indicates an agreement by the victim not to fight over the matter.

Conflict between persons or groups from different *dewa*s, which might easily result from a theft or a drunken fight in the county town, is always difficult to resolve, people told me. The process of mediation, in such cases, follows a set pattern and closely mirrors the accounts given by Ekvall for the pre-1958 period (Ekvall 1954, 1964, 1968).

Outsiders, such as monks, initially intervene to establish a temporary truce so the parties can talk. Then it is the task of the mediators, *zowa* (*gzu ba*), to carry out the mediation. These are likely to be the *gowa* from neighbouring *dewa* or senior monks from a local monastery.

A meeting is set up in a neutral place, now often the local town, with different groups in different rooms and the mediators acting as go-betweens. Their task, they told me, (and this is confirmed by Ekvall 1964) is not to determine the facts or apportion blame but to determine the appropriate level and nature of compensation. Blood money is calculated after the deaths of each side have been reckoned and set off against each other and depends on the identity of the victims and the nature of the killings.

A settlement may also involve apologies, other payments and offerings of religious books. In the case of the Ngulra-Chocomama fight, for example, Ngulra would not accept the normal blood money because men had been killed within their own encampment, but the case was settled by the intervention of a senior *lama*, who ordered a small, but symbolic, extra payment by way of apology. The mediators may also establish where boundaries should run, deciding on a just division of pastures depending on the local history of land use. Crucially, the mediators have to convince the parties that the proposed compensation takes into account all these relevant factors.

Mediation is seen as a difficult and not always successful undertaking. In Golok the *xhombo*, members of the former ruling families, have a special status and are often renowned for their oratorical skills.

Even here, however, the *lama*s are regularly appealed to in the most problematic cases. The most senior *lama*s at Labrang, Jamyang Zhepa and Khongtang (until his death in 2000), were very active, travelling throughout Amdo to settle major disputes. It was Khongtang who, as already mentioned, settled a long-running feud between two Golok tribes in the late 1990s, a conflict which had its roots in the period before 1958.

They are seen as able to resolve conflict that is beyond the capabilities of local mediators. Tibetans always tell the truth in front of them, my informants told me, and the *lama*s suggest just solutions, *jömdri* (*rgyu 'bras*), taking into account the history of the case. This was a very important concept and often attributed to the *lama*s' wisdom and knowledge of religious texts, history and precedent. The Tibetans always made the point to me that the *lama*s were successful because everyone 'believes in' and 'has faith in' them. They are seen as capable of persuading reluctant and obstinate parties by appealing to their own religious authority. In such cases, therefore, although a conflict may have been caused by a new pasture division, or occasioned by the availability of cheap alcohol in the new towns, the course of retaliation and mediation follow patterns already described by Ekvall.

Now, when there has been a killing or a serious fight, however, the police invariably get involved. Some pastoralists successfully elude their grasp but culprits are generally caught and punished. Some years ago, for example, some animals strayed from the family with whom I subsequently stayed onto the pastures of the neighbouring *repkor*. When one of the boys went to fetch them he was badly beaten by the neighbours. The result was a fight between men of the two *repkor*, during which one was killed by the boy's elder brother.

Revenge killings would almost certainly have been carried out had the *gowa* of the *dewa* not intervened collectively to secure a truce. In the mean time the boy's two elder brothers were arrested by the police and imprisoned. The younger was just held for a couple of months but the elder was incarcerated for eight years. Nevertheless, the mediators decided that their family should also pay blood money in an amount which amounted to more than the family's entire wealth and the whole *repkor* had to combine to raise the money. The mediators also decided that the family should be expelled from the area for three years, to remove them from contact with their neighbours. Following this, good relations were restored between the *repkor* and the family has now returned from exile without any lingering animosity.

The Chinese state system of criminal punishment is seen by the Tibetans, in such cases, as completely inadequate for achieving a final settlement to their disputes. 'They cannot produce just solutions they do not care about the history', my fieldwork assistant said dismissively. By treating violence and murder as crimes to be punished by the state, the police fail completely to engage with the nomads' norms of retaliation and compensation. Once fighting has erupted, the norms of retaliation rule supreme and the police, refusing to order compensation in accordance with these norms, are unable to settle them. This would, therefore, appear to be a case of resistance to Chinese authority..

RULE OF THE CHINESE COMMUNIST GOVERNMENT

The Chinese government claims for this time period are a matter of some controversy. For instance they claim to have "liberated the Tibetan serfs" but many Tibetans were nomads or owned their own land rent free, and for those who were under obligations, there is controversy about whether their status is similar to the European serf and how onerous the obligations were.

Also the system based on recognition of "reincarnated Lamas" meant that any children from any family (though mostly males) might become recognised as the religious and political leaders of the next generation. This unusual system of government has no analogy in the European system. There are other differences as well. Also starvation was common in China at the time, but was not common in Tibet. There are widely varying accounts of the effect of the takeover on welfare of Tibetans. See Serfdom in Tibet Controversy-Slavery, and Tibetan welfare after the Chinese takeover

In 1949, seeing that the Communists were gaining control of China, the Kashag expelled all Chinese connected with the Chinese government, over the protests of both the Kuomingtang and the Communists. The Chinese Communist government led by Mao Zedong which came to power in October lost little time in asserting a new Chinese presence in Tibet. In October 1950, the People's Liberation Army entered the Tibetan area of Chamdo, defeating sporadic resistance from the Tibetan army. In 1951, Tibetan representatives participated in negotiations in Beijing with the Chinese government. This resulted in a *Seventeen Point Agreement* which formalised China's sovereignty over Tibet.

From the beginning, it was obvious that incorporating Tibet into Communist China would bring two opposite social systems face-to-face. In Tibet, however, the Chinese Communists opted not to place social reform as an immediate priority. To the contrary, from 1951 to 1959, traditional Tibetan society with its lords and manorial estates continued to function unchanged. Despite the presence of twenty thousand PLA troops in Central Tibet, the Dalai Lama's government was permitted to maintain important symbols from its de facto independence period.

The Chinese quickly abolished slavery and serfdom in their traditional forms. They also claim to have reduced taxes, unemployment, and beggary, and to have started work projects. They established secular schools, thereby breaking the educational monopoly of the monasteries, and they constructed running water and electrical systems in Lhasa.

The Tibetan region of Eastern Kham, previously Xikang province, was incorporated in the province of Sichuan. Western

Kham was put under the Chamdo Military Committee. In these areas, land reform was implemented. This involved communist agitators designating "landlords" — sometimes arbitrarily chosen — for public humiliation in *thamzing* or "Struggle Sessions," torture, maiming, and even death.

By 1956 there was unrest in eastern Kham and Amdo, where land reform had been implemented in full. These rebellions eventually spread into western Kham and Ü-Tsang.

In 1956-57, armed Tibetan bands ambushed convoys of the Chinese Peoples Liberation Army. The uprising received extensive assistance from the U.S. Central Intelligence Agency (CIA), including military training, support camps in Nepal, and numerous airlifts. Meanwhile in the United States, the American Society for a Free Asia, a CIA-financed front, energetically publicized the cause of Tibetan resistance, with the Dalai Lama's eldest brother, Thubtan Norbu, playing an active role in that organization. The Dalai Lama's second-eldest brother, Gyalo Thondup, established an intelligence operation with the CIA as early as 1951. He later upgraded it into a CIA-trained guerrilla unit whose recruits parachuted back into Tibet.

Many Tibetan commandos and agents whom the CIA dropped into the country were chiefs of aristocratic clans or the sons of chiefs. Ninety percent of them were never heard from again, according to a report from the CIA itself, meaning they were most likely captured and killed. "Many lamas and lay members of the elite and much of the Tibetan army joined the uprising, but in the main the populace did not, assuring its failure," writes Hugh Deane. In their book on Tibet, Ginsburg and Mathos reach a similar conclusion: "As far as can be ascertained, the great bulk of the common people of Lhasa and of the adjoining countryside failed to join in the fighting against the Chinese both when it first began and as it progressed." Eventually the resistance crumbled.

In 1998, the Dalai Lama's organization itself issued a statement admitting that it had received millions of dollars from the CIA during the 1960s to send armed squads of exiles into Tibet to undermine the Maoist revolution. In 1959, China's military crackdown on rebels in Kham and Amdo led to the "Lhasa

Uprising." Full-scale resistance spread throughout Tibet. Fearing capture of the Dalai Lama, unarmed Tibetans surrounded his residence, and the Dalai Lama fled to India.

In 1965, the area that had been under the control of the Dalai Lama's government from the 1910s to 1959 (Ü-Tsang and western Kham) was renamed the Tibet Autonomous Region or TAR. Autonomy provided that the head of government would be an ethnic Tibetan; however, actual power in the TAR is held by the First Secretary of the Tibet Autonomous Regional Committee of the Chinese Communist Party, who has never been a Tibetan. The role of ethnic Tibetans in the higher levels of the TAR Communist Party remains very limited.

The destruction of most of Tibet's more than 6,000 monasteries occurred between 1959 and 1961. During the mid-1960s, the monastic estates were broken up and secular education introduced. During the Cultural Revolution, Red Guards inflicted a campaign of organized vandalism against cultural sites in the entire PRC, including Tibet's Buddhist heritage. According to at least one Chinese source, only a handful of the religiously or culturally most important monasteries remained without major damage, and thousands of Buddhist monks and nuns were killed, tortured or imprisoned.

In 1989, the Panchen Lama died of a massive heart attack at the age of 50. The PRC continues to portray its rule over Tibet as an unalloyed improvement, but a handful of foreign governments continue to make protests about aspects of PRC rule in Tibet as groups such as Human Rights Watch report alleged human rights violations. Most governments, however, recognize the PRC's sovereignty over Tibet today, and none have recognized the Government of Tibet in Exile in India.

Riots flared up again in 2008. Many ethnic Hans and Huis were attacked in the riot, their shops vandalized or burned. The Chinese government reacted swiftly, imposing curfews and strictly limiting access to Tibetan areas. The international response was likewise immediate and robust, with some leaders condemning the crackdown and large protests and some in support of China's actions.

Tibetans in Exile

Following the Lhasa uprising and the Dalai Lama's flight from Tibet in 1959, the government of India accepted the Tibetan refugees. India designated land for the refugees in the mountainous region of Dharamsala, India, where the Dalai Lama and the Tibetan government-in-exile are now based. The plight of the Tibetan refugees garnered international attention when the Dalai Lama, spiritual and religious leader of the Tibetan government in exile, won the Nobel Peace Prize in 1989. The Dalai Lama was awarded the Nobel Prize on the basis of his unswerving commitment to peaceful protest against the Chinese occupation of Tibet. He is highly regarded as a result and has since been received by government leaders throughout the world. Among the most recent ceremonies and awards, he was given the Congressional Gold Medal by President Bush in 2007, and in 2006 he was one of only five people to ever receive an honorary Canadian citizenship. The PRC consistently protests each official contact with the exiled Tibetan leader.

The community of Tibetans in exile established in Dharamsala and Karnataka, South India, has expanded since 1959. Tibetans have duplicated Tibetan monasteries in India and these now house tens of thousands of monks. They have also created Tibetan schools and hospitals, and founded the Library of Tibetan Works and Archives — all aimed at continuing Tibetan tradition and culture. Tibetan festivals such as Lama dances, celebration of Losar (the Tibetan New Year), and the Monlam Prayer Festival, continue in exile.

In 2006, Tenzin Gyatso, the 14th Dalai Lama declared that "Tibet wants autonomy, not independence." However, the Chinese distrust him, believing that he has not really given up the quest for Tibetan independence.

Talks between representatives of the Dalai Lama and the Chinese government began again in May, 2008 with little result.

THE INVASION AND ILLEGAL ANNEXATION OF TIBET

Treaties in international law are binding on the countries signing them, unless they are imposed by force or a country is coerced into signing the agreement by the threat of force. This is reflected in the Vienna Convention on the Law of Treaties, which is regarded as a reflection of customary international law.

The People's Republic of China (PRC) feels strongly about this principle, particularly as it applies to treaties and other agreements China was pressured to sign by Western powers at a time when China was weak. The PRC is particularly adamant that such "unequal" treaties and other agreements cannot be valid, no matter who signed them or for what reasons.

After the military invasion of Tibet had started and the small Tibetan army was defeated, the PRC imposed a treaty on the Tibetan Government under the terms of which Tibet was declared to be a part of China, albeit enjoying a large degree of autonomy. In the White Paper, China claims this treaty was entered into entirely voluntarily by the Tibetan Government, and that the Dalai Lama, his Government and the Tibetan people as a whole welcomed it.

The facts show a very different story, leading to the conclusion that the so-called "Seventeen-Point Agreement on Measures for the Peaceful Liberation of Tibet" was never validly concluded and was rejected by Tibetans. The Dalai Lama writes that the Tibetan Prime Minister, Lukhangwa, told Chinese General Zhang Jinwu in 1952: "It was absurd to refer to the terms of the Seventeen-Point Agreement. Our people did not accept the agreement and the Chinese themselves had repeatedly broken the terms of it. Their army was still in occupation of eastern Tibet; the area had not been returned to the government of Tibet, as it should have been."

Diplomatic activity and military threats

Soon after the Communist victory over the Guomindang and the founding of the PRC on October 1, 1949, Radio Beijing began to announce that "the People's Liberation Army must liberate all Chinese territories, including Tibet, Xinjiang, Hainan and Taiwan". Partly in response to this threat, and in order to resolve long-standing border disputes with China, the Foreign Office of the Tibetan Government, on November 2, 1949, wrote to Mao Zedong proposing negotiations to settle all territorial disputes. Copies of this letter were sent to the governments of India, Great Britain and the United States. Although these three governments considered the spread of Communism to be a threat to the stability of South Asia, they advised the Tibetan Government to enter into direct negotiations with the Chinese Government as any other course of action might provoke military retaliation.

The Tibetan Government decided to send two senior officials, Tsepon Shakabpa and Tsechag Thubten Gyalpo, to negotiate with representatives of the PRC in a third country, possibly the USSR, Singapore or Hong Kong. These officials were to take up with the Chinese Government the content of the Tibetan Foreign Office's letter to Chairman Mao Zedong and the threatening Chinese radio announcements still being made about an imminent "liberation of Tibet"; they were to secure an assurance that the territorial integrity of Tibet would not be violated and to state that Tibet would not tolerate interference.

When the Tibetan delegates applied for visas to Hong Kong in Delhi, the Chinese told them that the new Chinese Ambassador to India was due to arrive in the capital shortly and that negotiations should be opened through him.

In the course of negotiations, the Chinese Ambassador, Yuan Zhong Xian, demanded that the Tibetan delegation accept a Two-point Proposal: i) Tibetan national defence will be handled by China; and ii) Tibet should be recognized as a part of China. They were then to proceed to China in confirmation of the agreement. On being informed of the Chinese demands, the Tibetan Government instructed its delegates to reject the proposal. So negotiations were suspended.

On October 7, 1950, 40,000 Chinese troops under Political Commissar, Wang Qiemi, attacked Eastern Tibet's provincial capital, Chamdo, from eight directions. The small Tibetan force, consisting of 8,000 troops and militia, was defeated. After two days, Chamdo was taken and Kalon (Minister) Ngapo Ngawang Jigme, the Regional Governor, was captured. Over 4,000 Tibetan fighters were killed.

The Chinese aggression came as a rude shock to India. In a sharp note to Beijing on October 26, 1950, the Indian Foreign

Ministry wrote: "Now that the invasion of Tibet has been ordered by Chinese government, peaceful negotiations can hardly be synchronized with it and there naturally will be fear on the part of Tibetans that negotiations will be under duress. In the present context of world events, invasion by Chinese troops of Tibet cannot but be regarded as deplorable and in the considered judgement of the Government of India, not in the interest of China or peace." A number of countries, including the United States and Britain, expressed their support for the Indian position.

The Tibetan National Assembly convened an emergency session in November 1950 at which it requested the Dalai Lama, only fifteen at that time, to assume full authority as Head of State. The Dalai Lama was then requested to leave Lhasa for Dromo (Yatung), near the Indian border, so that he would be out of personal danger. At the same time the Tibetan Foreign Office issued the following statement: "Tibet is united as one man behind the Dalai Lama who has taken over full powers... We have appealed to the world for peaceful intervention in (the face of this) clear case of unprovoked aggression."

The Tibetan Government also wrote to the Secretary General of the United Nations on November 7, 1950, appealing for the world body's intervention.

The letter said, in part: "Tibet recognizes that it is in no position to resist the Chinese advance. It is thus that it agreed to negotiate on friendly terms with the Chinese Government...Though there is little hope that a nation dedicated to peace will be able to resist the brutal effort of men trained to war, we understand that the United Nations has decided to stop aggression wherever it takes place."

On November 17, 1950, El Salvador formally asked that the aggression against Tibet be put on the General Assembly agenda. However, the issue was not discussed in the UN General Assembly at the suggestion of the Indian delegation which asserted that a peaceful solution which was mutually advantageous to Tibet, India and China could be reached between the parties concerned. A second letter by the Tibetan delegation to the United Nations on December 8, 1950 did not change the situation.

Faced with the military occupation of Eastern and Northern Tibet, the defeat and destruction of its small army, the advance of tens of thousands of more PLA troops towards Central Tibet, and the lack of active support from the international community, the Dalai Lama and the Tibetan Government decided to send a delegation to Beijing for negotiations with the new Chinese leadership.

TIBET & THE DALAI LAMA UNDER CHINESE COMMUNIST PARTY RULE

From 1913 until Chinese annexation in 1950, Tibet was a de facto independent polity that controlled its own affairs. However, Tibetan elites failed to enact meaningful reforms that might have protected Tibet from external aggression. The Dalai Lama was only fourteen years old when the Chinese Communists came to power in 1949; Tibetan governmental authority was thus in the hands of his regent and the cabinet of ministers.

Historically, Tibet as a political entity was weaker when a regent ruled the country. Not all of the ruling elites agreed with the need to reform the political and economic landscape of Tibet, and the monastic elites were against any changes that would inhibit their leverage over the populace. Moreover, the Tibetan army was small, weak, and had few modern weapons.

Like the Qing and the Kuomintang rulers before them, Chinese Communist Party (CCP) leaders saw Tibet as an unalienable part of Chinese territory.

The annexation of Tibet was therefore less about liberating oppressed serfs and more about reclaiming "lost" territory that previous regimes had failed to control. CCP Chairman Mao Zedong realized that the "best strategy was to 'liberate' Tibet peacefully, i.e., with the agreement of the government of Tibet… [yet] military action would be needed to force Tibet to the negotiating table." Therefore, the PLA's 18th army attacked Chamdo, a location in Eastern Tibet, on 7 October 1950. The 10,000 weak troops stationed there could not withstand a Chinese attack. The Tibetan leadership thus decided to negotiate directly with the Chinese to avoid a full-scale invasion of the capital.

On 23 May 1951, Tibetan representatives signed the Seventeen-Point Agreement, which cited foreign imperialism as the root cause of Tibet's claims for independence. The agreement forced Tibetan leaders to formally acknowledge that Tibet was an integral part of China and must therefore accept Chinese rule. However, the agreement also stipulated that Tibet would maintain its "local" government until the people were willing to initiate socialist reforms.

During the first decade of Chinese involvement in Lhasa, the Chinese Government moved deliberately to introduce institutions and mechanisms that would allow it to eventually consolidate its rule and strengthen its legitimacy. However, Tibetans continued to view the Dalai Lama and the traditional Tibetan elites as the legitimate rulers of Tibet, and the Communists faced a great deal of resistance from both the traditional power structure and also many sectors of society in implementing basic reforms.

On 9 March 1955, the Communist authorities formed the Preparatory Committee for the Autonomous Region of Tibet (PCART). Beijing defined PCART as "an authoritative body for consultation and planning during the transitional period before the establishment of the Autonomous Region of Tibet." It was meant to lay the groundwork for future "democratic reforms" in a manner that would gain the support of the Tibetan people. The Tibetan elites continued to ostensibly rule Tibet, but the Chinese began to gain more and more power behind the scenes. A sizeable PLA garrison was also established in Lhasa, serving as the home for both the political and military CCP leadership.

Meanwhile, the Chinese Government had already commenced agricultural reforms in eastern Tibetan areas that had been incorporated into other provinces of China. The Party Secretary of Sichuan initiated Chinese "democratic" reforms in Tibetan areas of the province in late 1955. These reforms disrupted the Tibetan way of life to such an extent that a large-scale revolt erupted across eastern Tibet. Thousands of refugees from eastern Tibet poured into Lhasa and set up camp near the Dalai Lama's Potala Palace, bringing with them grim stories about the impact of the Chinese reforms.

The conditions throughout central Tibet also declined dramatically during this time. Chinese hard-liners argued that it was the responsibility of the CCP to implement reforms more quickly to destroy what they saw as the feudalistic and backwards practices of Tibetans. Mao Zedong was reportedly alarmed by the growing unrest in Tibetan areas and personally guaranteed the Dalai Lama that the Chinese would not implement any policy of land reform in Tibet for at least six years. However, the Dalai Lama could not control growing anti-Chinese sentiment in Tibet.

On 10 March 1959, amid rumors that the PLA intended to kidnap or assassinate the Dalai Lama if he attended a theatrical performance at the military garrison, Tibetans attempted to block PLA movements in the streets of Lhasa and clashed with Chinese soldiers. The situation on the streets of Lhasa grew increasingly tense and negotiations between the Tibetan and CCP leaders in Lhasa broke down in acrimony. On 17 March 1959, the Dalai Lama fled Lhasa to seek asylum in India, where he renounced the Seventeen-Point Agreement and attempted to garner support for Tibetan independence.

The leadership vacuum created by the revolt and exodus of many officials to India subsequently meant that the CCP no longer saw it necessary to focus on gaining the support of Tibetan elites. The period of quasi-self-rule in Tibet was over; PCART was formally designated as the regional government of Tibet, and the Chinese bestowed new posts upon Tibetan elites who had not participated in the uprising or fled. The Panchen Lama had remained in China, and the CCP appointed him Chairman of PCART. However, it was actually the PLA Military Control Committee that held power in Tibet. In September 1965, the PCART was officially transformed into the Tibet Autonomous Region.

During the disastrous Great Leap Forward from 1959-1962, Tibetans suffered from widespread famine and starvation. Radical political reforms were also set in motion. Likewise, the 1966-1976 Great Proletarian Cultural Revolution (GPCR) was a devastating and traumatic experience for Tibetans. In China proper, one could view the Cultural Revolution largely as an attack on authority, whereby the proletariat and Mao's Red Guards struggled against any "reactionaries" within the CCP who betrayed the cause of socialism by embarking upon a "capitalist road." In Tibet, the Cultural Revolution was perceived as nothing less than a full-scale attack upon the core of Tibetan culture and religion.

Red Guards destroyed religious artifacts and buildings; forcibly disrobed monks and nuns from monasteries across Tibet; and prohibited the people from engaging in many traditional religious practices. At the end of the Cultural Revolution, there were reportedly fewer than 1,000 monks in the eight functioning monasteries (out of an estimated 6,000 monasteries before 1949) that had not been destroyed. The physical, intellectual and spiritual foundations of Tibetan Buddhism were decimated.

Following Mao's death in 1976, Chinese policy in Tibet pulled back from these excesses. The Chinese Government appointed Ulanfu, a Mongol and the only ethnic minority in China to hold a senior position in the Party, as head of the United Front in July 1977. His selection as director indicated that the CCP was reverting to policies that displayed greater leniency towards minority peoples.

In May 1977, high-ranking ethnic Tibetan CCP official Ngawang Jigme announced that the Dalai Lama was welcome to return to Tibet as long as he eschewed separatism and did not otherwise act to destabilize the socialist regime in Tibet. By 1978, Deng Xiaoping had consolidated his power and launched the beginning of the Reform Era. The regime also started to rehabilitate religious leaders, such as the Panchen Lama.

Beijing invited a delegation representing the Dalai Lama to observe conditions in Tibet towards the end of 1979. At this point, many of the more liberal policies implemented at the centre had not yet trickled down into Tibet, and the population was still feeling the effects of Maoist policies. As the delegation toured through ethnographic Tibet, it received a sincere and fervent response from the people. The Communist Party apparently was shocked that twenty years after the Dalai Lama had fled to India, he was still revered as a symbol of Tibetan pride and nationalism despite all attempts to subvert and destroy socio-political system of traditional Tibet.

The CCP held a special work forum on the future of Tibet in April 1980 to assess its policy toward the TAR. The conference report noted: "We have been established for thirty years. Now the international situation is very complicated. If we do not seize the moment and immediately improve the relationship between the nationalities, we will make a serious mistake."

In order to emphasize that the Party was serious about implementing reforms in Tibet, CCP General Secretary Hu Yaobang arrived in Lhasa on 22 May 1980, intentionally chosen to coincide with the anniversary of the historic signing of the Seventeen-Point Agreement.

Hu bluntly admitted that the Communist Party had failed the Tibetan people, and promised to promote liberal reforms in the TAR as the renewed basis for Chinese legitimacy in Tibet. Following Hu Yaobang's trip, the CCP loosened strictures on religious practice in the TAR, perhaps hoping to allow Tibetans to express ethnic identity in a non-political fashion. While political dissent of any kind still was not tolerated, the early and mid-80s were a period of relative liberalization.

Overall, the relationship between the Chinese Government and Tibetans gradually improved during the Reform era, until a series of violent events shattered this relative calm. The Tibetan exile authorities in India had long been engaged in an effort to interest the international community in the plight of the Tibetan people, and by the mid-to-late 1980's this effort was finally beginning to bear fruit. Sensing an opening as economic reforms gathered steam and the Chinese leadership appeared increasingly open to the world, the Tibetans inaugurated an international campaign to leverage Western support for Tibet and pry additional concessions from Beijing. The new approach rapidly gained support in the United States. On 21 September 1987, the Dalai Lama spoke on Capitol Hill for the first time, at the invitation of the Congressional Human Rights Caucus, and articulated a five-point proposal for rectifying the Tibet issue.

These developments had an almost immediate effect on people inside Tibet. After a small monk-led protest in Lhasa on 27 September, thousands of Tibetans marched through the streets of

Lhasa on Chinese National Day and clashed with police. On March 1988, monks gathered in Lhasa for the Monlam religious festival and again launched protests that ended in violence. Protests continued throughout the year. By March 1989, as the thirtieth anniversary of the 1959 uprising approached, Lhasa was extremely tense and Chinese authorities retreated from their liberalized policies on cultural and religious expression. In a foreshadoing of events to come in Beijing, large scale protests in Lhasa on 10 March 1989 were violently put down by security forces using live fire on demonstrators; estimates of dead ranged from dozens to hundreds. Then-TAR Party Secretary Hu Jintao imposed martial law and imprisoned large numbers of monks and nuns.

HISTORICAL BACKGROUND AND ANALYSIS OF THE SELECTION PROCESS

The PRC and its predecessors in China have long struggled to maintain stability along its western periphery, where concentrated communities of ethnic and religious minorities reside. During the past four years, Beijing has been forced to contend with violent clashes between ethnically Turkic Uyghurs and Han migrants in Xinjiang; widespread protests by Tibetans throughout ethnographic Tibet (i.e. the present-day Tibet Autonomous Region and Tibetan areas of Qinghai, Gansu, Sichuan, and Yunnan provinces) that have at times flared into violence; andrecently, unprecedented protests by ethnic Mongols across the Inner Mongolian Autonomous Region.

Efforts to influence the selection of important Tibetan lamas have been a key element of the exercise and consolidation of political authority in Tibetan areas since the establishment of the theocratic state in Tibet, for both distant imperial authorities as well as Tibetans themselves. The history of theocratic rule in Tibet is intimately intertwined with Chinese imperial politics, with influence waxing and waning as empires rose and fell. At the time Tibet was incorporated into the Mongol Empire (and subsequently the Mongol-led Yuan Dynasty), imperial authorities cultivated lamas from the Sakya school of Tibetan Buddhism, which was pre-eminent in Tibet.

However, Tibet was rife with political and sectarian conflicts, into which both Mongol and Chinese imperial authorities often inserted themselves or were drawn by Tibetan parties. During the thirteenth and fourteenth centuries, the Gelukpa school rose to challenge the Sakya and Kagyu schools for political and religious leadership. After unseating the Sakya through alliance with a powerful secular Tibetan prince, the Geluk achieved an alliance with the Mongols and came to dominate political authority in Tibet. In 1578, the Mongol khan gave a senior Gelukpa monk named Sonam Gyatso the title Dalai Lama. By this time, however, Mongol rulers had long ceased to govern China and there is substantial dispute among scholars regarding the exact nature of Tibetan relations with then-ruling Ming court, with most Western scholars contending that the Ming did not exercise sovereignty or actual control over Tibet.

As Manchu warriors conquered the crumbling Ming Empire (1368-1644) and consolidated their rule in China, the Gelukpa sect was likewise further consolidating power in Tibet. Scholars differ on the significance of early relations between the emerging Tibetan and Qing imperial powers (Qing Dynasty: 1644-1911), but during this period, Tibet was generally under direct lamaist rule with some element of Mongol protection. In 1642, the Mongol khanate ceremoniously bestowed the conquered Tibetan lands upon the Fifth Dalai Lama, but reserved the title of king of Tibet for himself and his successors until the last such ruler died in the early eighteenth century, at which point the Qing emperor assumed the role of designating or at least recognizing Tibetan spiritual leaders. In 1652, the Qing Emperor Shunzhi invited the Fifth Dalai Lama to Beijing for an official visit. Some scholars believe that a priest-patron relationship subsequently emerged, whereby the Qing Emperor sought the spiritual patronage of the Fifth Dalai Lama much as its Yuan predecessors had done. Following the Dalai Lama's visit, reports from the Imperial Colonial Office note that it liaised with the Dalai Lama in his capacity as "spiritual leader and temporal adjudicator of selected affairs among the populations of eastern Mongolia and Qinghai." The Qing court began to monitor and even attempted to direct the Dalai Lamas, with limited success.

By 1661, the Imperial Colonial Office considered itself to be supervising the selection process of key lamas. Nonetheless, the Qing court felt threatened by the Dzungar tribes of the northwest, whose influence had permeated Tibet by the early eighteenth century, and launched multiple attacks on Lhasa between 1718 and 1720, in the name of defeating the Dzungars. Some scholars argue that when Qing leaders subsequently established a military garrison as well as installed imperial commissioners (ambans) in Lhasa, they dissolved the monarchy and effectively stripped Tibet of its sovereignty.

However, other scholars maintain that "under the influence of the Qing dynasty, the Dalai Lama's nominal leadership of Tibet continued in name with various restrictions, including the creation of a short-lived Tibetan monarchal institution." Although acknowledging the presence of ambans in Lhasa, Gray Tuttle's extensive study of this period asserts that "Gelukpa prelates largely served as the actual rulers of Tibet, in the capacity of regents for a series of young Dalai Lamas who died before, or shortly after, they reached maturity." Qing historian Evelyn S. Rawski and others also assert that the imperial presence in Lhasa was initially more indirect. Only after the murder of two ambans, stemming from their involvement in a local political dispute, did the Qing emperor take greater notice of the situation in Lhasa in 1750. The Qing emperor responded with a dual strategy of enlarging the garrison in Lhasa while again recognizing the secular and religious authority of the Dalai Lama. Qianlong also established a council of ministers and instructed the ambans to monitor Tibetan affairs more closely. Nonetheless, Tibet scholar Melvyn Goldstein argues that from the time the protectorate was created in 1727, actual Qing authority over Tibet remained limited despite a lack of Tibetan cohesive internal unity. The Qianlong Emperor himself remarked in 1792 that the quality of ambans sent to Lhasa was quite poor, and it was thus relatively easy for the Dalai Lama and his ministers to ignore them.

The Manchu military intervention and subsequent attempt to gain greater influence may have represented the apex of Qing power in Tibet. Weary of Tibetan intrigues, in 1792, the Qianlong

Emperor called for a complete restructuring of the Tibetan government in a document called "Twenty-Nine Regulations for Better Government in Tibet." It included a lottery system to assist in the selection of key incarnations, whereby Manchu officials would place the names of the candidate(s) – provided by ecclesiastical authorities, and divined through traditional methods – into a golden urn. An amban drew lots from the urn and chose the name of the successful candidate. The Qing reportedly developed this practice to avert manipulation of the selection process by politically prominent Tibetan families, as the discovery of an incarnate lama in such a family could certainly enhance its standing and political fortunes. Likewise, the regulations forbade relatives of high-ranking incarnate lamas from aspiring to public office. The emperor continued efforts to raise the status of the ambans in Tibet in order to assert greater influence over administrative decisions and key appointments. However, internal unrest in China during the second half of the nineteenth century largely undermined the ability of his successors to influence Tibetan affairs.

From 1792 until the end of the Republican period in 1949, in practice the Tibetans infrequently used the golden urn to select important reincarnate lamas, especially during times when authorities in Beijing were unable to assert effective influence over Tibetan affairs. Even modern PRC historians admit that the use of the urn process was inconsistent to the point of being nearly discretionary. Chinese scholar Ya Hanzhang notes that Tibetan authorities sought and apparently received permission from Qing authorities to forgo the normal procedures when there was only a single undisputed candidate, as was the case with the Ninth (Lungtok Gyatso, recognized in 1807) and Thirteenth (Thupten Gyatso, recognized in 1877) Dalai Lamas. The Fourteenth Dalai Lama, for his part, asserts that the urn method was used for the selection of only one of his predecessors, the Eleventh, and that in other cases it was either not used at all or only after-the-fact to placate Manchu authorities. In short, there is considerable debate about the degree to which Tibetan authorities utilized the golden urn process out of a sense of imperial obligation, as a convenient means of settling difficult internal disputes, or some combination of the two.

At the turn of the twentieth century, British attempts to expand their influence beyond India and into Tibet led to an "activist, annexationist Chinese policy toward Tibet" whereby the Qing court again attempted to directly intervene in Tibetan affairs. While the Younghusband Expedition initially resulted in negotiations between Tibetan and British authorities, the British Foreign Office quickly pulled them back and acknowledged Chinese preeminence in Tibet via the 1906 Anglo-Chinese Convention. After the British withdrawal, the Thirteenth Dalai Lama travelled to Beijing to negotiate directly with the Qing emperor over his and Tibet's status. The Manchu court treated him as a subordinate, and instructed him to "obey the laws of the Sovereign State China.... [and] exhort the Tibetans to be obedient." The Chinese even arranged all of the Dalai Lama's meetings with foreign officials in Beijing. As Goldstein succinctly states, the Chinese made it clear that "he was subordinate to the emperor and that his position in Tibet was dependent on their goodwill."

The situation worsened when the Dalai Lama subsequently attempted to return to Lhasa. The Qing authorized General Zhao Erfeng, who was named an amban in 1908, to dispatch two thousand soldiers to Lhasa to control the Dalai Lama. Realizing that he faced grave danger, the Dalai Lama fled to Darjeeling, India in early 1910. The Chinese acted to strip him of not only his authority, but also his incarnate status. The Dalai Lama appealed to the Chinese to allow the British to act as intermediaries to negotiate a solution to the political crisis in Tibet. Yet, before such an arrangement could be undertaken, the Qing Dynasty collapsed, leaving China in chaos. Chinese troops stationed in Tibet withdrew and departed overland through India. The Dalai Lama arrived back in Lhasa in January 1913. This was the first time since the early eighteenth century there were no Chinese soldiers on Tibetan soil.

During the Republican Period (1911-1949), turmoil in China allowed Tibet to assert de-facto independence. During his time in India, the Thirteenth Dalai Lama had become friends with Sir Charles Bell, the political officer in Sikkim for British India. Bell shaped his thoughts on the importance of creating modern political institutions, a modern bureaucracy, and a modern army in Tibet. Upon his return to Lhasa, the Dalai Lama began to implement these new ideas on how to develop a modern Tibetan state. These modernization efforts were frequently frustrated by the conservative Tibetan political and ecclesiastical elements, however, and failed to materialize as hoped.

Yuan Shikai, the Republic of China's Provisional President, sent the Dalai Lama a letter in fall 1912 that invited him to take up his post as spiritual leader of Tibet and serve the fledgling Chinese state. In response, the Dalai Lama stated that he did not require Yuan's permission to return to power, and fully intended to assert his rule in Tibet. Coupled with a proclamation issued twenty-two days later, these statements arguably constitute a declaration of Tibetan independence. However, subsequent negotiations between the British, Chinese, and Tibetans resulted in the 1914 Simla Convention, which proclaimed Chinese 'suzerainty' – but not sovereignty – over Tibet. Following the close of negotiations, it became clear this arrangement satisfied neither the Republic of China (ROC), which claimed Tibet as an integral part of its territory, nor Tibet, which saw itself as an independent state. The ROC disagreed with Lhasa authorities on where to draw the borders of Tibet and finally refused to sign the accord. Britain and Tibet decided to sign a bilateral note based on the convention, leaving the actual convention unsigned by any party.

Generalissimo Chiang Kai-shek saw the death of the Thirteenth Dalai Lama in 1933 as an opportunity to reassert Chinese authority at the time of the selection of the next reincarnation. An official ROC policy document promulgated on 10 February 1936, entitled "Methods for the Reincarnation of Lamas," contained thirteen articles describing the means by which the candidate selection process should occur for all high-ranking incarnate lamas. It stipulated that Republican leaders would play a role in the selection process, and also required the use of the golden urn. Yet, it appears that the Republican regulations had little impact in Tibet. Republican scholar Hsiao-ting Lin argues that even after the Kuomintang established a new mission in Lhasa in 1934, Nanjing remained largely unfocused on Tibet policy and failed to implement any concrete initiatives there. Following the death of the Thirteenth Dalai Lama in 1933, Tibetan religious leaders compiled a list of fourteen potential candidates using traditional methods of divination. They eventually selected a bright young boy named Lhamo Dondrup from a small village in the Tibetan area known as Amdo (present-day Qinghai province) as the Fourteenth Dalai Lama. The search team initially attempted to keep its selection secret. It feared that Ma Bufang, the local warlord in Qinghai, might either demand an exorbitant bribe before allowing the chosen candidate to leave or send a military escort with the boy to remain in Lhasa. When the team finally asked Ma permission to have the boy sent to Kumbum Monastery en route to Lhasa, the warlord repeatedly asked for large sums of money totaling 400,000 silver coins, as well as other favors.

Lhasa eventually asked the Kuomintang government whether it could convince Ma to free the young reincarnate from virtual house arrest. Nanjing subsequently responded by making its own demands, including the right to escort the Dalai Lama to Lhasa and also send a Chinese official representative to the ceremony, so that he could bestow a Chinese title upon the monk. Lhasa refused to agree to all of the initial terms set forth by Nanjing, but an agreement was eventually reached. On 29 March 1939, the Kuomintang announced that it would dispatch Wu Zhongxin, Chairman of the Commission for Mongolian and Tibetan Affairs, to Tibet as its official representative during the selection and enthronement ceremonies. Interestingly, the British Mission in Lhasa reported at the time that the ROC had previously requested Chinese representation at the enthronement of the Dalai Lama, but implied that Lhasa had rebuffed its request.

There is a strong continuity between Imperial and Republican approaches to the institution of the Dalai Lama. Even after the Qing Dynasty fell, it was a Chinese government priority to assert authority over all lands held during the height of the Qing Empire. Although the Republic of China was far too weak to establish effective control over Tibet during this time period, it never relinquished its claims there. In the end, the Chinese Republican leadership had no input into the selection process of the Fourteenth Dalai Lama, and possessed no function during the ceremony. The lack of Chinese official participation subsequently prompted the incoming Communist regime to strengthen existing policies and attempt to gain real control over the selection process in the future.

IMPERIAL CHINA'S EXERCISE OF AUTHORITY IN TIBET

Through its *Lifan Yuan* (Office of Border Affairs; after 1861, Zongli Yamen), the Chinese government handled Tibet's foreign and many of its domestic affairs. During the Qing, Tibet hosted imperial troops and border patrols, and the imperial court appointed Tibetan officials. The*Lifan Yuan* managed lama and nomad affairs, defined borders, ran a postal system, presided over meetings and ceremonies and supervised trade. It ratified the Dalai and Panchen Lamas, created joint rule by aristocrats and high lamas and elevated the Dalai Lama above the nobles.54 From 1728, the imperial representative in Tibet or *amban*handled Tibet's foreign and military affairs. From 1793, the *amban* had the right to identity the Dalai Lama and Panchen Lama, examine their incomes and expenses, supervise immigration, coinage, corvee labour, taxes and the penal system, as well as to appoint and pay the military. The*amban* certified monks and had to be present at key religious events, such as consecrations of reincarnated lamas (*tulku*). Monastic finances were under imperial control, but the emperor privileged monks over aristocrats in Tibet, so most monks were loyal to the Qing. Central-western Tibet was thus an administered territory of China under the Qing. In 1724, eastern Tibet was incorporated into existing Chinese provinces.

The Qing controlled Tibet for more than two centuries, but no fixed length of ties is needed for a State to legitimate its sovereignty in a territory. International law's answer to the query of how much of a historic tie a State needs for this purpose is: not nil, but not much. It cannot be otherwise: States such as the United States, Canada, India, Russia, the United Kingdom and France were constructed by force and the use of treaties made under duress. These States added contiguous territories to their cores that were soon treated as legal equivalents of pre-existing territory. This historic process is regarded as legitimate even where only short and vague ties to the added territory existed, because, under the inter-temporality principle, an act sufficient to confer title at the time it is performed establishes title even if the law subsequently changes. Imperial sovereignty in Tibet moreover provided protection and status to the Lhasa regime; thus the Dalai Lamas regarded it as legitimate and Tibetan elites saw themselves as imperial subjects.

Some pro-Tibet independence historians of Tibet, such as Elliot Sperling, recognize that Tibet was not independent, at least during the Yuan and Qing dynasties. Sperling however contends that Tibet, while not independent, was not part of China, because Yuan and Qing rulers were ethnic Mongols and Manchu who headed Mongol and Manchu empires and thus were not Chinese rulers. But soon after Mongols came to rule China, Han elites became strongly loyal to the Yuan and for three generations after its fall, refused to transfer their loyalty to the subsequent Han Chinese Ming Dynasty. Manchu were Chinese imperial subjects even before they took power and the Qing rulers identified their empire as Zhongguo (China).

Contending that Yuan and Qing dynasts were not Chinese rulers is like arguing that Britain's monarchs of the eighteenth and nineteenth centuries were not British because they were of German descent and practised, to varying degrees, German customs. It is also like the claim of present-day Hindu chauvinists that the Mughal emperors of India (1526–1858) were not Indian rulers because they descended from Central Asian princes. In fact, the Qing perceived itself as the successor to the dynasties of China that had come before it, which included being the political heir to its immediate, Han Chinese-led predecessor, the Ming, whose modes of governance and rituals it left largely intact. The Republic of China declared itself the Qing's legal successor and the People's Republic of China regards itself as the ROC's successor. A US federal court has found that to be a fact, in a case involving claims over responsibility to repay Qing government bonds.

After China plunged into chaos at the fall of the Qing, the ROC was not able to administer central-western Tibet for 38 years.

However, this hiatus did not diminish China's sovereignty over the territory. As Yale law professor Michael Reisman notes, international law "has traditionally tolerated temporary lapses in the control of central authorities over peripheral territories caused by internal disruptions". International law thus refutes claims of a right to re-establish a pre-existing Tibet independence. Yet, a widespread belief in it exists, especially in the West. How does this belief affect China's relations with the major powers most concerned with Tibet: India and the United States?

CHINA AND THE PEACEFUL LIBERATION OF TIBET

The People's Republic of China (PRC) was founded on October 1, 1949, and the Central People's Government under the leadership of the Communist Party of China (CPC) became the sole legitimate government of China. This government immediately won extensive recognition from many countries, and won the natural qualification to exercise sovereignty over the whole of the Chinese territory.

From the winter of 1949 to the spring of 1950, the Central People's Government planned the peaceful liberation of Tibet. In the spring and summer of 1950, the Chinese People's Liberation Army (PLA) marched toward Tibet. After having overcome foreign obstructions, put to rout the resistance by Tibetan separatists and beaten the harsh highland environment, the PLA advance troops arrived in Lhasa and various major towns and border areas in 1951. China's five-star red flag fluttered over the Himalayas. China thus succeeded in the peaceful liberation of Tibet, completing the holy task of unifying the mainland. From then on, Tibet no longer operated under the yoke of foreign forces, and returned to the big family of the motherland known for its national unity and fraternity. The peaceful liberation of Tibet is a joyful historic event for the Tibetans and peoples of other nationalities in China. Xagabba and Van Praag, however, term the move "aggression." They even create the "theory of Chinese Communist invasion of Tibet" to shock the world.

"Aggression" or "invasion" has strict meaning and cannot be applied indiscriminately. It involves standards concerning military behaviour of various countries in the world as well as many political issues in the international community. The UN resolution on the meaning of invasion, adopted at the 29th UN General Assembly in December 1974, stipulates that invasion refers to a country which violates, with military forces, another country's sovereignty, territorial integrity or political independence, or uses other forms of military forces which do not conform with the UN Constitution as contained in this resolution. The resolution specifies seven types of behaviour: invading, attacking, occupying, annexing, bombing, blockading, stationing troops and other forms of military behaviour. This should be the most authoritative explanation on invasion or aggression.

The above shows the word aggression or invasion contains two fundamental points: First, the invasion or aggression is possible only when the military move takes place between two countries and when one country takes action against another. No action taken on home soil can be termed invasion or aggression; second, the invasion or aggression is possible only when the military move aims at plundering and enslaving the other country, an action which infringes upon territorial integrity and sovereignty of another country.

World history shows many actions constitute invasion, which are aimed at another country's territory and sovereignty and geared to plunder and enslave people of another country. They include the British invasion of India in 1767, the British invasion of China in 1840, the Eight-Power invasion of China in 1900, the Italian invasion of Ethiopia in 1935, the Japanese invasion of China in 1937, the German invasion of Austria, Czechoslovakia and Poland in 1938-39, the German invasion of the Soviet Union in 1941, and the US invasion of Panama in 1989. All these actions constitute one country's encroachment upon another country's territory and sovereignty, and plundering and enslaving of people of another country.

Civil armed conflicts taking place within the same country, though varied in forms, do not fall into the category of invasion. They include conflicts between the Central Government and local government, between various regions, between various nationalities, between various religious factions and between various political groups. Tibet is a part of Chinese territory. Conflicts, including armed conflicts, between Tibet and fraternal regions in China or between the Central Government and the local government of Tibet are the internal affairs of China. Examples include the Qing imperial army sent to suppress the Zungar invasions in Tibet in 1718 and 1720. As the Qing imperial court exercised jurisdiction over Tibet, no one in the world called the two military moves "aggression" or "invasion."

In the early days of the People's Republic of China, PLA advance troops were sent into Tibet to drive imperialist forces out of the region for consolidated national defense and the defense of China's own territory. This constituted the Chinese government's exercise of jurisdiction over Tibet. It was a domestic, instead of an international behaviour, hence legal from beginning to end. Xagabba and Van Praag say nothing of the British military invasion of Tibet in 1888 and 1904. However, they forcibly termed the PLA move in Tibet "aggression." They did so with a view to fundamentally refuting the legality, reasonability and justice of China's peaceful liberation of Tibet. Facts slap them in the face.

In the summer and autumn of 1949, when the liberation war gained much ground in China and was approaching China's Tibetan areas, Britain, the United States and some other countries plotted actively for "Tibetan independence." In April 1949, US Secretary of State Dean Acheson sent a cable to the American Embassy in India: Washington wishes to see Tibet's military resistance capability secretly beefed up. (A. Tom Grunfeld [Canada]: The Making of Modern Tibet, p.143-144, translated by Wu Kunmin and others) In July, the Tibet Office of the Commission for Mongolian and Tibetan Affairs under the Kuomintang Government was expelled from Tibet by the Gaxag government. In August, Xagabba managed to have Lowell Thomas, a commentator with the Columbia Radio Station of the United States, enter Tibet together with his son. The Gaxag government attempted to stir up an opinion for "Tibetan independence" by relying on the American radio station. During their stay in Lhasa, they held secret talks with the Prince Regent Dagzha and Hugh Richardson, and met with high Tibetan officials, urging the Tibetan side to organize trained guerrillas to stem the

PLA advance troops. In September, the Gaxag government decided to expand its army by 10,000 and reinforce Qamdo and Nagqu. Lowell Thomas and his son called Tibet as "country" and appealed to the US government to offer military aid to Tibet and send diplomatic missions to Lhasa. Upon their return to the United States, they called for the United States to shoulder responsibility for the defense of Tibet.

Reginald Fox, a British spy, plotted construction of the Qamdo Radio Station for Tibet. In July 1949, Robert Ford had it built in Qamdo, and started collecting information concerning the Communist Party of China and the PLA's liberation war. Information thus collected from Xikang and Qinghai was supplied to Lowell Thomas, his son and the Gaxag government. Hugh Richardson and Reginald Fox were responsible for re-sending the information to Britain. At the instigation of Hugh Richardson and some others, the "foreign affairs bureau" of the Gaxag government sent a cable to Chairman Mao Zedong in November 1949: "Please do not send troops to cross the border into Tibet." At the suggestion of Hugh Richardson, Prince Regent Dagzha ordered the Gaxag government to draft a "Tibetan independence declaration" which was revised and turned into English by Hugh Richardson. The English version was brought to the United Nations by Xagabba and Gyalo Toinzhub to seek UN support. Through repeated discussions, Hugh Richardson, Lowell Thomas and his son, and Prince Regent Dagzha sent a "goodwill mission" composed of Tibetan officials to the United States, Britain, India and Nepal in early 1950, seeking their aid and support for "Tibetan independence."

On January 17, Reginald Fox sent a letter to the headquarters of the Tibetan army, making suggestions for its resistance against the PLA advance troops: "It should be extremely difficult for the Communist Party to send troops into Tibet. In order to slow down the advance of the Communist army, various official routes, highways and bridges should be damaged thoroughly. Mines should be planted at various strategically important positions, places where the Communist troops may be ambushed, major rivers with no bridges and mountain entries. Some Communist spies are highly likely to be sent into Tibet to confuse border residents by creating rumors and saying something which will make them change their mind. They will also collect and send information concerning deployment of Tibetan troops to the Communist Party.

"In order to check the possible spread of Communism among residents who are loyal to the 14th Dalai Lama, and in order to stabilize various parts of Tibet, they should be told immediately to prepare for a retreat of at least 20 miles. This is a point of extreme importance. The troops should be deployed in places where the Communist army can hardly cut their escape route and besiege them. Decisions concerning defense matters should be made immediately."

On January 19, the commander-in-chief of the Tibetan army sent a reply to Reginald Fox, expressing sincere thanks for his good suggestion, which he said would "lie embedded in the mind for ever."

Thereafter, the Tibetan army operated basically in accordance with the suggestion made by Reginald Fox. The above facts show how much efforts the British and American forces had made for the control of the Gaxag government. They also show the necessity and urgency for the People's Republic of China to exercise jurisdiction over Tibet.

Patriotic Tibetans, however, ardently demanded and supported the PLA advance troops?entry into Tibet. On October 1, 1949, the 10th Panchen Erdeni sent a cable to Chairman Mao Zedong and Commander-in-Chief Zhu De: "Northwest China has been liberated and the Central People's Government has been formed. All people who are full of sap feel encouraged. There is hope for the people to lead a happy life and for the country to rejuvenate. Tibet is expected to be liberated at an early date." (Selected Materials on the History of Tibet, p.376)

On December 2, 1949, Kampus Yexei Curchen, who was close to the former Prince Regent Living Buddha Razheng, murdered by the pro-British elements in the upper echelon of Tibet ruling class in 1947, went to the PLA troops in Xining, Qinghai, condemning imperialist crimes in instigating hatred for the Han and sabotaging internal unity of Tibet. He demanded immediate liberation of Tibet.

At a mass rally in Lanzhou on January 26, 1950, the Tibetans protested against foreign forces in their plot to invade Tibet, opposed the "goodwill missions" sent by the Gaxag government of Tibet to preach "Tibetan independence" in foreign countries, and expressed resolute support for the PLA advance troops to march into Tibet. Huang Zhenqing, a famous Tibetan in Gannan, said: "We will mobilize the Tibetan people to welcome with broad arms and support the PLA advance troops in their march into Tibet." (People's Daily, January 28, 1950)

In February, the Living Buddha Geda with the Baili Monastery in Garze, Dege Headman Xage Daodain, and Wanggyai, representative of Kangnan merchant Bangda Doje, and other famous Tibetan figures in Xikang Province went to Beijing to tell the Central People's Government that they would support the PLA advance troops to march into Tibet just like what the Boba Soviet government did in supporting the Red Army to resist the Japanese aggressors in the past.

TIBET AND CHINA

The entire North Indian cities and important industrial belts are within the devastatingly striking distance from the Tibetan plateau, which is the highest area in the world. During the last two hundred years, the world was dominated by the British and the Americans. "The supremacy of any one nation or civilization", Friedmann writes, "is a passing phenomenon, covering at best a span of a few centuries" (1960: 218). The West has seen that China is going to be the next super power in less than fifty years. The Dalai Lama was the greatest votary of China hosting Olympic. His Holiness is a man of compassion and there is no place in his heart for hatred. He has been trained from childhood to love all sentient beings. No two countries in history have such an intimate relation as between China and Tibet. In fact the title 'Dalai Lama' was given to the fifth Dalai Lama by a Chinese emperor of Mongolian origin. The Ming emperors and the Dalai Lama had mutual interests; the former wanted the influence of the Lama to rein in his Buddhists subjects and the latter to secure himself against any possible challenge to his authority.

The possession of India made Britain the greatest and mightiest power in history. The possession of Tibet by China will facilitate it towards its goal of the sole super power. The European countries and USA have rightly condemned the Chinese action in Tibet as a violation of human rights. But if we consider European peoples' actions in the present day United States, Mexico, Australia, Brazil, etc., it will be a pathetic story. For instance, the so-called Red Indians were ruthlessly wiped out in the American continent. "By destroying the buffalo herds, the whites were destroying the Indians' main source of food and supplies" (Newmann 2004: 8). On October 2, 1932, Jawaharlal Nehru wrote to his daughter: The Red Indians "were practically exterminated, and most of them died off under the new conditions. There are not many left today of these people who once inhabited a whole continent" (1949: 356). In modern parlance, the crime of genocide was committed in the Australian, North and South American continents in the 18th and 19 centuries. It is unfortunate that the original Americans are not called Americans; they are called 'Indians' and the settlers are called 'Americans'. Similarly the native people in present day Mexico were wiped out. The same is the story in Australia and South America.

However I do not intend to give the impression that the Chinese brutality should be condoned. For their present plight, the Tibetans themselves are responsible to a considerable extent. The British Government in India wanted to open up Tibet for trade; and several attempts were made through 'the suzerain power', China, but failed. Then Lord Curzon, Viceroy of India, who rightly understood that 'the Chinese suzerainty' was a 'constitutional fiction' wrote to the Dalai Lama; but the letters were returned unopened. If Tibet had responded to the British overtures, the whole of Tibet perhaps would have been independent. Even if the entire Tibet could not have been independent, it can be said with certainty that Outer Tibet would have been independent in the same way as Outer Mongolia, which is much nearer to Beijing than Tibet, is independent today. At the time of the collapse of the Manchu empire, both Tibet and Mongolia were constituent units of China. Both had Outer and Inner areas, called Outer and Inner Tibet and Outer and Inner Mongolia, Inner Mongolia is still a part of China. With the help of the two-year old USSR, the Mongolian People's Republic was proclaimed in 1924. In 1945, another Sino-Russian Treaty was concluded according to which the Chiang Kai-shek government of Nationalist China recognized the complete independence of Outer Mongolia. The action of the British empire in India would have similarly led to the independence of Outer Tibet. The British empire, wanted an independent Outer Tibet, not because of love for Tibet; but because it did not want China on its threshold. A quarrelsome and powerful neighbor is a perpetual headache. Despite repeated attempts from the British-Indian Government, Tibet kept aloof on the grounds that the British "were harboring ulterior designs on their country and their religion" (Bell 1924: 62). But the British policy in India was to annex only those territories which were fertile and rich in mineral resources and leave the rest under the largely autonomous Princely States which were in their largest number in the semi-desert areas of Rajputana (now Rajasthan and the Hyderabad region). Britain's interest in Tibet was to gain access to the vast Chinese market and to maintain the buffer zone to prevent any possible collision between the two empires. "In 1910, the Tibetan Government would have welcomed a British Protectorate," the Tibetan Ministers remarked: "The Indian States were in an ideal position, for each was safe from external aggression and free from interference as regards its internal administration. They sighed as they added, 'That is how we should like Tibet to be'" (Bell 1924: 246-7). Bell continues: "But it was recognized on our side from the first that this would have devolved far too heavy a burden upon us, the responsibility of protecting the distant and difficult expanses of Tibet" *(ibid.:* 247).

'The first communication of the Government of independent India to the Foreign Office of the Tibetan Government was to request the latter to ratify the Simla Convention." Unfortunately, "Lhasa refused to ratify the Simla Convention until territories such as Darjeeling and Kalimpong were returned" (Apri 2004: 11). The Simla Convention was finally ratified by the Governments of Tibet and India in 1948 *(ibid.:* 123).

It was not in the interest of Tibet to refuse to recognize the independent government of India as "the legal inheritor of the treaties, rights and obligations of British India." By the time it was too late, Tibet recognized the Indian Government as the successor to the British-Indian government on 11 June, 1948 *(ibid.:* 12). Moreover, Nehru was unhappy with the Tibetan view on 'lost territories'. These factors contributed to Nehru's policy towards Tibet. The possibility of militarily defending Tibet was formally discussed at that time, by the US and British governments. The conclusion was that it was not easy to help the Tibetans as the terrain was not favorable and in any case it was up to the Indian Government to decide since the arms or equipment would have to transit through India *(ibid.:* 19ff).

The Government of India made it clear that "it cannot, however, render active military assistance in form of dispatch of troops to Lhasa" *(ibid.:* 19ff). If India had taken the required initiative, it was likely that the Western countries would have helped Tibet in consonance with their policy of containment of communism anywhere and everywhere, as incorporated in the Truman Doctrine in the name of the US President Harry S Truman on March 12, 1947.

The Treaty between the Republic of India and the People's Republic of China on Trade and Intercourse between 'the Tibet region of China' and India was signed on 29th April, 1954 at the Ministry of Foreign Affairs in Beijing by the Indian Ambassador N Raghavan and Chang Han-fu, the Chinese Deputy Foreign Minister. Normally, a treaty is signed between two countries without mentioning any particular area within the country. But the Chinese diplomacy succeeded in mentioning Tibet as 'the Tibet region of China'. Never before was Tibet referred to as 'the Tibet region of China'. Thus, Tibet was sacrificed at the altar of Sino-Indian friendship. The treaty was then ratified on 4 June 1954 *(ibid.:* 211). Subsequent events demonstrated that the treaty was the source of perennial border problems. The Chinese government complained on 29 June 1954—only after 25 days of the ratification of the treaty— that Indian troops with rifles had crossed into the Tibet region of China and intruded into Wu-je area. It appears that India negotiated the 1954 Treaty out of compulsion. The Prime minister, JL Nehru said: "We must give up these facilities such as telegraph lines; if we do not give them up voluntarily, then we shall be forced to give them up. The fact is that if we did not like to give up those things, we would have been forced to give them up. We must accept this fact" (Prime Minister's speech in the Lok Sabha, 18 May, 1954 (Chakravarty 1961: 60).

But if China is aspiring to be the super power it should behave responsibly and allow full autonomy to the Tibetans without compromising its national security and unity. It should withdraw the People's Liberation Army from Tibet and the Sino-Indian international border, keeping only border check posts to prevent illegal ingress or egress into China.

TIBET AS A REGION OF CHINA

Tibet—a comparatively vast area—is the roof of the world and its possession gives China geopolitical advantage in its cherished aim of dominating the Asian continent and ultimately the world. The might of the erstwhile British empire, as stated above, was founded upon the resources and strategic importance of India. Britain was relegated to a minor power after the loss of the Indian empire. Similarly, Tibet as a part of China will give the latter strategic importance and security. If Tibet either falls into the hand of or becomes an ally of, another major power, the security of China will be gravely threatened.

The importance of the Tibet region also lies in the fact that most of the major and minor rivers in China and Southeast Asia including the Indian sub-continent originate there. For instances, the 2,897 kilometre long Indus river of India and Pakistan, which is one of the largest irrigation systems in the world ; the 2,704 kilometre long Brahmaputra which is an important waterway of southern Asia; and the 2,400-kilometre long Salween, the major river of Southeast Asia and the longest in Myanmar. Other major rivers—Mekong and Yangtze—flow through Tibet.

Only in the event of China degenerating into a condition similar to the one obtaining in the first decade of the last century can Tibet hope to regain its de facto or full independence—a possibility which does not seem likely. In the interest of the Tibetans themselves, therefore, they should cooperate with the Chinese and convince them that the meaningful autonomy will not in any way harm the Chinese national interest. The Dalai Lama said his faith in the Chinese officials was becoming "thinner and thinner" while his faith in the Chinese people was "growing stronger and stronger" and he advised the Tibetans to "develop good relations" with the Han Chinese people. The advice of the Dalai Lama is timely. The Tibetans should try to win the hearts of the Hans who should exert pressure on their government to grant meaningful autonomy to Tibet. The Dalai Lama also rightly pointed out that people showing concern and sympathy for the Tibetan cause should not be seen as "pro-Tibetan" but as "advocates of justice" *(ibid.).'China,* the future super power, should act magnanimously and give absolute autonomy to Tibet retaining only external affairs, defense, communication, currency, and citizenship. The Central Government should not interfere with the Tibetan social, religious and customary practices, unless they hinder the political, civil and human rights of the Tibetans. All civilian posts in Tibet should be manned by the Tibetans with the Dalai Lama as the spiritual and temporal Head of the government of the Tibet region of China. Their peaceful coexistence will be in the interest of both—especially the Tibetans. A happy Tibet will strengthen the hand of China in its bid towards gaining the super power status. With some exceptions, history has been a witness to the coexistence of a theocratic Tibet under the thirteen incarnations of the Dalai Lama and the imperial China. Let the millennium herald the peaceful and exemplary coexistence between a theist Tibet and an atheist China within the Chinese constitutional framework.

THE WORLD TODAY

In order to find a way out of the seemingly perennial Tibetan dilemma, His Holiness The Fourteenth Dalai Lama called a special meeting for the third time, November 17-22, 2008 at Dharamsala, without Himself participating in it, in order to give the delegates absolute freedom to express their opinion without any reservations. The first two such meetings were held in 1951 and 1959. For more than half a century, the Dalai Lama has been trying to find a mutually acceptable solution to the vexed issue. As a septuagenarian, he has, however, justifiably lost hope. He said: "As far as I am concerned, I have given up." Yet the Chinese charge that the Tibetans are 'splittists' is untenable; for they do not want to split the country. All that they want is a meaningful autonomy within China and within the framework of the Chinese constitution. However, this writer does not see any possibility of any fruitful discussion with the Chinese government unless the mindset of the Han leaders undergoes a rational transformation.

Four decades ago, I wrote an article 'Tibet Today: A Nation in Chains' which was published in the Tibetan Review in November 1968. The paper was serialised in *Now!* November 19-21, 2008. The response from the people has encouraged me to pen my thought on the subject in the world of 2008. In 1968,1 thought that Tibet might be able to regain her pre-October, 1950 *de facto* independent status in view of the power politics among the major Powers of the world. During the interlude of forty years, there has, however, been a sea change in the international politics, diplomacy and power equations in the comity of nations. The bi-polar interpretation of world politics in terms of a struggle between the United States of America and the Union of Soviet Socialist Republics for world supremacy metamorphosed into a unipolar planet after the disintegration of the latter on December 25,1991.

Harold Joseph Laski (1893-1950), the celebrated British political scientist from the London School of Economics and Political Science, had written as early as 1925: "Russia cannot exist as a Communist State when she is surrounded by capitalist communities" (1960: 537). Yet during the period, 1968-2008, China steadily advanced towards the status of a major power in the world. The respective Gross Domestic Products in trillion dollars (2002 estimate) of USA, China and Japan are $10.45, $5,989 and $ 3.651. By the second half of this century, China will be the richest and the most powerful country in history, replacing the United States of America. As early as 1960, Friedmann wrote: "The most important change in the world balance of power results from the emergence of Communist China as the third world Power" (1960: 87-8)—the first two were USA and USSR. As the twentieth century was ushered in, John Milton Hay (1838-1905), who was Secretary of State for the USA from 1898 to 1905, asserted: "The world's peace rests with China, and whoever understands China, holds the key to world politics during the next five centuries" (Bowles 1955: 69). Very truly did Napoleon Bonaparte (1769-1821) say: "China -there lies a sleeping giant. Let him sleep, for when he wakes he shall shake the world" *(ibid.:* 67). Writing in 1960, Friedmann argued: "After centuries of unchallenged Western supremacy, it is not easy for the people of the West to adjust their thoughts and actions to a world situation in which the balance of world politics would be determined by Asia rather than Europe or even North America" *(ibid.:* 218). During the last two hundred years, the world was dominated first by the British with the help of the British Navy and the British-Indian Army and then the Americans by way of the possession of 'weapons of mass destruction'. The American domination of the world, represented by the recent swashbuckling occupant of the White House has been resented to such an extent, even by the Americans themselves, that the "approval rating of US President George Bush, on the last leg of his second term, had reached an all-time low in modern opinion polls since 1938, with a record number of Americans saying the country is on the 'wrong track'." He had to be strictly kept indoors during the election campaign of the new presidential candidate of his Republican party. John McCain had to bear the cross of the existing Republican President Bush and he lost the election to a relatively younger and inexperienced first 'black' candidate.

Laski also wrote: "It must be remembered that any great power is a menace to the peace of the world if it has ambitions it cannot fulfill except by the making of war. That was once true of Spain; it was once true of France; it is true in our own day of Germany and Japan. But we have to remember that, in the next age, it may be true of the United States if the character of its economic system pushes it, as may well be the case, to imperialism" (1968: 228). The Laskian vista may well be true also of China in less than fifty years. Consequent upon the meteoric rise of China and its influence in international arena and the concomitant weakening of the American influence, the United Nations Organization had no alternative but to admit the People's Republic of China as a member and rightfully allot to it permanent seat as one of the Five Big Powers—USA, UK, USSR (Russia since 1991), France and China—in the Security Council in 1971. Prior to this that seat was unjustifiably occupied by the tiny island of Taiwan—with the support of the United States which was hoping that the Government in Taiwan might one day take over mainland China. The year 1972 witnessed the unprecedented visit of US President Richard MQhous Nixon (1913-1994) to China as the communist country had become too important to be ignored any longer in the American national interest. The Sino-American rapprochement led to the gradual withdrawal of covert CIA funding to the Dalai Lama's office and the Tibetan resistance against the Chinese in Tibet ceased. "The Dalai Lama sent a taped message to the Mustang fighters ordering them to lay down their arms, but rather than surrender, many preferred to die" (French 2003: 264).

China's meteoric rise is not due to, but in spite of, eommunism. It is due to incandescent patriotism, an uncompromising sense of national unity and determination to surpass the advanced countries in everything - be it in Olympic gold medals, Olympic-sized airports and other modern infrastructure, the health profile of its citizens or in any other parameter of development. It is this spirit of nationalism, among all the age-groups of the population, that is feeding China's determination to become the greatest nation on the planet. Moreover, the founding fathers of the Chinese republic were dedicated and devoted men and women. Bowles (1955: 105) writes: The administration of the country is carried on by men who live under strict discipline, whether civilian or military. Many are paid no salaries, but are given only board and lodging, a bare minimum of clothing, some cigarettes, free education for their children and medical attention. Selfless young Chinese have returned from abroad to lead hard and austere lives. 'The administration is absolutely honest', writes a recently expelled Catholic priest who warned against underestimating the strength of the Peking Government. 'I imagine that under the present regime it would be more difficult to buy a Chinese official than an official in the Western countries'. Where salaries are paid, they are extremely low. Mao Tse-tung is said to receive less than the equivalent of $150 a month. And the earnings of his subordinates are proportionately lower. An awed Indian official once said to me, 'Mao himself has only one suit, and his wife works for a weekly wage'.

TIBET PAST, PRESENT AND FUTURE

Tibet during the British rule in India enjoyed virtual independence from China. The representative of the Manchu dynasty in Lhasa called the Amban had no effective power. The imperial authority declined to such an extent that in 1856 when Nepal attacked Tibet, China had no role to play. On the conclusion of the war, Nepal and Tibet signed in 1856 a treaty which was not objected to by China. But the British, to keep off other imperial powers—especially the Russian—invented the so-called 'Roman concept' of Chinese suzerainty which worked well in their imperial interests. A year before the fall of the Manchu dynasty, when the Chinese Imperial army entered into Tibet "to facilitate the maintenance of order and for the protection of the existing foreign trade marts" the Dalai Lama fled Lhasa in the night on February 12, 1910. The Dalai Lama entered into Sikkim through either Jelep La or Nathula—most likely through Jelep La—and "the Maharaj Kumar met him at Rhenock and accompanied His Holiness to Darjeeling and Calcutta."

In October 1911 the revolution against the Ch'ing began; on 12 February 1912 the last Ch'ing emperor abdicated, and, on the 15 Yuan Shih-k'ai was elected president of the new Chinese Republic. Chinese troops in Tibet mutinied and looted Lhasa. In April the Chinese garrison in Lhasa surrendered to the Tibetans but refused to be repatriated to China in the hopes that an expedition from the east would come to their rescue. The Chinese Republican government attempted to make the Chinese garrison commander in Lhasa their representative, but this move was resisted by the Tibetans, who demanded the evacuation of all Chinese soldiers and officials from Tibet. Chinese troops were finally removed from Tibet, via India, at the end of 1912 (Smith 1997: 181).

His Holiness remained in Darjeeling till July 1912 when He reentered Tibet "taking up residence at Samdong Monastery near the lake Yamdrok Yumtso until the last of the Chinese garrison could be removed" *(ibid.)*. The Chinese were repatriated from Tibet to China through Sikkim and Calcutta sea port. Owing to the repatriation, from Tibet through Sikkim to China, of 1,263 men, 93 women and 46 children, subjects of China, the Sikkim Darbar was called upon to supply transport, et cetera. This involved heavy expenditure. It was borne by the Government of India.

"In January 1913 the Dalai Lama finally returned to Lhasa. Tibet was free of the Chinese for the first time since 1720." In January, 1913, the Dalai Lama proclaimed that Tibet was independent and signed a treaty with Mongolia (Bell 124: 304). There were no Chinese in Tibet till October 7, 1950.

On the 7th of October, 1950, forty thousand Chinese soldiers invaded Kham in Eastern Tibet (French 2003: 259). Exactly one month after the invasion, Sardar Vallabhai Patel (1875-1950), Deputy Prime Minister and Home Minister of India, wrote a prophetic letter to the Prime Minister Nehru on November 7, 1950 stating that very soon they [the Chinese] will disown all the stipulations which Tibet has entered into with us in the past. That throws into the melting pot a frontier and commercial settlements with Tibet on which we have been functioning and acting during the last half a century. The undefined state of the frontier and the existence on our side of a population with its affinities to the Tibetans or Chinese have all the elements of the potential trouble between China and ourselves (Arpi 2004: 225).

The Sardar proposed that India should send a token Indian force to help the Tibetans in resisting the Chinese invaders (Thomas 1960: 210). His proposal, however, fell through. In the fifties, India had to withdraw all the rights it had acquired since 1904 as forewarned by Sardar Patel. The situation on the peaceful pre-independence Sino-Indian border—as peaceful as the US-Canadian border—changed overnight and became volatile for the first time in the history of the two biggest Asian countries.

It was a grievous mistake committed by the first Prime Minister of India who deviated from the time-honoured policy of keeping

China out of Tibet by gainsaying Chinese sovereignty over Tibet. Once India accepted Tibet as "the Tibet region of China" for the first time in 1954 in the treaty between India and China, it became difficult to controvert the Chinese claim over territories which had been once a part of Tibet. It is an incontrovertible historical fact that the Himalayan areas—some in India and some outside India—were once a part of Tibet in the past. For instance, there is a place called Sadiya, Assam, India. The original name was Sa-di-ley- ya. 'Sa' means land; 'di' means this; 'ley' means from; 'ya' means up. The word is Tibetan and Sadiya marked the boundary of Tibet in the south. Moreover, parts of Sikkim, Bhutan and other areas on the Tibetan periphery were once a part of Tibet in the past. It may be recalled that on February 27, 1947, Sikkim had sent to the Government of India a memorandum prepared by Sirdar D K Sen, laying a claim over Darjeeling (Moktan 2004: 113-27). Sikkim was "a former tributary of Tibet" and "originally under Tibetan rule" (Moraes 1966: 191-92). Even as late as 1873, John Ware Edgar, Deputy Commissioner, Darjeeling, during his visit to Kabi, presently Kabi-Tingda in North Sikkim—spelt 'Kubbi' by Edgar—found that "the people of this village pay their chief revenue to Thibet, but are bound to do certain services for the Sikhim Rajah, and to supply some food for his household" (Edgar 1969: 55). Sir Charles Bell wrote: Sikkim is "a State of Tibetan origin and originally part of Tibet" (1924: 170). Bell was "Late British Political Representative in Tibet, Bhutan and Sikkim" from 1908 to 1919. He was the greatest authority on the history of the region under his charge. It may be noted that the British protectorate over Sikkim was in accordance with the treaty between the Emperor of China and the Queen of the United Kingdom of Great Britain and Ireland and Empress of India in March 1890.

Bibliography

Atar Singh Jadoan: *Military Geography of South East Asia*, Anmol, Delhi, 2001.

Aziz, Barbara: *Tibetan Frontier Families*. New Delhi: Manohar Publications, 1978.

Bosson, James E. : *Tibetan Treasury of Aphoristic Jewels*, Bloomington, IN: Indiana University Press, 1968.

Clifford, Terry : *Tibetan Buddhist Medicine and Psychiatry: The Diamond Healing*, York Beach, ME: 1984.

Cole, Alan : *Mothers and Sons in Chinese Buddhism*, Stanford, CA: Stanford University Press, 1998.

Dalai Lama: *My Land and My People: Memoirs of the Dalai Lama of Tibet*. New York: McGraw Hill, 1962.

Donnet, Pierre-Antoine: *Tibet: Survival in Question*. London: Zed Books, 1994.

Gaur, Mahendra : *Indian Policy of Neighbour*, Delhi, Kalpaz Pub., 2006.

Geshe Kelsang : *Buddhism in the Tibetan Tradition: A Guide*, London: Tharpa, 1984.

Goodman, Steven D. : *Tibetan Buddhism: Reason and Revelation*, Albany, NY: State University of New York Press, 1992.

Gyatso, Geshe Kelsang : *Buddhism in the Tibetan Tradition: A Guide*, London: Tharpa, 1984.

Havnevik, Hanna : *Tibetan Buddhist Nuns*, Oslo: Norwegian University Press, 1990.

Jackson, David P. : *Tibetan Thangka Painting: Methods and Materials*, London: Serindia Publ., 1984.

Jagannath P. Panda: *China's Path to Power : Party, Military and the Politics of State Transition*, Pentagon, Delhi, 2010.

James E. : *Tibetan Treasury of Aphoristic Jewels*, Bloomington, IN: Indiana University Press, 1968.

Janice A. Jackson : *Tibetan Thangka Painting: Methods and Materials,* London: Serindia Publ., 1984.

Keane J.: *Democracy and Civil Liberty,* London, Verso, 1988.

Lamrimpa, Gen : *Calming the Mind: Tibetan Buddhist Teachings on Cultivating Meditative Quiescence,* Ithaca, NY: Snow Lion, 1995.

Lauf, Detlef Ingo : *Tibetan Sacred Art: The Heritage of Tantra,* Berkeley, CA: Shambhala, 1976.

Mary, W.: *Military Space Force: the Cultural Dimensions of Authority,* Cambridge, Belknap Press, 1985.

Prabir De: *India and China in an Era of Globalisation : Essays on Economic Cooperation,* Bookwell, Delhi, 2005.

Rinpoche, Sogyal : *The Tibetan Book of Living and Dying,* San Francisco, CA: Harper, 1992.

Ronald M. Davidson : *Tibetan Buddhism: Reason and Revelation,* Albany, NY: State University of New York Press, 1992.

Singer, Jane Casey : *Tibetan Art: Towards a Definition of Style,* London: Laurence King/Alan Marcuson, 1997.

Thampi, Madhavi : *India and China in the Colonial World,* Social Science Press, Delhi, 2010.

Tulku, Tarthang : *Sacred Art of Tibet,* Berkeley, CA: Dharma Publ., revised ed., 1988.

William Theodore : T*he Buddhist Tradition in India, China and Japan,* New York: Vintage Books, 1972.

Index

❑❑❑